GOTTI'S
RULES

ALSO BY GEORGE ANASTASIA

Blood and Honor

Mob Father

The Goodfella Tapes

The Summer Wind

The Big Hustle

The Last Gangster

GOTTI'S RULES

The Story of John Alite, Junior Gotti,
and the Demise of the American Mafia

GEORGE ANASTASIA

DEY ST.
AN IMPRINT OF
WILLIAM MORROW PUBLISHERS

Gotti's Rules is a journalistic account of John Alite's involvement with the Gambino crime family and his role in the federal trials of John Gotti Jr. and Charles Carneglia. Scenes and dialogue have been reconstructed based on quoted trial testimony, court-related documents, interviews, FBI and other law enforcement documentation, and published news stories.

GOTTI'S RULES. Copyright © 2015 by George Anastasia. All rights reserved. Printed in the United States of America. No part of this book may be used or reproduced in any manner whatsoever without written permission except in the case of brief quotations embodied in critical articles and reviews. For information address HarperCollins Publishers, 195 Broadway, New York, NY 10007.

HarperCollins books may be purchased for educational, business, or sales promotional use. For information please e-mail the Special Markets Department at SPsales@harpercollins.com.

FIRST EDITION

Designed by Renato Stanisic

Library of Congress Cataloging-in-Publication Data has been applied for.

ISBN 978-0-06-234687-2

15 16 17 18 19   OV/RRD   10 9 8 7 6 5 4 3 2 1

FOR ANGELINA, JULIET, NICOLAS, AND GEORGE

John Alite was a murderer, drug dealer, and thug.

Over the course of a twenty-five-year career as a gangster he brutalized people: stabbing them, shooting them, beating them with pipes, blackjacks, and baseball bats. He's not proud of that, but he doesn't try to hide from it, either. It's who he was.

But it's not who he is.

At least that's his position today, in 2014, as he tries to put his life back together, a fifty-year-old former mob associate and hit man trying to live a normal life, trying to figure out how he got off track, and trying to get back on.

"Sometimes I wonder what happened," he says.

A lot of people do.

The simple answer is that he did what he did to make money, to live well and to enhance his position in the Gambino crime family. He did most of it, he says, on the orders of John A. Gotti (known as Junior) and sometimes on the orders of John J. Gotti, Junior's father. Two federal court juries in New York heard Alite tell parts of his story. One came back with a conviction. The other couldn't decide.

Alite's story, from where he is sitting, is a graphic and often brutal look at organized crime. Take a step back, however, and his experiences, detailed in debriefing sessions with the FBI, in testimony from the witness stand, and in hours of interviews for this book, are part of the bloody and treacherous tapestry that describes the demise of the American Mafia. The once powerful, monolithic, and highly secretive criminal organization has lost most of its clout in the American underworld, a victim of multi-pronged federal prosecutions and the deterioration of a "value" system that held it together for decades.

Alite (pronounced Ā-Lite) took the stand in 2009 at the trials of mob soldier Charles Carneglia and mob boss Junior Gotti. Carneglia was convicted of racketeering and murder. He is serving a life term. Gotti beat the case after a jury hung, almost evenly deadlocked on all three counts. Like Alite, Junior is now a free man and putting his own spin on this story. He denies most of the allegations made by Alite, including charges that he dealt drugs and killed, or ordered the murders of, several individuals.

Junior also has denied that he ever cooperated with authorities. There is an FBI document that will be detailed later in this book that refutes that claim. Known as a "302"—the numerical designation for a memo summarizing a debriefing session—the five-page memo outlines a meeting on January 18, 2005, in which Gotti Jr. and two of his defense attorneys met with federal prosecutors and FBI agents at the U.S. Attorney's Office on Pearl Street in lower Manhattan.

Jerry Capeci, the dean of mob reporters in America, broke the first story about Junior's attempt to cooperate. The 302, which had never before been made public, expands and confirms Capeci's report, which was based on sources. The meeting was described as a "proffer session," a negotiation in which a target or potential defendant agrees to tell authorities what he knows in an attempt to work out a plea and cooperation deal. Nothing that is said during one of these sessions can be used against the target or against anyone else if an agreement is not worked out.

Junior and his lawyers apparently never completed the deal,

but that didn't keep them from trying. And, as the document indicates, it didn't stop Junior Gotti from giving up information about murders, corrupt cops and politicians, his crime family's influence in the Queens District Attorney's Office, and his own wheeling and dealing, including a plan he and an associate had to turn a city garbage dump into the site for a new Bronx House of Detention, which he would sell to the city for $20 million.

Let Junior Gotti and his lawyers spin that information any way they choose. The document speaks for itself. There was no attempt while writing this book to interview anyone in the Gotti camp. To turn Alite's story into a "he said, they said" narrative would serve no purpose.

The Gottis deny virtually everything Alite alleges. Alite, on the other hand, denies very little. His version of the events that marked his life—a version that federal authorities adopted when they put him under oath on the witness stand—is a story of murder, money, and betrayal. It's one man's life of crime, a seduction of sorts that made him rich, turned him terribly violent, and very nearly got him killed on a dozen different occasions.

It may also be a story of redemption, but that's a question that can't be answered at this point.

The backdrop is the Gotti family and the American Mafia; more accurately, the Gotti family and the demise of the American Mafia. No one individual has had more to do with the once secret society coming apart at the seams than John J. Gotti.

Gotti was a mob boss who loved the spotlight, a celebrity gangster who thumbed his nose at the conventional wisdom of the old-time wiseguys. Their idea was to make money, not headlines. Gotti thought he could do both. For a long time he did. He and his son embodied the Me generation of the mob. Junior (for the purpose of this story he's referred to as Junior even though he and his father had different middle names) was a spoiled, self-absorbed second-generation gangster whose sense of entitlement was his undoing. He was all about status and power. He liked the idea of being a mobster, but never really understood how it worked.

Smug and arrogant, bullies in expensive suits, the Gottis played by their own set of rules, rules that allowed them to do whatever they wanted to whomever they wanted.

That was part of the hypocrisy of the Gotti crime family. The image they projected didn't mesh with the reality. Even the Dapper Don moniker was phony, according to Alite. If Gotti Sr. didn't have an associate picking out his clothes and telling him how to dress, the former thug and hijacker would have dressed like, well, a thug and hijacker, clashing plaids and stripes and colors rather than the cool, sophisticated elegance that became his trademark.

The media, of course, helped create the image. John J. Gotti on the cover of *Time* magazine; in boldface on Page Six of the *New York Post;* a sound bite, a pithy quote, leading the evening news. John Gotti was the face of the American Mafia at the end of the twentieth century.

And his son, coming on his heels, extending the reign.

It could be argued that Cosa Nostra was on the way out even before the Gottis got onstage. Second- and third-generation Italian Americans, in fact, make lousy gangsters. The best and the brightest in that community are now doctors, lawyers, educators. The mob is scraping the bottom of the gene pool.

That's where the Gottis were located.

Add more sophisticated law enforcement, high-tech electronic surveillance, and the RICO Act and it's clear the deck was stacked against the American Mafia. Throw in the death of omertà, the code of silence that was the foundation for the wall of secrecy that once protected the honored society. And also consider this: the Mafia was always a front, a façade, a *fugazy* if you will. Mario Puzo, Francis Ford Coppola, and Martin Scorsese have built stories around *the life,* and the public has developed a perception based on those wonderfully written, directed, and acted fictions.

The reality is that if there ever was nobility and honor—and I'm not sure there was—it disappeared two or three generations ago. The American Mafia took the value system of the Italian-American community and bastardized it for its own benefit. The concepts of honor, fierce family loyalty, and respect, concepts that were and are as common and as expected in most Italian-American homes as spaghetti and meatballs for dinner on Sunday, were twisted into a code of conduct that lent power and status to outlaws and thugs.

Gotti Sr. played those cards well. Gotti Jr. took advantage of them but never really figured out the game. Ironically Alite, born of Albanian parents, understood it better than Junior. He saw all of this as he came of age. At first he was fascinated and awestruck by the Mafia and drawn to the power and charisma that was the Gotti family. Then he was abused by it. And finally he broke away from it. Did he become a witness to save his own skin? Without question. That's part of his story.

But there is so much more.

The everyday struggle to survive while growing up on the streets of Woodhaven, Queens. His chance to make it out by playing baseball in college. The lure of the drug trade. The money and the violence on the fringe and then at the epicenter of the mob. And finally his life on the run, a fascinating and then harrowing three-year experience that took him into and out of a dozen different countries before he settled in Brazil. First there were the sunny beaches and beautiful women of Copacabana. Then there were the rats and the dank, fetid cells of two of that country's most notorious prisons. Alite spent two years in that hell before being extradited back to the United States to face racketeering-murder charges.

Shortly after he was returned, in March 2007, he cut a deal and agreed to cooperate. Two years later he was on the witness stand.

"I believed in something that didn't exist," he now says in explaining his decision to turn on the mob. It's the same explanation he offered to two federal juries and one that he comes back to again and again in ongoing weekly sessions with a therapist.

The rules that are referred to repeatedly in this book come from Alite's own analysis of his life with the Gambino crime family. These were the codes and protocols, enunciated by John Gotti Sr., that Alite and everyone else in the organization had to live by. They weren't written down. There were no underworld tablets of stone. But they were hard and fast commandments nonetheless. And to violate any of them was to court death. Unless, of course, your name was Gotti.

I've spent most of my life working as a journalist. I've been taught to structure a story around the answers to four key questions, the four W's they teach in journalism school—Who? What? Where? When? I've always felt the most important question, however, and the one that brings more to any story, is the fifth W— Why? Why did Alite do what he did? The question applies to both his life on the streets and his decision to cooperate.

This book may provide an answer. Or it may, like his testimony, result in a hung jury.

What it certainly will do is deconstruct the myth that is the Gotti family. Honor, loyalty, nobility? Go read *The Godfather*. As this is being written, there is again talk of a movie to be produced by Junior and his media-savvy sister Victoria.

In the Shadow of My Father is the working title.

John Alite lived in the shadow of both Gottis. His story is decidedly different than the fantasy that Junior and Vicky Gotti are trying to spin.

George Anastasia
June 2014

CHAPTER 1

He wrapped the blade of the knife in tape, covered it with a greasy rag, taped it again, and finally slathered the entire weapon with oil. Then he very carefully inserted it, handle first, into his rectum. He was beyond the point of thinking about how crazy that might seem. It was about survival. And at the end of the day, John Alite always did what he had to do to survive.

He figured if he was going to die, he would go out fighting. All he wanted was a chance and the knife gave him that. He had been in Presídio Ary Franco, one of the worst hellholes in the Brazilian prison system, for about six months. He had learned how to get by and even prosper. Status and money worked on the inside as well as, and sometimes better than, they did on the streets.

But now he was jammed up. The corrupt warden of the prison had targeted him as a troublemaker. Alite and some of the other prisoners had organized a boycott. They weren't buying the contraband that the warden's minions brought into the prison each day. What's more, they had put out the word that any other prisoner who did would be beaten.

It was just one of the many power plays that took place every day in Ary Franco, but this one was costing the warden money, big money; maybe two or three thousand American dollars a week.

So he had decided that Alite, the cocky Mafioso from New York, would be punished.

In a few hours three or four guards and inmate trustees, prisoners loyal to the warden who served as his enforcers, would be coming for him. A prison guard who was in Alite's camp, who was a friend of both Alite and the leaders of the Commando Vermelho, had tipped him off. He knew what was coming, but there wasn't much he or his friends in the Red Command, a prominent Brazilian criminal organization that had power both on the streets and in the prisons, could do about it. The knife was his only option.

The guards and trustees would take him to a special cell in the bowels of the prison and deal with him. It happened all the time to inmates who had fallen out of favor. At the very least, Alite figured he was in for a severe beating. There was, he knew, a real chance that he could be killed.

He had thought his notoriety as an American prisoner—and a Mafioso at that—would offer him some protection, but he may have miscalculated. If he died in this rat's nest of a prison, the official explanation would exonerate the authorities. A knife fight among inmates? A dispute over contraband drugs? An accident? There were dozens of ways to explain the death. Who would really know? Or care?

Back in the States, the feds were continuing to target Junior Gotti and those around him. Had Alite, Gotti's one-time enforcer and business partner, not gone on the run, he would have been sitting in an American prison. Instead, as he had done for most of his life, he had chosen to fight on his own terms, in his own way. That's what led him to Brazil and to the prison cell where he now sat waiting.

Ary Franco had a reputation as the worst of the worst. Several years later, in 2011, a special United Nations investigation into prison problems in Brazil recommended that the prison be closed and its estimated fifteen hundred inmates relocated. When the findings of the U.N. panel were made public—stories of systemic corruption, filthy, bug-infested cells, cases of torture and abuse, wanton violence, and inmate murders—Brazil's justice minister, José Eduardo Cardozo, had this to say: "If I had to spend many years in one of our prisons, I would rather die."

Alite was long gone by the time that report was issued, but he didn't need a U.N. panel to tell him how bad things were. He had experienced it all firsthand. As he waited that day for the guards to come for him, he knew that death was an option.

It's almost impossible to describe the disconnect he was experiencing.

He was an American mobster arrested on an Interpol warrant after spending more than a year bouncing from the United States to Europe to Africa and then Central and South America. Along the way he had made three stops in Cuba. In retrospect, Alite thought as he tried to get comfortable with the foreign object stuck in his ass, he probably should have stayed in Havana. Interpol had no connections there and the chance of being extradited was minimal.

He had enough money and enough Cuban friends to make his life secure.

Instead, he had chosen Brazil. Not a bad choice when you think about it. He lived in a neighborhood in the Copacabana section of Rio, had developed friendships, taught boxing at a local gym, and had a girlfriend who was everything any guy thought about when he fantasized about the sensual, passionate, and beautiful women of that country.

But he had stayed too long. He knew it. He sensed it in the days leading up to his arrest. John Alite had lived and worked and committed crimes in many places and he was always aware of the world around him. Whether he was on a street corner in the Queens neighborhood where he grew up or on a train from Amsterdam to Paris, he could sense trouble. And in most cases, he could do something to avoid—or confront—it.

As he sat in his prison cell, he thought about all of that. What could have been. What should have been. In the short term, he knew he should have moved on. In fact, he was planning to do so. He was heading for Venezuela or Argentina or Colombia. The pieces were all in place. And then he found himself surrounded on a street corner not far from his apartment. A heavily armed SWAT team of Brazilian military police had appeared from nowhere, popping up from behind cars and out of alleyways. A helicopter circled overhead.

The news reports said it all. A dangerous American Mafia leader, wanted for murder, extortion, and racketeering, had been arrested on a street corner in Copacabana. "King of Crime in New York Arrested in Rio," screamed a headline in Portuguese the next day. The "king" reference was a little over-the-top, Alite knew, but it helped him once he was dumped in Ary Franco. All the inmates knew about John Alite and many wanted to befriend him. They had read or heard the stories about this top associate of John "Junior" Gotti, this high-ranking member of the Gambino crime family who had been taken into custody and was facing extradition to Tampa, Florida, where a multiple-count racketeering and murder indictment and a possible death sentence awaited him.

He was a wealthy American gangster, a gringo with cash and connections. Somebody worth knowing. That helped him make his way in the violent prison underworld.

His plan was to get bail while in Brazil, fight the extradition, and then skip the country if things didn't work out. Getting bail proved to be nearly impossible, however, so he had settled in and plotted an escape. Life was miserable, but not unbearable. Like any prison anywhere in the world, money helped. And he had plenty of that.

There was cash from the drug trade and the extortions. And there was money from his family, who, on his orders, had sold the properties he owned in New Jersey and wired the proceeds to his associates in Brazil.

Six months after his arrest on the Interpol warrant, Alite was still fighting extradition, still an inmate at Ary Franco. He knew that if he went back to Tampa he'd have few cards to play. It was a tough, conservative jurisdiction with no-nonsense judges and juries that had little time for New York gangsters. Life in prison or a lethal injection were his likely options if he returned. So he was toughing it out in Brazil, figuring out how to work the system and what his next move would be. Escape was a possibility, but not from Ary Franco. He'd have to arrange to be moved to a less secure facility. Money could make that happen.

While in Ary Franco, he also had lots of time to think and it might have been then that the idea of playing a final trump card surfaced. He would do whatever he had to do to survive, but whatever he did would be for himself and his family. That's family with a small *f*. He had four children from two different relationships. He had a girlfriend, more than one in fact. He had his mother and father and his brother and sisters and nieces and nephews and uncles and aunts. That was who he cared about and who he thought about.

The idea of the Mafia as "Family" was no longer relevant. He had come to that conclusion a long time ago, but never really had to face up to it. As he sat in prison going over where he'd been, what he'd done, and whether he'd ever be able to do any of it again, he began to think the unthinkable. Was he just looking for some self-justification for what he might eventually decide to do? Maybe. That's certainly how some people might interpret things after the fact. John Alite doesn't care.

"People who know me know why I did what I did," he said

several years later as he sat in a restaurant in southern New Jersey not far from Philadelphia, sipping a coffee and playing with an English muffin. "Other people should just mind their own business."

Other people hadn't seen what John Alite had seen. They hadn't experienced what he had experienced. Alite ultimately decided to become a witness for the U.S. Justice Department, testifying against Gotti Jr. and another former associate.

He got out of jail after ten years and is now putting his life back together.

That was the card he played and now he has to live with the results. He is okay with that. The money is gone, but in some circles, the status remains. He moves around the same way he had before he left New York. Still solidly built and in good shape—albeit years older and, he would say, wiser. With dark hair and piercing brown eyes, the five-foot-eight, heavily tattooed wiseguy walks with his head up and looks everyone squarely in the eye. He is not hiding, has no intention of doing so. He has been back to the old neighborhood and he has partied with old friends at popular nightspots in Queens and in Manhattan. He gets stares from some people, but others accept him for who he is.

Willie Boy Johnson, a mob associate not unlike himself, had given him one piece of advice as he moved toward the inner circle of the Gotti organization.

"Keep your eyes open and your mouth shut," said Johnson who, like Alite, turned on the Gottis. Willie Boy ended up dead as a result. John Alite is still very much alive.

Angelo Ruggiero, a made member of the crime family and at one point Gotti Sr.'s best friend, had also laid it out for him. Ruggiero was on his deathbed, ostracized by Gotti and persona non grata in the family.

"Johnny only cares about himself," Ruggiero had said. "Get away from him and his son."

Alite was thousands of miles from New York as he thought about those conversations and the other events in his life that had led to Ary Franco. While he could never be formally initiated into the Mafia because he was of Albanian descent, he knew that on the streets he was a smarter and more effective mobster than Gotti Jr. and most of the crime family crew that he worked with. He also knew that the Gottis were more form than substance; that the father had developed a media persona that had little to do with reality; that the son was a screwup who, had he had different bloodlines, would have been beaten silly or killed by someone long ago; and that the daughter, Victoria, was a spoiled Mafia princess who cared only about herself.

The Gottis were a soap opera long before Vicky got her own reality TV show. Alite had had a part, a long-running and highly lucrative part, in the story. But he knew that like Willie Boy and Ruggiero, he was expendable—a piece that the Gottis would discard if and when it benefited them. So deciding to cooperate, when he thought about it in those terms, was not that difficult. It was about survival. He would have to break the rules of the underworld if he cut a deal with the feds, but the Gottis, father and son, brothers and uncles, were breaking those rules long before Alite ever thought about it.

The Mafia doesn't deal drugs? Gotti Sr. made a fortune from the heroin trade and turned on associates who were in the business not because he opposed drug trafficking, but because they got caught. Alite knows this because Gotti Sr. used him to expand the drug business and because Ruggiero, one of those drug dealers, later confided in him.

Gotti Sr. was a man of honor? Ask Paul Castellano about that.

Ask the former mob boss of the Gambino crime family if he ever trusted the flashy mob capo out of Queens who had Castellano gunned down outside of Sparks Steak House in Midtown one cold December night.

The Gottis, Alite began to realize as he sat in his Brazilian prison cell, were a dysfunctional group of Mafia misfits who wrested control of one of the biggest crime syndicates in America and tore it apart. Nepotism, greed, and treachery replaced honor and loyalty when John J. Gotti took over. Junior Gotti followed in his father's footsteps. Manipulative like his dad, but surprisingly devoid of street smarts, "Blinkie" turned and ran on more than one occasion when he and Alite were on the streets together.

"They like to say I was his best friend," Alite says of the media reports about his relationship with the younger Gotti. "That's not true. I was his babysitter."

From Alite's perspective, Junior Gotti was a cheap-shot artist with a penchant for stabbing or gunning down unsuspecting victims, then scrambling to blame someone else when the heat came. He had a sense of entitlement that was not unlike that of other rich, spoiled sons of famous fathers.

These were some of the things that Alite thought about while he was on the run for more than a year and hearing reports that Gotti Jr. was trying to cut a deal with the government by giving up information at proffer sessions with federal prosecutors. Those same thoughts haunted him during quiet times in his Brazilian prison cell.

The guards came and got him late that afternoon. The first thing they told him to do was to strip naked. He knew that was part of the routine. Then they pulled him out of the crowded cell and led him down a hallway, through a doorway, and down a set of stairs. He tried to walk normally. He didn't want his gait to betray the fact that he was armed.

There were four guards with guns and two prison trustees who were carrying blackjacks. He recognized one of the trustees, Bomba, a burly lifer who was usually hopped up on steroids. He was the warden's guy. He did whatever he was told. In this case, Alite was sure, he was the one who would administer the beating.

It made sense. The guards would need deniability. There already was a lot of heat and bad publicity over a Chinese businessman who had been arrested at the airport with thirty thousand dollars stashed in his clothing. He was picked up on a currency violation. The businessman was on his way to the United States, where his wife and daughter had already relocated. Instead, he was sent to Ary Franco. Four days later he was dead. The autopsy report said he had been brutally beaten and tortured. Alite figured the businessman balked at paying off some guards. Seven of them had been charged. It had become an international incident.

This wasn't going to be another.

Trustees were merely inmates with semiofficial status. But they were still inmates and a fight between inmates was neither unusual nor surprising.

The guards and trustees led him to an isolated "dry cell," a cell without a toilet or a sink or electricity. It was under a stairwell in a remote area of the prison. They unlocked the door and pushed him in. The door was slammed shut. Alite stood in the dark, left alone to wait and wonder.

It took a while for his eyes to get acclimated. The cell was small, about ten feet by ten feet, and it had the foul smell of shit and piss and blood, the residue, he assumed, of the last session trustees had had with an inmate.

Leaving him alone was designed to instill fear. But Alite was strangely calm. He walked around the cell to get a better idea of his surroundings. It was difficult to see, but his eyes were adjusting. He moved to a corner, squatted, and pulled the knife out.

"When we wrapped the knife, we left a piece of string dangling from the tape," he said, explaining how several Brazilian inmates with the Red Command had helped him. "It was like a tampon. I just pulled on the string and the knife came out."

It had a small handle and blade of five or six inches that had been sharpened on stone and was almost razorlike.

Alite carefully unwrapped it. He threw the soiled rag and tape into another corner, out of the way. He didn't want to slip on them. Then he began to exercise with the knife in his hand, shadowboxing, doing squat thrusts and some push-ups.

His adrenaline was flowing when he heard the door opening.

"Are you ready, gringo?" said Bomba, the first one through the door.

Alite pounced, slamming the door shut on the other trustee and then lashing out at Bomba, whose eyes could not adapt quickly enough to the darkness. The first thrust of the knife went for the hand in which he held the blackjack. The blackjack fell to the floor.

The trustee screamed in fear and in surprise and in anger. Alite was on him now, slashing and stabbing. Although it seemed much longer, the attack was over in minutes. Bomba lay moaning on the floor as Alite pushed open the cell door. The other trustee stared in horror as the naked, blood-soaked prisoner came toward him. He screamed for help from the guards, but they were long gone. They didn't want to be held accountable for the beating they knew Alite was going to take from the two burly trustees. They were out of earshot. Alite slashed the second trustee across the stomach, a glancing blow, but enough to send him running.

Then it got quiet.

Alite walked alone back toward the cell block. The other prisoners looked up in surprise and then several began to cheer. One reached out his hand.

"Gringo," he said, "the knife."

Alite didn't understand at first, didn't even realize he was still holding the weapon. But then it came to him. He handed the inmate the knife and continued walking back toward his own cell. When other guards came to search, as he knew they would, they wouldn't find it.

"You do what you have to do to survive," John Alite said years later, sitting in a diner in South Jersey. "And unless you've been there, you don't really understand what that means."

It was impossible to tell if Alite was talking about the incident at Ary Franco or about his life as a Mafia enforcer, murderer, drug dealer, and extortionist turned government witness.

Maybe he was talking about both.

CHAPTER 2

John Gotti was livid. His son and several members of his young crew had gotten into a fight outside the Arena, a popular club on Metropolitan Avenue in Queens. It wasn't bad enough that Junior and his guys were acting like jerks. That was a fairly common occurrence. What was more troubling was that the Arena was linked to a high-ranking member of the Genovese crime family. Acting up at a place like that was a sign of disrespect.

But Junior and his crew never thought in those terms. Punching, shoving, and shouting, a bunch of young guys were having at it. It happened more often than you'd imagine. This time someone from the Gotti crew pulled a gun and shot a kid in the thigh. Everyone scattered.

The victim happened to be the nephew of Genovese crime family capo Ciro Perrone.

"It was a punk-ass thing to do!" Gotti screamed. "You gonna shoot somebody, shoot 'em. Don't punk-shoot 'em. Who did it?"

Gotti was talking to John Alite, one of the newer members of his son's crew. Alite said he didn't know. Junior Gotti sat at his father's side, silent. Several other members of the Gotti organization, including Angelo Ruggiero, Gotti's best friend and Junior's godfather, and Willie Boy Johnson stood off to the side, waiting.

"Everybody in the room knew it was his fuckin' son who had

done the shooting," Alite said as he recounted a story that defined his life with the Gottis. "I had stepped in front of Junior during the fight. I got between him and this other kid. From behind me, Junior pulls out this derringer, reaches around my body and shoots the kid. A cheap shot. His father was right. It was a punk thing to do. But I'm not gonna tell him it was his son. I'm taking the heat. I don't say shit."

After Gotti finished his tirade, he called Ruggiero and Johnson to the side and had a whispered conversation. They then escorted Alite across the street to the Bergin Hunt and Fish Club, the family's mob clubhouse.

"Angelo told me they were supposed to give me a beating," said Alite, who at that point was still recovering from an assault that had left him hospitalized for nearly a month. "They told me to just take off, to not come around the clubhouse for a couple of weeks. They were gonna tell John they gave me a beatin' and I was in the hospital. Angelo knew what had happened. 'My fuckin' godson's no good,' he said, 'but what are we gonna do?'

"This is the kind of shit I had to deal with, day in and day out. The father was a tyrant and the son was a pussy. And I was in the middle. That's what people don't know about the Gottis. That's what they were really like."

Gotti Sr. controlled the crime family with an iron fist. There was a strict and often bizarre set of rules that Alite learned early on. But the primary rule was this: the Gottis did whatever they wanted, to whomever they wanted, whenever they wanted. The rules didn't apply to them.

___

John Gotti's Rules of Leadership: Whenever possible, underlings must take the weight of a crime pending against Gotti or his family.

___

It wasn't the first time that Alite was left hanging by Junior. But it was the first time that some older members of the organization privately expressed their opinions. Alite had been around the Gottis for less than a year and was still feeling his way. This was supposed to be a special organization built around honor and loyalty. He was beginning to wonder.

The Gottis talked the talk, but their actions said something else. The father was charismatic and had a loyal group of followers, guys that Alite looked up to. The son? That was a different story.

Alite got involved with Junior sometime in 1983. He had met him before that, but it was just a casual hello, how ya doin' kind of thing. Of course he knew who Junior was. More important, who his father was. You didn't live in Woodhaven, Ozone Park, or Howard Beach in the 1980s without knowing who John Gotti was.

And if you were moving small amounts of cocaine, as Alite was at the time, you would come under the Gotti umbrella. Alite had been dealing with guys who were part of Junior's crew. He also had a relationship with Sonny DiGiorgio, who worked for Angelo Ruggiero. DiGiorgio was the cousin of John Gotti's wife, Victoria. Alite, who had his own small cocaine operation, would occasionally help DiGiorgio in low-level heroin deals. DiGiorgio had a connection at Rikers Island, a prison guard. They used the guard to smuggle smack into the prison, where there was a ready and captive market. Alite was little more than a mule, taking the drugs to the guard and the money back to DiGiorgio, but he was able to pick up some extra cash and it was another important neighborhood connection.

Later he would learn that the heroin deals at Rikers were part of Ruggiero's bigger drug operation, an operation that Gotti claimed to know nothing about but from which he was making tens of thousands of dollars each week.

"Turns out everybody in that crew was involved in drugs,"

Alite said. "They were all making big money. Nobody was supposed to talk about it, but everybody knew."

Alite wasn't making a lot of money at this point, but hoped to. The mob, he knew, could help him get to where he wanted to be. He and the guys he was around were moving marijuana and cocaine through the bars in their neighborhood in Queens. That's how he made the connection with Junior Gotti, according to his testimony at two different trials.

They first met around 1981. It was a casual friendship. They were around the same age—Alite was nineteen, Junior was eighteen—and moved in the same circles, hanging in bars and clubs in the neighborhood. Two years later, they started doing business together.

Johnny Gebert, a kid Alite had grown up with, set things up. It was the summer of 1983. Alite had just gotten back from California, banished there by his father, who had tried to get him away from the streets. It didn't work. He came back to Queens and went back to dealing drugs.

Gebert told Alite that Junior wanted to see him. Alite knew right away what it was about. He also suspected that Gebert had pushed the issue, telling Junior that Alite was making money bigtime. It wasn't true. Alite might have been grossing about two grand a week, but not even half of that ended up in his pocket. When Junior said he wanted a weekly kick of five hundred dollars, Alite shook his head and laughed.

"I told him I wasn't making that kind of money," Alite said. "I don't know if he believed me or if he even cared. All Junior ever cared about was his end. The point of meeting me was that he was going to get something from me."

Junior knew Alite had been to college and used that to bust his balls, called him "College Boy," not as a term of endearment, but as a way to belittle him. After some negotiating, it was agreed that Alite would give Gebert two hundred dollars a week to pass on to Junior. At the time, Alite wasn't moving weight. He might grab a quarter kilo of cocaine from a source, break it down, step on it, and put together small ten-dollar packages that three or four people who worked for him would sell in selected bars along Jamaica Avenue.

Alite would later describe Gebert as a "rabid dog" who had been "a criminal from the age of eleven." He didn't trust him or particularly like him, but he was happy to make the Gotti connection through him. Once Alite started kicking up, he moved closer to Junior, who would stop around the neighborhood from time to time. Alite knew how to make money and that attracted Junior.

The first job they pulled together should have been a warning to Alite that things weren't what they seemed. Gebert had a beef with a crew of Jamaican drug dealers who had ripped him off. They set up a marijuana deal, but when he showed up, they beat him with brass knuckles and stole his cash. He was out several thousand dollars and he wanted revenge. He also wanted to establish the pecking order on the street. Gebert was with Junior. Junior was with his father. Nobody fucked with John Gotti. The fact that Gotti might not have been aware of what was going on was of no matter. His name was thrown around by all kinds of hustlers and wannabe gangsters. Gebert was a little more than a poseur, however, because he had a legitimate link to the son. That's the way Alite saw it anyway.

"This was my first chance to make an impression on the Gottis, which was something I wanted to do," he said. According to Alite, Junior set it up. "Gebert knew the storefront where the Jamaicans hung out. We were going to drive by and shoot 'em."

The plan was simple. Alite would be the driver in the lead car. Gebert would be the shooter in the front passenger seat. Junior and an associate named Jerry were to follow in a blocking car, a standard mob move in any shooting. The blocking car was there to jam up traffic in the event the cops showed up. This would give the shooter a chance to get away. Not really a complicated plan and one that should have gone off without a hitch. But on the night the shooting was to go down, Gebert showed up high. He had been smoking angel dust. He apparently needed the drug to amp up his courage.

Alite just shook his head.

It was early evening. The storefront where the Jamaicans hung out was at 117th Street and Jamaica Avenue in the Richmond Hill section of Queens. Junior had his own social club at 113th Street and Liberty Avenue, which was where they met. Alite said Junior supplied a stolen car for Alite to drive and handed Gebert a .38-caliber pistol.

They made one pass of the storefront and then circled back around. Alite slowed the car as they approached the location a second time and Gebert leaned out the open window. He got off five or six shots. Alite saw three or four guys who had been standing in front of the clubhouse scatter. He wasn't sure if anyone had been hit.

"Drive!" shouted Gebert in a panicked laugh.

Almost immediately, Alite heard police sirens. He tried to stay calm, to drive normally. The plan was to turn left at the second street past the storefront, head toward Atlantic Avenue, and then work their way back to Junior's social club. Alite made the left, but when he looked in the rearview mirror he saw Junior, in the blocking car, continue down Jamaica Avenue, away from the shooting scene. Then, at the next stop sign, Gebert jumped out of the car and took off on foot, leaving the gun on the floor below the passenger seat.

"Son of a bitch, I'm all alone," Alite said. "I hear the sirens. I got no blocker. I know I gotta ditch the car and the gun. What the fuck? At that point, I wanted to kill Gebert. And I wasn't too crazy about Junior, either."

He drove two more blocks, turned down a narrow street, and stopped. He left the car in the middle of the street, opened both front doors to block the cops from maneuvering around the vehicle, and took off on foot. He dumped the gun in a nearby trash can, stopped at a store to buy a soda, then took off his shirt and began to casually jog back toward the clubhouse.

The run gave him time to think and also allowed him to calm down. He was just a kid out for a run. Nothing unusual about that if the cops came on him. They didn't. But no thanks to either Gebert or Junior.

The drive-by shooting of the Jamaicans gave Alite an idea of the kind of people he was dealing with. When he asked Junior what had happened (Gebert was nowhere to be found), Junior blamed Jerry for the mix-up. He said he got confused and panicked when he heard the police sirens. Alite knew it was bullshit, but he wasn't about to challenge Junior. He had his foot in the door with the Gotti organization and he wanted to stay there. He was making decent money on the street and knew that with the Gambino organization behind him, he could make even more.

Dealing drugs and booking sports were two things he knew very well. On his own, he could make a living, but he would always have to kick up to the Gottis. But if he worked with Junior, it would be others who kicked up to him. Alite knew all of this intuitively. He didn't sit down one day and say to himself, I'm gonna connect with Junior Gotti and make myself a fortune, but that's what he did.

Alite had grown up in a lower-middle-class section of Woodhaven. His upbringing was hardly the same as the pampered, organized-crime-funded childhood of Junior Gotti, who grew up just a few miles away, in Howard Beach. 'There were six of us living in a four-room apartment," Alite said of his home. "When my sneakers wore out I had to use tape to hold them together."

He was a product of the streets, where he learned that you took the opportunities that presented themselves. No one was going to hand you money. If you were smart and if you weren't afraid to take chances, you could get ahead. If you had the mob behind you, you could go even further.

Alite, twenty-two years old and on the make, decided that the Gottis offered him the best opportunity for advancement. He jumped at the chance. It was a life of money, murder, and mayhem. He adapted quite easily.

One of the first benefits of the Jamaican escapade was his enhanced standing with Junior. Now he was hanging out on a regular basis with the young wiseguy. Three, four, sometimes five days a week. As Alite would later tell the FBI, they were working deals, talking about money and business ventures, setting up their own sports book, and, allegedly, according to Alite, expanding the drug business. And Junior stopped calling him "College Boy."

Eventually word got back to the father that Alite was a new member of Junior's crew. A few weeks later, Alite was told that John Gotti Sr. wanted to meet him. He was ordered to show up at the Bergin Hunt and Fish Club one afternoon. When he arrived, Gotti Sr. said, "Let's take a walk."

They hit it off.

"He told me he liked me," Alite recalled.

John Gotti's Rules of Leadership: No member of any crew, in the presence of the boss, may wear sunglasses.

"I knew Junior had a bunch of wannabes around him and the father knew that, too. He saw me as somebody who was different. I wasn't afraid of anything or anybody. And I'd do anything. He liked that. We're in the middle of a conversation, we're walking on the street, he stops, and it's like he's looking at me for the first time."

Alite didn't know what to think. His mind raced. He was trying to determine if he had said something wrong.

" 'Hey, John,' Gotti said, 'take off those fuckin' sunglasses. Only rats wear shades so you can't look in their eyes when they're talking.' "

Alite quickly complied and Gotti picked up the thread of his earlier conversation. He wanted Alite to look out for his son, to work with him.

"Get one thing straight," Gotti said. "I've already lost one son. I'm not losing another." (Frankie Gotti, just twelve, was killed when the motorbike he was riding was accidentally struck by a neighbor's car.)

"I really don't know you yet," Gotti continued. "My son somehow always seems to pick friends who are useless junk piles. . . . So far, I don't see you as one of the usual garbage bags, far from it, but you still need to convince me."

Alite jumped at the chance. The son brought him to the father. The father had power and status. That's what life in the underworld was all about.

Or so Alite thought.

Life with the Gottis was much more.

"It was a soap opera," he says. "Nobody knows the real story. Nobody would believe it."

In addition to Junior, Alite met Vicky Gotti, the younger daughter of the mob boss, a Mafia princess who had an over-the-top sense of entitlement. There was also Mrs. Gotti, the elder Victoria, whom her husband referred to as "Butch." A cigarette held between two fingers, a string of expletives spewing from her mouth, she was a mob matriarch who said whatever came into her mind, no matter the consequences.

There were also Gotti's brothers: Pete, who was referred to as "the Garbage Man" because he had once worked in the Sanitation Department; and Richie, known as "Pea Brain" for what became obvious reasons.

Alite spent a lot of time with the Gotti family and, looking back on it now, realizes he was there mostly to clean up the mess and keep Junior Gotti out of harm's way. If that meant Alite had to take a fall or a beating, so be it. He quickly learned to anticipate problems. And with the Gottis there were always problems. *Time* magazine might have had the father's picture on its cover and the entertainment and movie business may have glorified the "Teflon Don," but that wasn't the man or the family that Alite came to know. Years later, Vicky's obnoxious reality TV show *Growing Up Gotti* was surprisingly closer to the truth than Armand Assante's portrayal of the Don in a television movie.

"They say it was about honor and loyalty, but it never was," Alite said. "They only cared about money and didn't care how you made it. They told me one of the rules was you couldn't deal drugs. What they meant was if you got caught, you were on your own. But they wanted their end.

"The father was getting a hundred thousand dollars a month from a big-time heroin dealer named Mark Reiter. I was friends with his son Greg. And Junior had a piece of everybody's action on the street." Alite would tell a federal jury that Junior started setting Alite up with some suppliers.

Alite heard the same refrain from both Junior and Angelo Ruggiero—if you're gonna deal drugs, go big-time. Don't be a penny-ante street corner hustler. Junior told him not to be a "nickel-and-dime junk dealer." He pointed to his uncle Gene, his godfather, Angelo Ruggiero, and Johnny Carneglia. They were big-time heroin dealers and top associates of his father. There was a ban on dealing drugs within the crime family, but those guys just ignored the rule. And Gotti Sr., who had a financial interest, didn't seem to care.

Junior told Alite those guys lived well. They traveled. They had private jets that brought the stuff up to New York.

"He told me if you're gonna get in, get in," Alite would tell the jury.

The upside was obvious. The money was staggering. But the price could be significant. If you got jammed up, you were on your own. Ruggiero would learn that the hard way.

But those were things Alite would deal with later. For now he was sitting on top of the world. He had a network in place and he had the power of the mob behind him. For a kid who grew up poor, it was like hitting the lottery.

"I liked the attention," he would tell a federal jury. "I liked the money. I liked everything about the life."

Part of that life was built around his reputation as a brawler who would never back down. He was only five foot eight, but he worked out regularly and knew how to box. More important, he was fearless. He'd take on anyone, anytime and anyplace.

The White Castle on Rockaway Boulevard was the scene of one of his more memorable confrontations.

One summer night in 1984 Alite was driving around in his father's Monte Carlo when he spotted Monique, a girl from the neighborhood he sometimes dated and often hung out with at O'Brother's and the White Horse, two bars along Jamaica Avenue. It was two in the morning. He asked her if she wanted a ride. They were both bored.

"Let's go get some burgers at the White Castle," she said.

When they pulled up, Alite spotted a friend, Mitch Sanders. Alite stayed in the car and Monique went to get the burgers. A few minutes later, Junior pulled up in another car with Johnny Boy Ruggiero, Angelo's son; a kid named Frankie; and Joe O'Kane. They were all part of Junior's crew.

As they were talking, Alite looked into the White Castle and saw a group of guys hassling Monique. There were five or six of them. They were drinking beers and being obnoxious. One turned around, pulled down his jeans, and flashed his ass in her face.

Alite didn't say anything to Junior or the others. He just got out of his car and walked into the restaurant. He approached the flasher.

"You got a problem keepin' your pants on?" he asked.

"Fuck you" was the reply.

Alite punched the guy in the face. One of the others hit him over the head with a beer bottle and at some point he was stabbed in the face with an ice pick. Junior and the others came running and a brawl broke out inside the restaurant. The other patrons scattered and the manager called the police.

With the sirens, the fighting stopped. Alite's face had blown up like a balloon. He and Monique got into the Monte Carlo and headed up 101st Street toward Woodhaven Boulevard. She was looking at Alite, telling him he had to get to a hospital, that there was something wrong with his face. Then she screamed, "Look out!"

Alite looked to his left and saw a monster pickup truck bearing down on him.

"It was three of the guys from the White Castle," he said. "They rammed my car. Those big wheels went right up on the hood, drove me off the road and into a tree. We were pinned inside."

The three brawlers got out of the truck with baseball bats and started to whale away at the windshield. Alite put Monique under him and tried to fend off the bats as he crawled out through the hole where the windshield had been. Junior pulled up with the other guys, but when another driver stopped and said he was call-ing the police, they took off. So did two of the guys in the truck.

Alite saw it all in a blur. He remembers Joe O'Kane, a young kid, maybe seventeen years old, staying to help him fight off the guys with the baseball bats. He remembers running after one of the guys, a burly, three-hundred-pound thug, and beating him with his own bat. Then he collapsed. He was rushed to Jamaica Hospital in an ambulance and underwent emergency surgery. He had a broken arm, his insides were caved in—his pancreas was se-verely damaged—and it took more than a hundred stitches to sew up the gashes on his face, head, and body. Before they wheeled him into surgery he regained consciousness. One of the last things he saw was his father and other members of his family in a fist-fight in the hospital with the family members of the guy from the monster truck whom he and O'Kane had pummeled.

Alite was in intensive care for two weeks and then spent an-other week in recovery. Junior and the others visited him and laughed and joked about what had happened. They were pumped up about some other development as well. Junior couldn't keep his mouth shut.

He told Alite how some friends of his father had "helped" a guy named John Cennamo commit suicide. About a year earlier Cennamo had been in the Silver Fox Bar when another brawl broke out. Junior apparently stabbed a kid named Danny Silva. Silva died.

Junior used to talk about the stabbing as if it were some-thing to be proud of, Alite recalled. He boasted about killing Silva, saying "I put him down." It sounded like he was talking about an animal. A federal prosecutor later told a jury that after the brawl, Junior Gotti went back to the bar where Silva lay on the floor bleeding out. Gotti, according to the prosecutor and a witness at the scene, looked down at Silva, and in a Porky Pig voice said, "That's all folks." He then left the murder scene for a second time.

Cennamo was the only witness who fingered Junior as the person who had stabbed Silva. Junior denied the allegation and privately said it was Mark Caputo, another member of his crew, who had committed the murder. Alite would testify that this was a typical Gotti move, but one that he was seeing for the first time. It didn't really matter, because the murder case never went anywhere.

Cennamo wasn't able to testify. Several months after the March 1983 murder of Danny Silva, he was found hanging by the neck from a tree behind a Laundromat in St. Albans, Queens.

The death was ruled a suicide, but Cennamo's family never believed it. No one has ever been charged, but as he lay in the hospital bed recovering from the White Castle brawl, Alite later told a jury, he watched and listened as Junior joked about it.

"He went to the window. My room looked out over the Van Wyck Expressway, and he pretended to see something," Alite said. "He laughed. The other guys laughed. He said something like, 'Hey, look. Can you see him hanging from that tree?'" Alite said Junior joked about how the kid had had help getting the noose around his neck.

Alite would later tell authorities that Junior said his father had taken care of it and that Angelo Ruggiero, Willie Boy Johnson, and John Carneglia committed the "suicide." To Alite, the lesson was simple. Everyone in the neighborhood understood—no one testified against a Gotti.

"I was in intensive care for two weeks and in and out of the hospital for the next two months," Alite said. "I was walking with a cane. In fact, I had the cane the night we got into that fight at the

Arena." That was the night when Alite said Junior stood behind him and shot Ciro Perrone's nephew with the derringer.

Alite didn't bring the cane to the meeting with Gotti Sr. He didn't want to look any more vulnerable than he was. He also knew going in that he wasn't going to give up Junior. He didn't want to end up like John Cennamo, with a noose around his neck, hanging from a tree.

CHAPTER 3

It was a hostile takeover, in the purest sense of that term.

On a cold night in December 1985, Paul Castellano, the boss of the Gambino crime family, was gunned down in front of Sparks Steak House, a posh Midtown restaurant. Castellano was on his way to a meeting with Frank DeCicco. He never made it to the door. Big Paulie and his bodyguard and driver, Tommy Bilotti, were executed as they got out of their Lincoln Town Car. Four gunmen, dressed in white trench coats and wearing thick, black, Russian-style winter hats, took both of them out.

John Gotti and Salvatore "Sammy the Bull" Gravano watched it all go down from their car, which was parked about a half block away. Within two weeks, John J. Gotti, then just forty-five years old, was the new boss of the biggest crime family in New York, and, by extension, the country.

The hit was against all rules of the Mafia. No one takes down a sitting boss without the approval of the Commission, a Mafia tribunal made up of the leaders of the five New York crime families. Gotti ignored the prohibition. He couldn't seek Commission approval because what the hit really was about was drugs.

His brother Gene, his best friend Angelo Ruggiero, and a top associate, John Carneglia, had been indicted for dealing heroin.

Wiretapped conversations, which were part of the case and would eventually be made public, had sealed the deal for the feds.

On one tape, recorded in 1982, Ruggiero and Gene Gotti discussed the situation and the jeopardy they both were in. Ruggiero told Gene Gotti that Castellano and Vincent "the Chin" Gigante, the leader of the powerful Genovese crime family, were in agreement. Anyone dealing drugs would be killed, no questions asked.

The two mob bosses had "made a pact," Ruggiero explained.

"Any friend of ours that gets pinched for junk, or that they hear of anything about junk, they kill him," Ruggiero said as the FBI tape rolled. "No administration meetings, no nothing. Just gonna kill him. They're not warning nobody, not telling nobody because they feel the guy is gonna rat."

There were dozens of other tapes that clearly put all three in the "junk" business. Ruggiero was the most talkative. As the case moved toward trial, the defense attorneys, under the rules of pretrial discovery, were being given all the evidence the feds had gathered, including transcripts of the incriminating wiretapped conversations. It was just a matter of time before Castellano got access to them.

The Gotti crew had also lost an ally who might have been able to hold Castellano off. Longtime crime family underboss Aniello Dellacroce had died of cancer on December 2, 1985, two weeks before the Castellano shooting. Dellacroce was in many ways more highly regarded in the family than Castellano. He was a "gangster," while Castellano was a "racketeer." The perception was that Big Paulie was more interested in the business end of the underworld than in the day-in, day-out struggle to survive that was the life of most guys under him.

Castellano had taken over the family when his brother-in-law Carlo Gambino died in 1976. Guys like Ruggiero, the Gotti brothers, and Carneglia didn't respect him as much as they did

Dellacroce. They understood the pecking order and recognized Castellano as boss, but they thought he had inherited the spot. He didn't earn it. He also had more money than anyone and his prohibition on drug dealing was based at least in part on the fact that he didn't need the money.

It wasn't a moral question. That was an issue built out of a romantic vision of the Mafia painted by Mario Puzo. The reality was that the prohibition was a pragmatic decision. If you were secure in your position in the underworld, dealing drugs was a high-risk proposition. You were coming in contact with low-life narcotics traffickers who would sell you out in a minute. You ran the risk of using your own product or having members of your organization use it, in which case they became undependable. And you exposed yourself to more serious law enforcement scrutiny.

Those were the real reasons for the ban on dealing drugs.

The tapes of Gene Gotti, Ruggiero, and Carneglia gave the government a solid case on which to build a drug trafficking racketeering indictment. More important, they gave Castellano what he was looking for. With the death of Dellacroce, Castellano decided to break up the Gotti crew. He was correctly suspicious of the loyalty there. With the drug charges, he had the justification for permanently eliminating some of John Gotti's top associates.

The tapes confirmed beyond any doubt that John Gotti's guys had been major players in the drug underworld, big-time heroin dealers. The situation left Gotti with few choices. He could take out his top three guys, or go down with them.

He decided a preemptive strike was the better course of action. He'd deal with the ramifications later. It was a risky move. Five years earlier a similar situation had existed in Philadelphia. In March 1980, Angelo Bruno, the longtime boss of the Philadelphia–South Jersey crime family and a close friend of the late Carlo Gambino and Castellano, had been shotgunned to death outside his South Philadelphia row house. The hit went down on a rainy Friday night.

It was orchestrated by Antonio "Tony Bananas" Caponigro, Bruno's Newark-based consigliere. Like Ruggiero, Carneglia, and Gene Gotti, Caponigro had been dealing heroin and found Bruno's stance against drug trafficking hypocritical.

One of Bruno's top associates, Raymond "Long John" Martorano, was a major player in the meth trade in the City of Brotherly Love and the consensus was that Bruno got a piece of that action through a phony position as a "salesman" for a vending machine company that Martorano and his brother owned.

Bruno had also allowed Giuseppe and Rosario Gambino, distant Sicilian cousins of Carlo, to set up shop in Cherry Hill, New Jersey, just across the river from Philadelphia. The brothers opened a restaurant called Valentino's, but their real business was heroin trafficking. They were part of what later became known as the Pizza Connection.

The Gambino brothers had been invited to Bruno's home for Easter dinner. Caponigro and others around him were certain they came bearing an envelope full of cash. And they were just as certain that cash came from dealing *babania*.

What Caponigro hadn't anticipated, and what Gotti would have to deal with as well, was the treachery within the underworld. Caponigro thought he had Commission approval to take out Bruno. He was led to believe this by several leaders of the Genovese organization who saw a way to remove both Bruno and Caponigro from the scene, thereby destabilizing the Philadelphia family at a time when the casino gambling boom in Atlantic City was just beginning. Philadelphia had long controlled the seaside resort, but until casinos, no one thought the city was worth much. Now there was money to be made.

Caponigro went to New York for a meeting about a week after

Bruno was killed. He thought he was coming back as the new boss. Two days later his body was found in the trunk of a car abandoned in the South Bronx. He had been beaten and tortured before he was killed. Twenty-dollar bills were stuffed in his mouth and his anus, a sign, underworld watchers said, that he had been killed because he had gotten too greedy. More important, the murder of Caponigro (and three of his associates believed to have been involved in the Bruno hit) was a way to maintain underworld order. You don't kill a boss without Commission approval.

John Gotti would have problems with that same Genovese crime family in the wake of the Castellano hit. But he managed to avoid Caponigro's fate. Gravano later testified about the situation.

"Every family sent their blessings and they accepted it," he said of Gotti's ascension to the top spot, "except the Genovese family." Instead, there was a warning. The rules had been broken and "someday somebody would have to answer for that," Gravano said he was told.

By the time the Castellano hit went down, Alite had worked his way back into favor with Gotti Sr. The Arena shooting incident was forgotten. Alite was spending part of each day with Junior and was a regular at both the Bergin Hunt and Fish Club in Queens and the Ravenite, a social club on Mulberry Street that became Gotti's Manhattan base.

One day late in November 1985, about a month before the Castellano murder, Alite was asked to take a ride with Junior and his father. The elder Gotti drove, which was unusual to begin with. And he seemed jumpy. Alite said Gotti was very talkative during the car ride, which was out of character.

"He was just acting funny," Alite said. "He took me and Junior with him and drove out to Staten Island to Castellano's house. He had to drop off some Christmas presents. He was trying to act casual, but he was kidding around more than he ever did. To me, he seemed uptight. I think he took us because he wanted somebody there when he went in the house. Probably told Paul he had two kids in the car outside. We waited about an hour before he came out and drove back to the city."

About a week later, the same scene was replayed. This time Gotti asked Bobby Boriello and Alite to drive out with him. Again they waited in the car while Gotti met with Castellano.

Whether those meetings were discussions about the drug case is open to speculation. But it would make sense. Gotti might have been trying to take Castellano's temperature. Dellacroce was dying and it would just be a matter of time before Castellano made a move.

"After the shooting—everybody knew who was behind it—we were on call twenty-four-seven," Alite said. "And everyone was told to bring their guns. Before that, whenever you went to one of the clubhouses, you weren't supposed to have a gun. But for those weeks after the Castellano murder, it was high alert."

But along with the caution came arrogance, Alite said.

"Everybody was more cocky, all of us," he said. "It was all over the news. It was everywhere. He was the new boss of bosses."

As he looks back on it now, Alite is still amazed that Gotti was able to pull off the coup and then survive the aftermath.

"He talked about the rules, he talked about honor, but here he was breaking the biggest rule of all, killing a boss, and nobody did nothin'," Alite said. "We were kids. We weren't schooled in all that stuff. But those older guys, they shoulda known. They shoulda done something. Instead, they all rolled over for him."

It was just one more example of the Gottis talking the talk, but then doing whatever was in their own best interest. Alite had seen it on a smaller scale for more than a year. Shortly after the drive-by shooting of the Jamaicans, there was a situation with another local drug dealer, named Kevin Bonner.

Bonner was in the coke business with a guy named George

Grosso, who happened to be John Gebert's brother-in-law. They were moving product in the same general area as Alite, in the bars and pubs along Jamaica Avenue, and, according to both Kevin Bonner's and Alite's trial testimony, they were kicking up to Junior. But, as Alite would tell the court, that didn't matter when Junior saw a chance to make an even bigger score.

Johnny Boy Ruggiero, Angelo's son, was part of Junior's crew. Since Angelo was Junior's godfather, Junior and Johnny Boy were like cousins. The younger Ruggiero was always talking about "expanding" the business, Alite said. Alite testified that he and Junior made a connection with a supplier named Tony Kelly, who would sell them weight, a kilo or more at a time. Alite was still dealing in quarter kilos.

Junior brought up the idea, once again teasing Alite about being penny ante, then prodding him about going big. The plan was to go in as partners with Kevin Bonner. Kilos went for about forty thousand dollars at that time. Junior, Alite, and Bonner would each put up one-third.

Alite was fine with the idea, but Bonner balked.

"He didn't want to leave George Grosso," Alite said.

So Junior sent some friends to persuade him.

"I'm on Jamaica Avenue one day when Junior drives up with some guys from his crew, including Johnny Boy and Greg Reiter, a tough kid who was a friend of mine," Alite said. "Junior asks if Bonner is still balking. When I tell him he is, Junior says stay on the avenue. We'll be back in a few minutes."

Bonner had two guys selling cocaine out of the White Horse Tavern and Nino's Pub. A few minutes later, Alite would tell the court, he saw Junior's car pull up on the two guys, who were standing outside the tavern. Junior got out of the car and watched as the others, armed with baseball bats, went after Bonner's two drug dealers.

"They baseball-batted them," Alite said. "They threw one of the kids through the window of a bridal shop on Eighty-Sixth Street. Then they got in the car and drove away. Nobody said a thing."

That wasn't entirely accurate. The next day, according to Alite, Kevin Bonner said, "Okay."

The first purchase went down a few days later at Shell Bank in Howard Beach. Bonner fronted some of the money. The rest would be paid after the fact. Tony Kelly went to the trunk of his car, pulled out a package, and handed it to Alite. It was a kilo of coke. They headed back to an apartment, where they split the package. Bonner took a third and Alite kept the rest. According to Alite, he and Junior would share in the profits from the sale of the two-thirds of a kilo after he cut and packaged it.

Alite would later tell a jury that this was the start of an expansion that would eventually generate more than $100,000 a month in profits for each of them. He said they cornered the coke market up and down Jamaica Avenue and in several other neighborhoods in Queens. Anyone else who was dealing had to buy from them or kick up to them. At its high point, the business was moving up to eight kilos of coke a week, he said. It was a heady time for Alite, who couldn't believe his good fortune. And he traced it all back to his association with John Gotti Jr.

"I grew up, my father was a taxi driver," he would later explain to a jury. "I had no money. I wore tee-shirts and chinos. When I got to know him [Junior], it was a big thing. I would walk around, people knew who he was, who his father was, knew what the Gambino family was. Everyday people, the public like yourselves would treat us a lot different. When I went to restaurants, I didn't wait. When I went to shows, I got the best seats. I went to tailors. Had my shirts made at David Nadler's in Brooklyn. We went to stores and got suits custom-made. We got treated like we were celebrities. It was something I wasn't used to when I grew up."

Alite gave up a part of who he was in order to live that life. At first he was willing, happy even, to make the trade-off. Later he would see it for what it really was. He was being used and abused by the Gottis. Trying to explain it in simple street terms at Junior Gotti's trial, he told a jury, "The only way to understand it was, I was a prostitute and he was a pimp."

Today Alite looks back at some of the things he agreed to do and cringes. Not the murders and the violence per se. That was part of his character, part of the image he wanted to project. And it was part of the world in which he was living. Everyone knew that violence was part of the life. If you dealt drugs, if you associated with mobsters, if you ran cons or tried to scam and hustle someone in the underworld, you could get rich or you could get hurt. It was Willie Lomanesque. It came with the territory. Alite admits that he was "wild" and used it to his advantage.

It was the petty stuff, the "unnecessary violence," that still bothers him.

"I always thought of myself as the good bad guy," he said.

There was another drug supplier, a neighborhood kid, from whom Alite used to buy quarter and half kilos of cocaine. After they established the connection with Kelly, the kid was irrelevant.

"He was a decent guy, not into violence, even though he was in the drug business," Alite recalled as he told the story from the witness stand. "I grew up with him. He was a friend of my sister's. Junior says, 'Let's rob him.'"

So, according to Alite, they did. Alite said he set up what was supposed to be a buy at an apartment the kid and his partner kept on Ninety-Eighth Street off Jamaica Avenue. Alite went up first, but left the door open. Gotti and an associate came up minutes later waving guns around. The kid was pistol-whipped. Alite fell on the floor and, as they had planned, Gotti kicked him in the face. He ended up with a black eye. The move was to convince the kid that Alite had nothing to do with the robbery. They grabbed a quarter kilo of coke, which Alite cut, packaged, and put on the street. Alite testified that he and Gotti shared the revenue, which amounted to 100 percent profit. All that Alite had had to do was give up a friend.

But in the Gotti organization, friends were nothing more than pawns, interchangeable parts to be used and then discarded.

Angelo Ruggiero was John Gotti's lifelong friend. Yet Gotti put him on the shelf. Ruggiero and Gotti used to hijack trucks together when they were first coming up. Ruggiero introduced Gotti to Dellacroce and helped get him made. But Gotti was all about public perception, both in the media and in the underworld. Angelo Ruggiero had been picked up on dozens of FBI tapes talking about the heroin business. Never mind that Gotti's brother Gene and John Carneglia were part of the same case. Gotti was going to make an example of Ruggiero. It was his way to establish the new administration.

"He needed a fall guy," said Alite. "It wasn't about dealing drugs, it was about getting caught. Gotti was making a fortune in the drug business, but no one was supposed to know it. In the beginning, I think Junior and his sister Vicky really believed their father wasn't involved in drugs. Hell, everybody in our crew, everybody around Senior, was dealing. But he wanted to make an example of Ruggiero."

Ruggiero was dying of cancer when Gotti banished him from the organization, ordered that no one should be around him, even considered having him killed. Alite couldn't believe it. Despite the ban, he visited Ruggiero frequently. He remembered that Angelo had looked out for him after the Arena incident. He wasn't going to turn his back on him.

"He sent word he wanted to see me," Alite said. "He was staying at his mother's house in Howard Beach. They had a bed in the living room. He was on a morphine drip and was taking all kinds of antibiotics. He was shrunken up. When he spoke it was like his throat was full of fluid. But he still was a tough son of a bitch. And he was pissed off."

At that first meeting, Ruggiero asked Alite to help make some collections for him, money that was still owed him. But even after making those collections, Alite continued to visit. No one was supposed to associate with Ruggiero, whom Gotti had taken to calling a "junk-mouth *babania* dealer." It was during those meetings that Ruggiero cautioned Alite about the Gottis.

"They're no good," he said. "They only care about themselves. John's the boss? He can't even control his own wife. How's he gonna run a family? He's a motherfucker. And Junior, my scumbag godson, is even worse. Get away from them."

Ruggiero couldn't understand why he had been put on the shelf. He was dying of liver cancer and told Alite he would have readily taken the fall for the heroin pinch. Then he went into a rant about Gotti, about how he always wanted his end from the heroin business but never wanted to get his hands dirty; about how when Gotti decided that he wanted to toughen Junior up by sending him to military school, he told Ruggiero that he had to pay Junior's tuition.

Junior attended, but didn't graduate from, the New York Military Academy, a private boarding school in Cornwall-on-Hudson, about sixty miles north of New York City. Tuition, room, and board at the time was more than twenty grand a year. The cost came out of Ruggiero's end of the heroin business, not Gotti's. Ruggiero said again that the Gottis were no good, that he had introduced Gotti into the life and that he deserved some respect.

"It would have been nice to be asked," he said quietly as he once again said he was willing to take the fall in the drug case. "This cancer is killing me anyway, so it don't matter. But I would have liked to be asked instead of being put on the shelf like some piece of shit."

Loyalty was a one-way street with the Gottis. Ruggiero was reinforcing that perception. But for Alite, walking away wasn't an option. He was in and, to be honest, he was enjoying the financial benefits. He knew he was smarter and tougher than Junior. And he was starting to see John Gotti for who he really was. The game now for Alite was to benefit from the association. And, more important, to survive.

A few months after Gotti took over as boss, he sent for Alite. He had an assignment for him. Joe Gallo, one of the old-timers in the family, was still the consigliere. He had come up under Albert Anastasia (no relation to the author of this book) and had served in the administrations of both Carlo Gambino and Paul Castellano. That's how far back Gallo went with the crime family. He had quietly helped usher in the Gotti administration, overseeing the meetings at which all the captains elected a new boss after Big Paulie was killed.

Gallo wasn't part of the plot to kill Castellano, but he was smart enough to realize how it went down. Gravano would later testify that Gallo had cautioned all the captains not to discuss family business with anyone from any other mob family and not to talk about the murder. The only response to give anyone who asked was that he, Gallo, and others were trying to get to the bottom of what had happened and that the captains all agreed on who their new boss should be.

A few months later, that new boss decided Gallo should "retire," step down, give up his spot in the hierarchy. Frank DeCicco, who had helped set up the Castellano hit at Sparks, was Gotti's underboss at the time and DeCicco's uncle was going to be tapped as the new consigliere.

Gotti told Alite to go to Gallo and tell him what the plan was.

"I wasn't even a made guy," Alite said, "and he's sending me to tell Gallo, an old-timer who knew all about this stuff. I'm supposed to tell him that he was done. It was a sign of disrespect. I went and talked to the old guy. He was a gentleman."

Alite said he believed Gallo picked up on the fact that he was uncomfortable delivering the message.

"He looked at me and said, 'Don't worry about it, kid,'" Alite recalled.

Gallo quietly stepped down. Gotti was solidifying his hold on the organization.

Money continued to roll in. Now Gotti was getting a piece of everyone's action, not just the guys in his crew. It was the financial way of the underworld. Money flowed up. Of course, there was very little in the way of bookkeeping, and finances were often fluid. As Alite would later explain to a jury, Junior Gotti was supposed to get half of everything Alite was making. Sometimes Alite would play with the numbers.

"I tell him I give him half, but I keep more than that," he explained years later to a federal jury. It was, he said, a way of life on the street.

"Everybody does it. We cheat each other. That's the life. It's treacherous."

Alite figured the guys under him were lying as well. That's just the way things were. You weren't going to change it. But at that point, in the mid to late 1980s, it almost didn't matter. There was so much money coming in from so many different deals and scams and ripoffs that nobody complained.

"All Junior cared about was his end," Alite said. "And if it was big enough, he never really questioned me. Maybe we did a score where we made a hundred thousand dollars. I'd tell him it was eighty thousand. He was happy with the forty grand I gave him. I kept sixty. This happened all the time."

Alite figured he deserved the bigger end because more often than not he was the one putting himself at risk. Alite testified that Junior came up with another connection who had counterfeit money. According to Alite, they paid twelve cents on the dollar for a stack of hundred dollar bills, about three hundred grand in all. Now, to parlay that into an even bigger score, Alite said they decided to use some of the counterfeit money to buy cocaine from a group of Colombians.

Alite testified that he set up the deal through a contact of his. Junior and another associate waited in a car while Alite and a kid named Vinny, another of Junior's friends, went into the house on 118th Street and Rockaway Boulevard.

Alite had two guns tucked into his waistband, one on his hip and the other in his back. Vinny, a big, 270-pound kid, also was armed.

"He was supposed to have my back while I did the deal," Alite said. "We were buying two kilos for eighty grand. Most of the cash was counterfeit but I had mixed in some real bills just in case. The counterfeit bills were good quality, but I wanted some real money in case anyone was smart enough to really check."

There were three Colombians in the kitchen as the deal went down. Another was standing in the doorway to a back room. They all had guns. They began to count the money while Alite examined the two kilos of coke. At that point, Vinny panicked and said, "I'm gonna wait outside."

Alite couldn't believe it.

"This was another one of Junior's guys and he's supposed to have my fuckin' back. Instead, he's running out on me."

The Colombians looked at one another. Alite just nodded and told Vinny, "Go ahead. I'll be out in a minute." But he was steaming. He had two guns. There were four Colombians. They each had a gun. He decided to play it out. He continued to examine the cocaine. They counted out the bills. The deal went down.

As he exited the house, sweat dripping down his back, Alite saw that Vinny's car was gone. Down the street Junior was in the second car with a kid named Jerry.

"I trotted over to the car and jumped in the backseat," he said. "The first thing I said was, 'I'm gonna kill that fuckin' Vinny.'"

The next day Alite set out to do just that.

"Junior arranged to pick him up," Alite said of Vinny. "We drove over to a friend's house where Vinny was staying and then the three of us took a ride. Vinny was scared, but not scared enough to disobey when Junior told him to get behind the wheel and drive."

Alite was in the backseat. Junior sat in the front passenger seat. They drove around Howard Beach, which was not unusual. As they drove, Junior tried to get Vinny to relax. He spoke in a calm, conciliatory way.

"What happened up there?" he asked. "Why'd you leave?"

Vinny offered a half-assed response. Alite could see he was nervous. He kept looking in the rearview mirror, checking Alite out. Ironically, Alite testified that it was Junior who had a gun that day, not Alite.

"I wanted to shoot him," Alite said. "But I think Junior knew I would kill him. I'm not sure Junior had the guts or the stomach to do it. We drove around for about a half hour and ended up over near 164th Street and Howard Beach. It's a swampy area, lots of tall grass and marshes."

Alite would tell a federal jury that "it's a known spot to shoot guys and dump them there."

Vinny knew that as well. When Junior told him to pull over for a second, the hulking young wannabe slowed the car down, but instead of pulling over, he quickly opened his door and rolled out.

The car slowed to a stop. Alite testified that Junior pulled out a .25-caliber pistol and got off one shot.

"I heard Vinny yelp," Alite said, "but he kept running. We never saw him around the neighborhood again."

CHAPTER 4

The train ride from Amsterdam to Paris takes a little over three hours, a high-speed journey with a stop in Brussels before arriving at the Gare du Nord in the City of Light. It's a comfortable, pleasant ride that for the most part goes through bucolic countryside dotted with rolling green hills and well-maintained farms and vineyards.

Alite took the train with his common-law wife, Claudia, in 2003. He was on the run at the time and had arranged for her to meet him in Europe. He was using a fake passport. He had eight different identities, with matching documentation purchased on the black market in Senegal. He financed his travels with money wired by friends back home to various cities. The cash often was funneled through banks in Canada, a system Alite had set up before he fled. Claudia brought money as well. He arranged her trip because he wanted to spend some time with her, explain what he was doing and why. And he wanted her to tell everyone that he cared about—their two sons; his son and daughter from his first marriage, to wife Carol; his parents and his grandparents—that he was okay. He wanted them to know that he was trying to work things out, trying to stay alive, trying to stay one step ahead of the mobsters who wanted him dead and the federal authorities who wanted him in jail.

It was on that train ride that Alite started to assess where he was and where he was going. It wasn't a geographic question. It was—and the irony was not lost given that he was on his way to France—an existential one. What was the meaning of it all? It was there, in a comfortable first-class compartment, with Claudia sitting next to him, that the seeds of what would eventually follow were planted. It was there that he asked himself a basic question.

How did all this happen?

The simple answer is to say that Alite was the product of his environment, that he grew up poor in a section of Woodhaven, Queens, where the Mafia was an institution. And that he was drawn to the wealth, the status, and the power that that institution embodied. But if he was being honest with himself, and the farther he got from New York and the Gottis the easier it was to look at things honestly, he had to admit that he had made the choices that had ultimately resulted in him sitting on that train under an assumed name wondering if a bullet or a badge would be waiting for him at the next stop.

He was one of four children of Albanian-American parents who settled in Woodhaven in the 1960s. His father, Matthew, was a cabdriver who loved to gamble. His mother, Delva, worked as a secretary. His grandparents, Albanian immigrants, lived with the family, which included an older brother, Jimmy, and two sisters: Denise, who was three years older; and Marie, who was a year younger.

John was only a year younger than Jimmy, but as a kid he was decidedly smaller and less athletic. Although their father saw Jimmy as the kid who had a shot at making something of himself through athletics, it was John who became a standout high school athlete and won a baseball scholarship to the University of Tampa.

As kids growing up their father was adamant about sports. He didn't care much for school. He was a high school dropout. But athletics were important. He instilled in both boys the need to train, to practice, and to never back down. Baseball and boxing were the two sports that he emphasized, and while Jimmy soon grew tired of the grueling training routine every day after school, John couldn't get enough.

Sports taught you about life—that was the education Matthew Alite was giving to his sons. Sports was about preparation and opportunity. It was about always being ready because you never knew—on the baseball field or in a boxing ring—when your chance might come. You had to grab it because there might not be another. Life was like that, and while Matthew Alite might not have been a success in terms of wealth and status, he knew there was more to being a man and he wanted his boys to understand, too.

Sports would teach that lesson.

So would the streets.

John Alite remembers being eight years old and walking home from school one day when two older kids—ten-year-olds—bullied him. They were standing on a corner near his house as he headed home. They had played hooky. They were smoking cigarettes and they asked him for money. He said he didn't have any, which was true, but they roughed him up, searched him, and then sent him on his way. As he left, one of the kids flicked a cigarette butt that hit him in the forehead.

Alite ran home and told his father what had happened.

"Did you fight them?" Matthew Alite asked.

John looked at the floor, knowing that he didn't have the right answer.

His father lifted his head and looked him in the eyes.

"I want you to go back out there," he said. "Find the kid who flicked the cigarette butt at you and punch him in the face."

Alite hesitated, then argued that they were older and bigger. What's more, he said, there were two of them. His father, anticipating what John was going to say, told him to go across the street and get his cousin Gregory, who was also ten.

"Take him with you," he said. "He'll make sure it's a fair fight."

Then his father added, "If you let it go this time, it will happen again and again. You'll get a reputation as soft."

Alite did as he was told. He took the first shot, hitting the bully squarely in the face. But after the surprise, the bully answered back, effectively pummeling eight-year-old John Alite. The fight ended only because the older boy got tired. Alite and his cousin trudged back home. When they told his father what had happened, Matthew smiled.

"You did the right thing. I'm proud of you," he said. "Bullies live off fear and look for easy targets. Now everyone knows you're no easy target."

A week later, Alite was again walking home from school when he crossed paths with the same two ten-year-olds. The one he had punched smiled and said, "Hey, kid, if I try to take your money are you gonna fight me again?"

"Have to," said Alite.

The older boy laughed and put his arm on Alite's shoulder. He looked at his friend and said, "I like this little guy. He's got guts."

That was a memory that came back as the train sped from the Netherlands to France. His father was right. You had to stand up for yourself. No one else would. No one else could. But Mathew Alite also offered John his initial glimpse into the world of organized crime. And John Alite never forgot that, either.

"My father had a cousin who ran a card game with Charlie Luciano, a soldier in the Gambino family," he said. "The game would go from ten at night to six in the morning. They played in the back room of this parking garage in the Bronx. Some nights my father would take me and my brother. I loved it."

The room was filled with cigar smoke. The background noise was the clicking of chips, the rustle of decks being shuffled, the laughter of winners, and the moans and shouts of losers. Most of the players were wiseguys or mob associates.

"My father would proudly introduce us," Alite said. "He worked the room before settling in at a table. We'd roam around, ending up in another room, a little kitchen off the main room, where there was soda and ice cream and potato chips. Most nights the guys who were winning would call us over and give us a 'tip.' It might be a twenty-dollar bill, big money. A few times it was a hundred-dollar bill. We couldn't believe it."

If he knew about the money, Matthew Alite would tell his sons to give it back, which would invariably result in mock indignation from the wiseguy benefactor, who more often than not prevailed upon the elder Alite to let his sons keep the cash. Sometimes, if their father's luck was not running, the boys went home with more money than he did.

But for John Alite it wasn't about the money, it was about the life. He was fascinated with the men in that room, guys with names like Little Al, Vito, Old Man Frankie, Big Jack, and Blackie. They dressed well and acted as if they didn't have a care in the world. More important, and this was something an eight-year-old John Alite could feel, they oozed confidence and a sense of belonging to something important and powerful.

It would be years before Alite realized that it was all a façade, that the honor and loyalty, the camaraderie and brotherhood that the mobsters preached was meaningless. As he rode in the train to Paris he could see that clearly. But as a young boy, every time he left that back room in that Bronx parking garage John Alite had one thought—he wanted to be like those guys at the poker game.

When he was in high school he got a job after school working at Dick's Deli on the corner of Seventy-Ninth Street and Jamaica

Avenue. There was a mob clubhouse across the street run by the Luchese crime family and two or three guys from that clubhouse would come into the deli every day and use the phone in the back. By that point Alite was smart enough to realize what was going on. They were taking bets for a sports book. From time to time someone would come in the deli and leave an envelope for the guys across the street. Alite eventually was assigned the job of running the envelope over to the clubhouse.

He was enrolled in Franklin K. Lane High School in Queens, the same high school that John Gotti Sr. had attended. Gotti left in his sophomore year, a constant truant who had a reputation for bullying other students.

Alite wasn't a model student, but he got decent grades and was a standout baseball player, a second baseman who could hit. He was a starter on the varsity team all four years and captain in both his junior and senior years. But he continued to work at the deli when he had time, a situation that exposed him to the world that Gotti Sr. was so much a part of. And it was there that he got his initial lesson in the power of the organization.

"There was this guy in the neighborhood named Patty Antiques," Alite said. "He was a mob guy and he had an antique store on Jamaica Avenue where he sold a lot of stolen goods. One day he came into the deli. I was talking to some friends who were there. One of them told a joke and I started laughing. For some reason Patty Antiques thought I was laughing at him. He was a little bit crazy."

He started screaming at Alite, threatening to kill him. One of the guys from the clubhouse across the street happened to be in the deli and stepped in, telling Patty Antiques that Alite was a friend of his and the other guys from the clubhouse and that he should just let it go.

Alite thought that was the end of it. The next day, after he had finished a workout at a small, makeshift gym a few doors from the deli, Alite was standing on the corner when Patty Antiques pulled up in his old, rusted white van, jumped out, and waved a handgun at him. Alite took off as the demented wiseguy got off four or five shots. None hit the target. Alite sprinted up a small side street that he knew the van would not be able to negotiate and then took a circuitous route home. Two hours later, Patty Antiques was outside Alite's house brandishing an even larger gun, one that Alite's grandmother and sister would call a machine gun.

Antiques was waving the gun and shouting, "Johnny Alite! Johnny Alite! Where are you? Why don't you come out and play?"

Alite's sister and grandmother were on the porch. They screamed at Antiques, telling him they were calling the police. Antiques, a convicted felon who couldn't possess a weapon, took off. But Alite stopped his sister from calling the cops. Instead, he dialed the home phone number of his former Little League baseball coach, Albert Ruggiano.

Ruggiano had coached him as a twelve-year-old and now occasionally worked out with him at the corner gym. Ruggiano's father, Anthony "Fat Andy" Ruggiano, was a capo in the Gambino crime family and was the guy who ran the neighborhood. Anybody with a problem went to him.

"He was like president of the United States as far as we were concerned in our neighborhood," Alite would tell a federal jury years later. "If there was a problem, you go to him. You don't go to the police. So that's what I did."

After Alite explained the situation, Albert Ruggiano said he would talk with his father. A few minutes later, he called Alite back and told him, "Don't worry about it. We'll take care of it."

The next day he got word that Patty Antiques had been spoken to and that he wouldn't bother Alite again. But two days later, Alite was again running away from the crazy mobster who had spotted him on the street and opened fire. As soon as he got home, Alite called Albert Ruggiano. Ruggiano couldn't believe it, but knew his father wouldn't stand for that kind of disrespect. He told Alite to meet him at the Finish Line, a sports bar in Ozone Park where a lot of wiseguys hung out.

Alite got there first. While he was waiting, John Gotti Jr. and a few others walked in. Alite had met Gotti a few times casually. They knew each other, but weren't friends, hadn't yet struck up any kind of business relationship.

Junior was in military school at the time, but everyone knew his pedigree. His father was, like Fat Andy, a capo in the Gambino family. Junior wanted to know what Alite was doing at the bar. He explained that he had to meet with Albert Ruggiano about something. He wasn't about to share the specifics with Gotti or anyone else. They talked for about ten minutes, sports and street talk. Then Ruggiano arrived and signaled Alite over.

Ruggiano shook Alite's hand as they sat down at a table in the corner. But before he even brought up the Patty Antiques situation, he asked Alite about Junior Gotti, did he know him, was he doing anything with him, those kinds of things.

When Alite told him it was just a casual, hello, how ya doin' kind of relationship, Ruggiano told him to keep it that.

"Here's some advice from a friend," Albert said. "Avoid that guy, you hear? He's a punk, a loud-mouth. He thinks he's a tough guy. No one respects him. No one ever will."

Alite didn't know what to make of the warning. He knew the name Gotti carried weight in the neighborhood and he wasn't sure where Albert Ruggiano was coming from. So he just nodded and said he would remember. It was the first time anyone had warned him off the Gottis. It wouldn't be the last.

Ruggiano quickly shifted to the matter at hand. He told Alite to make sure he was out in a public place with some friends the next night. At first, Alite didn't get it. Ruggiano shook his head and smiled.

"It's important that you have an alibi," his former baseball coach said.

The plan was to grab Patty Antiques and either beat him or kill him. Murder was more likely because Antiques was acting crazy and because he had disregarded Fat Andy's clear edict to leave Alite alone. But Antiques must have gotten word. He disappeared. So the next night, some of Fat Andy's guys grabbed Antiques's stepson, a twenty-year-old who was always hanging around the neighborhood.

"They took him up to the roof of a building and threw him off," Alite said. "He survived, but broke his back, his arm, both legs, sprained his neck. He was in bad shape. He ended up in a body cast for about a year."

The incident left Alite with mixed feelings. On the one hand, he felt a strange sense of pride in the fact that Ruggiano and his family—the mob—stepped up on his behalf. It was something that everyone in the neighborhood would know about and it would give him status and a degree of respect.

On the other hand, Alite couldn't justify what happened to the stepson. He wasn't the one stalking John Alite; it was his crazy stepfather. Yet he paid the price. It said something about the Mafia that Alite wasn't yet ready to acknowledge. It wasn't about honor and loyalty. Those were just words. It was about absolute power. That's what the mob wanted. And it did whatever was necessary to get it.

As the train rumbled through the French countryside, Alite's thoughts drifted back again to those card games in the Bronx and how on the ride home one morning he had innocently asked his father who those men were.

Matthew Alite tried to explain to his young son that those men were part of a separate world. It was hard to make an eight-year-old understand, but John Alite remembered one thing his father had told him.

"Don't ever ask them for a favor," Matthew Alite said. "Because if you do and if they grant it, you'll be in their debt. Then they'll own you."

That's the situation Alite was in after the Patty Antiques incident, but sports almost saved him. He got a baseball scholarship to the University of Tampa and that September, much to his father's satisfaction, he left Queens for Florida. He spent one semester down south, but injured his elbow that fall season. He came home and underwent Tommy John surgery, but it didn't work. Every time he threw a baseball, he got an excruciating pain that ran from his elbow to his shoulder.

His career as a baseball player was over. He enrolled in Queens College and became a fixture in the neighborhood. He stayed in shape by working out regularly at a local gym, where he connected with some guys he had grown up with: Billy Estrema, who was working as muscle and a collector for a Luchese crew; Patsy Andriano, who was Alite's cousin and was working for Ciro Perrone, the Genovese capo; and Mikey Merlo, who had been part of the 7N9 Gang when they were kids.

The gang took its name from the neighborhood around Seventy-Ninth Street and Jamaica Avenue. John Gebert, George Grosso, and Kevin Bonner were also part of that group. Alite knew them all, but didn't run with them when he was young. Now he found himself moving in their circles.

Merlo was dealing drugs on a small scale but had big plans. Estrema and Andriano were also ambitious. They talked with Alite about branching out, about setting up their own little organization and generating some cash. They pulled a couple of robberies and did some strong-arm shakedowns, spin-offs of the stuff they were already doing for the mob. Alite had a minor role in that action, which may have saved his life.

Within three months, Estrema, Andriano, and Merlo were dead. (Andriano's son, also named Patsy, would later become a young, teenage member of Alite's mob crew.)

Estrema was shot in the head, his hogtied body found in a dumpster. Andriano answer a knock on his door one night and was greeted with a shotgun blast to the face. Another to the back of his head finished the job. Merlo also was shotgunned to death. The word on the street was that his shooting was in retaliation for the robbery of a drug dealer whom he was suspected of setting up.

The motives for the murders of Estrema and Andriano were never made clear, but the message Alite took from the violence was that individual entrepreneurship wasn't welcome on the streets. It was important to be connected. Your life might depend on it.

That point was driven home again when his sister's then boyfriend came to him for help. He and another guy had been moving drugs, small quantities of cocaine, in the neighborhood and were paid a visit by a couple of mob associates who demanded a street tax. It was a classic mob shakedown.

"This guy who was dating my sister asked me to go see my friend, Albert Ruggiano," Alite said. "So that's what I did."

Ruggiano was almost apologetic when Alite told him the story. He didn't know, he said, that they were friends of Alite. Then he told him, "Look, if you can make a score, go ahead and do it. I don't want anything, but tell them to pay you a hundred a week for taking care of their problem. Tell them they got nothing to worry about."

It was easy money and Alite jumped at the chance. Once again his connection to Ruggiano had brought him a benefit. He felt protected in the neighborhood and saw an opportunity to make even more money. That's when he started moving cocaine on his own.

He was stashing the drugs under his bed, using his bedroom to cut and package the product before he put it out on the street. Nothing big, but enough to generate a couple hundred each week in profit.

He made another connection with Sonny DiGiorgio, who worked for Angelo Ruggiero. Ruggiero had brought John J. Gotti into the mob. Both operated under the umbrella of Aniello Dellacroce, the crime family underboss. Alite had heard all those names but had no perspective at that point.

He was a kid, a twenty-year-old whose dream of playing baseball, maybe even making it a professional career, was over. But his chance to be a wiseguy was very real and he wasn't about to let the opportunity pass. His father, however, had other ideas. He discovered the drugs and a gun under his son's bed and shipped him off to live with an uncle in California.

"I was there about a year," Alite said. "I was living in Valencia and had enrolled in College of the Canyons."

It was a second chance to have a college career, but it didn't work out. There was a fight in a bar with a guy who turned out to be an off-duty police officer. And then a stabbing in a follow-up incident tied to the first fight. Alite was arrested and charged with assault, and pleaded guilty. He caught a break. The judge told him to go home, to leave California and never come back.

By the summer of 1983, a year after heading west, Alite was back in Queens, back in the old neighborhood, back dealing with some of the guys he had grown up with and with the mobsters who held sway. Shortly after he returned, Gebert made the connection for him with Junior Gotti. It was a business and personal relationship that would change Alite's life forever.

As the train pulled into the station at the Gare du Nord in Paris, Alite noticed several police officials coming on board. They began to question passengers, paying particular interest to him and his wife.

"I spoke a little French, they spoke some English," he said. "I had a fake passport. I was never sure who it was that they were looking for. But they let us go."

It would be another eighteen months, with stops in a dozen other countries, before Alite was arrested in Brazil. As he walked from the train in Paris that day back in 2003, John Alite thought he could run forever.

CHAPTER 5

Four months after the Paul Castellano murder, John Gotti's underboss Frank DeCicco was killed when a bomb planted under his car was detonated as he opened the driver's-side door.

The blast left a two-foot-wide crater in the street and shattered windows in nearby homes and businesses along Eighty-Sixth Street in the Bensonhurt section of Brooklyn. DeCicco was ripped apart. Another mobster who was standing next to him was seriously injured.

The bomber thought that man was John Gotti. It wasn't.

Gotti was supposed to attend a meeting that Sunday afternoon with DeCicco at the Veterans and Friends Club, a mob hangout on Eighty-Sixth Street near Fourteenth Avenue. At the last minute, he canceled. He had more important things on his mind. He had just beaten an assault case in state court but had a racketeering indictment hanging over him. That trial was due to start later in the year. The feds were also preparing for opening arguments in the highly publicized Mafia Commission trial, in which the leaders of all five mob families had been indicted. Castellano and Dellacroce were two of the original eleven defendants. They obviously would not be tried, but the case itself was indicative of what was going on in the underworld at the time.

Gotti had taken over the biggest Mafia family in New York

at the same time that U.S. Attorney Rudolph Giuliani was using mob prosecutions to build a reputation and a political career. The feds had finally figured out how to use the RICO statute that Bobby's Kennedy's pompous pal Robert Blakey had sculpted a decade earlier. Now prosecutions were focused on criminal enterprises and the crimes that advanced the agendas of those enterprises. Leaders could be held accountable for every "predicate act" that was cited in a RICO indictment. The Mafia Commission case included 151 counts.

These were not the best of times for the American Mafia. Gotti would have a brief if meteoric run at the top, but all the while he was looking over his shoulder, ducking both the feds and mobsters. The Genovese family was not going to ignore the Castellano murder. Someone would have to answer for what happened to Big Paulie.

DeCicco may have been the first victim of that vendetta, but John Gotti was the primary target.

Everyone knew the bombing was retaliation for the murder of Castellano, but at first no one was sure where it had come from. Gotti and Gravano, who replaced DeCicco as underboss, speculated that the murder had been carried out by a group of Sicilian mobsters who operated in New York and had been close to Castellano.

The Siggies used bombs all the time. What's more, everyone knew it was against the rules for American Mafiosi to use explosives. The chance of innocent bystanders getting hurt was too great. In fact the DeCicco bomb had injured a neighborhood woman on her way to her elderly mother's birthday party in a house across the street from where DeCicco's Buick Electra had been parked. The woman sustained minor injuries.

The irony in Gotti's thinking wasn't lost on Alite, who at that point was spending almost every day with Junior and who saw Gotti at least twice a week. On Wednesday nights everyone had to show up at the Ravenite, the Mulberry Street social club in Little

Italy that Gotti had taken over after Dellacroce died. And on Saturday nights everyone was expected to check in at the Bergin Hunt and Fish Club in Queens.

Alite was watching and listening and trying to learn. He knew his future depended on it. Even he, a novice in the business at that time, saw the flaw in Gotti's thinking. Gotti had broken the primary rule of the American Mafia by killing a sitting boss without Commission approval, yet he was looking to those same rules in trying to figure out who had killed his underboss.

Later word got out that members of the Genovese crime family, not some crazy Sicilians, were responsible for the bombing. Members of the Luchese organization were also in on the plot along with Danny Marino, a Gambino capo who headed a faction of the family that didn't want to fall in line under Gotti.

"We're all on alert again," Alite said. "Although at the time nobody knew the bomb was supposed to be for John."

John Gotti's Rules of Leadership: Members and associates are not to speak to the media. Granting interviews or appearing on television is prohibited.

While he might have been naïve in his thinking, Gotti was also clever in the way he responded once he saw himself as a possible target. Instead of heading for the shadows, Gotti ran to the spotlight. No one was supposed to talk to the media, but Gotti had certain reporters, like the highly regarded TV investigative reporter John Miller, whom he favored. He wouldn't grant lengthy interviews, but he was always ready with a sound bite or a quip as he entered or exited a courthouse or was approached in a bar or restaurant or on the street.

He also ratcheted up his "involvement" in the community. The famous Fourth of July barbecue, block party, and fireworks in

Queens grew out of this publicity campaign. Part of it fit with Gotti's temperament and was genuine. But part of it, Alite believes, was also a defense mechanism.

"He figured he was less likely to be targeted if he was around the media or if he had a lot of innocent people around him," Alite said. "It was a smart move."

If he had had his own publicist, Gotti couldn't have worked it any better. Over the next four years, as Alite watched in amazement, John Gotti became the face of the American Mafia. He was the country's celebrity gangster, an almost iconic figure the likes of which had not been seen since Al Capone.

While law enforcement investigators shook their heads at the bravado and arrogance and old-time mobsters cringed, those familiar with Italian culture nodded knowingly. Like Capone, Gotti traced his ethnic roots to Naples, not Sicily. The stereotypical male in Naples is a rooster who likes to look good and, as important, wants everyone to know it.

Facia una bella figura is the Italian expression that describes this behavior. "Make a good physical impression" is the literal translation but what it means is that while it's important to do well, it's just as important to look good while you're doing it. It's the antithesis of the dark, hide in a cave, stay in the shadows Sicilian temperament that extolled secrecy above all else and for generations was the standard for any Mafioso.

In September, six months after the DeCicco bombing, Gotti made the cover of *Time* magazine. He was on trial for racketeering at the time. The cover artwork, done by Andy Warhol, was a handsome John Gotti with a full head of neatly coiffed hair. He was wearing a double-breasted, dark suit jacket. His hands were adjusting one of the jacket buttons. There was a watch on his left wrist, under a shirt cuff that peeked out from the sleeve of the jacket. He wore a dark tie and a high-collared white shirt.

Now Gotti's name was appearing in the gossip columns almost as often as in the news sections of the papers. His appearances at clubs and restaurants were regularly chronicled. One account, a clear attempt to humanize the mob boss, was that he would occasionally show up at Regine's, a nightclub in Manhattan, with his own entourage and that one of his minions would tip the piano player a hundred dollars every time he played Gotti's favorite song, "Wind Beneath My Wings." It was all part of the growing legend. This, of course, was before Facebook and Twitter. God only knows how the publicity machine would have worked if social media had been available.

Gotti loved the *Time* cover. He had it framed and hung in his social club. (A framed copy of the cover is now available on eBay. The asking price? Around two hundred dollars.) He would also appear on the covers of *People,* the *New York Times Magazine,* and *New York* magazine during his bloody run as Gambino crime family boss.

The great Jack Newfield, in an obituary written in *New York* magazine after Gotti died in 2002, described him this way: "John Gotti was the don-as-diva. He was in love with himself and equated his ego with all of La Cosa Nostra. He was a throwback to the first narcissistic, star struck hoodlums—Bugsy Siegel and Al Capone, who didn't understand boundaries and were addicted to publicity."

That was an accurate assessment, but it came after the fact. In 1986, Gotti was just beginning to build his image. The first book written about him, by Jerry Capeci and Gene Mustain, was aptly titled *Mob Star.* That's who Gotti was to those on the outside. Alite saw a different Gotti, one more reflected in Newfield's description.

"I used to spend time over [at] the house," Alite said. "Sometimes I would sleep over on the couch. I saw and heard a lot of things that people didn't know about."

For example, Alite said John Gotti "was a terrible dresser." Left to his own devices, Alite said the Dapper Don would dress like the Steve Martin character in the "Wild and Crazy Guys" skits on *Saturday Night Live*. After he became boss, Alite said, Gotti had an associate named Fat Bob pick out his clothes. At that point Gotti could afford the two-thousand-dollar suits and five-hundred-dollar Italian leather shoes; he just didn't have the fashion sense to put it all together.

"Fat Bob dressed him," Alite said.

The Gotti family dynamic also surprised Alite. He knew from Junior that there were problems at home, but being in the house, a modest two-story in the Howard Beach section of Queens, gave him a firsthand view of how everyone interacted.

He overheard shouting matches in which Victoria Gotti matched her husband expletive for expletive. Usually the argument would end with a door being slammed. Neither Gotti nor his son had an enlightened view of the role of women in society. Alite, not particularly enlightened in that regard himself, was still surprised by the attitude and the violence.

In 1984, when Alite first started to get close to the Gottis, Junior was dating Kim Albanese, whom he would eventually marry. Alite and Junior were hanging out in front of Albanese house one day when another car with two guys inside pulled up. Junior and Alite had walked down the block and were talking with a kid from the neighborhood. The guys in the car were shouting out to someone in the house, flirting. Junior went nuts. He started screaming at the two guys, who quickly pulled away.

Junior was convinced that they had come by to see Kim. In fact, it was her sister Dina whom they were after, but that didn't matter. Junior recognized one of the guys in the car as Gene Foster and told Alite he wanted him beaten up.

"I'm still recovering from that White Castle fight at the time,"

Alite said. "I hadn't put on any weight and I was out of shape. But he tells me to give the kid a beating. For what? But that's the way he was and it's the way his father was."

Alite dragged his feet and, to his surprise, he got called on the carpet by Gotti Sr.

"Did my son tell you to do something?" Gotti asked him angrily after calling him to the Bergin one day. "What's the problem?"

Alite, who would later recount the story from the witness stand, put the word out in the neighborhood that he was looking for Gene Foster. One afternoon he was at Rockaway Beach with Joe O'Kane when Foster approached him.

"I'm carrying a folding chair," Alite said. "I always took it to the beach so I could sit down in the sand. I was still recovering. And I had started carrying this small pipe, which I kept in the folding chair. I'm walking down the steps toward the beach when this guy approaches me."

"You John Alite?" he said.

Alite said he was.

"I'm Gene Foster. I heard you're looking for me?"

With that, Alite said he dropped the folding beach chair and cracked Foster over the head with the metal pipe. Foster went down and Alite continued to pound him. A crowd gathered around. Some were friends of Foster. Others, Alite said, "were just Samaritans."

As the crowd started to press in on him, Alite handed O'Kane the keys to his car and told him to get it and bring it around. O'Kane was only seventeen at the time. He didn't have a license and barely knew how to drive.

"Just get the car," Alite told him.

Alite said he faced off six or seven guys who had come to Foster's aid. Foster was moaning as he lay in the sand. Blood was pouring from the gash in his head. Several of his ribs were cracked and one of his lungs was punctured. One of the bigger guys in the crowd was urging everyone on.

"Let's get him," he said.

Alite said he reached into his jockstrap and pulled out a derringer, pointing the small gun at the guy who was talking tough. Someone in the crowd laughed.

"That's not even a real gun," the guy said.

Alite pointed it at him.

"You wanna find out?" he asked. "You'll be the first one I shoot."

With that the crowd backed off. When O'Kane pulled up, he put the car in park and slid over to the passenger side. Alite said he threw his beach chair in the backseat, got in behind the wheel, and drove away. When he told Junior what had happened, Alite said Junior smiled. Alite never understood Junior's logic. Foster had come to see Dina, not Kim. Once Junior realized that, what was the point of the beating?

"He was happy that Foster took a beating," Alite said. "I still don't know why. That's the kind of guy he was. He liked to give orders. Never did much himself, but he liked to be in charge."

At the time, given the benefits, Alite was only too happy to oblige.

But being around the family also offered him a chance to see how the Gottis really operated. It wasn't pretty.

Alite was sleeping on the couch once when John Gotti started in on his son. It was a constant refrain, the father telling the son how to act, how to treat people, really how to use people.

"Fuck all your friends," Gotti told Junior. "Never let them forget you're the boss. They need to be afraid of you. You use them and when you're done with them, you throw them to the curb."

Then he spotted Alite on the couch.

"How ya doin', kid?" he asked, before returning to his harangue, telling Junior the guys he hung around with were "junk piles" and "garbage" and that he had better wise up and realize that.

"It didn't even matter that I was there or that I was one of those guys," Alite said. "Or maybe I was supposed to think I wasn't one of those guys. Gotti never broke stride. He just went on and on."

The only person in the house who would answer back was Gotti's wife, Victoria. Alite said their arguments were classic verbal clashes that brought out the worst in both of them. Victoria Gotti had the same temperament as her husband, but with a twist. She was half Italian and half Russian-Jewish. Her aggressiveness came from both those bloodlines. She was smart and tough, but could be mean and vindictive.

While Gotti was coming up in the mob, she was the one who held the family together. They had five children, two girls and three boys: Angela and Vicky, John, Frankie, and Peter.

Gotti spent two stints in prison while moving up the mob ladder. He did time for truck hijacking in the late 1960s and then did a bit for attempted manslaughter in 1975. He was part of a hit team (Angelo Ruggiero was also involved) assigned to take out James McBratney, a member of the notorious Westies, an Irish gang from the West Side of Manhattan. McBratney was suspected of orchestrating the kidnapping and murder of a nephew of Carlo Gambino, then the crime family boss.

McBratney was drinking in Snoopy's Bar & Grill on Staten Island in May 1973 when he was accosted by three men. He was shot and killed. Gotti was able to plead out to a lesser charge in that case and was sentenced to four years. When he returned home, he was formally initiated into the crime family.

The Gottis had established themselves in Howard Beach, living in a modest, middle-class neighborhood. Gotti was a soldier and then the capo of a crew that operated out of Queens. But there are those who say that it was his wife who was boss inside the house.

On March 18, 1980, the family was rocked when twelve-year-old Frankie was struck and killed while riding a motorized minibike around the neighborhood. Witnesses said the young boy had pulled out into the street from between two cars. A neighbor, John Favara, driving home from work, said he was blinded by the sun and never saw Frankie Gotti or the bike he was riding.

It was an accident.

It is easy to imagine the anguish felt by John and Victoria Gotti. Any parent who has lost a child knows the sorrow, anger, and bitterness that such a loss brings. But what does it say about a couple who turn that bitterness into rage and who, according to both law enforcement and underworld accounts, extract their own vengeance?

Word that Favara, himself a father and husband, had a serious problem began to circulate around the Howard Beach neighborhood. He was verbally assaulted by Victoria Gotti at one point. Others advised him that he'd be wise to move.

That summer, Favara put his house up for sale. But it was too late. On July 25, John and Victoria Gotti left for a trip to Florida. Three days later, Favara was abducted by four men who grabbed him outside a diner in Queens. He was never seen again.

"I was told they dismembered his body," Alite said. "The Gottis wanted revenge. I never understood that. The thing about it was that it was Kevin McMahon's minibike. He was letting Frankie use it. But John Gotti never held Kevin accountable because he was making money with Kevin. Kevin was part of the drug network. So it was okay. Everybody around the Gottis served a purpose. And as long as you were doing something for them, you got a pass. Favara was just a neighborhood guy. He wasn't any more responsible for Frankie Gotti being killed than Kevin, but Kevin was helping John Gotti make money. That's what it was all about."

When he started cooperating, Alite was asked by the FBI about the Favara murder. He said Junior had told him that his father ordered the hit in an attempt to assuage the grief and anger of his wife Victoria.

"Vicky Gotti not only blamed Favarra for the accident," the report reads in part, "she was also enraged that Favarra never offered the family an apology and didn't attend or send flowers to the child's wake or funeral." (The FBI memo that summarized Alite's comments misspelled Favara's name, adding an extra *r*.)

Years later, prosecutors in the racketeering murder case of Charles Carneglia would file a pretrial motion indicating that Carneglia was part of the Favara hit team and that he had disposed of the body by dropping it in a barrel of acid.

In a strange and twisted way that put the lie to the concept of "men of honor," the disappearance and apparent murder of John Favara gave Gotti status in certain underworld circles. "You don't mess with John Gotti" was the takeaway message. "Look what happened to that poor fuck who hit his kid on the minibike."

Once he became boss, Gotti was even more conscious of his image and the public's perception of him. No one was allowed to dress better than he when they were out together. When someone approached a group at a bar or restaurant, he would have to acknowledge Gotti first before saying anything to anyone else in the crowd. When Gotti was riding in a car, someone else would have to drive. He would sit in the front passenger seat. Anyone else rode in the back. Those were some of the protocols.

Alite was being schooled in the ways of the wiseguy and even though he could never be formally made, he was required to follow those rules as he moved around the underworld as an associate of the Gambino crime family.

Another rule was that wives were to behave in public. A

woman's behavior was a direct reflection on her husband. If a man couldn't keep his wife in line, the thinking went, how could he handle more serious business?

John Gotti's Rules of Leadership: Wives and girlfriends are to remain low-key. They are not to speak in public or call attention to themselves.

Gotti's wife was the exception to the rule. She was outspoken and opinionated and never tried to hide it. John Gotti may have been the boss of the biggest crime family in New York, but Victoria Gotti ruled the house in Queens. By spending time in that home, Alite had a unique view of family dynamics. Unlike the tough guys who were part of Gotti's crew, Victoria Gotti wasn't afraid to stand up to her husband.

It was a phenomenon that played out in more mob families than you might imagine. Alite could admire that. He liked women who had a little bit of an edge, an attitude; who weren't afraid to say what was on their mind.

Women are always more practical and have a better understanding of the way things work. Wiseguys have to preen and posture and show how tough they are. Maybe it's the testosterone.

In a world where death is a daily part of the equation, women are often more realistic.

There's a classic story about a mob hit in Philadelphia and the response the daughter of a jailed mob underboss offered unknowingly on an FBI wiretap. The woman's brother had been wounded and his best friend killed.

"What are they fighting over?" she asked as the feds listened in. Then she answered her own question. "Jail time or coffins."

In another Philadelphia case, two wives were sitting in a

restaurant a day after their husbands had been convicted in a major racketeering trial. The case had been built around the testimony of Big Ron Previte, a former Philadelphia cop turned wiseguy (under the old rules, a cop could never be a mobster, but times have changed). Previte wore a wire for the FBI for more than a year after he began cooperating.

To his former mob associates, Previte was a rat, a lowlife, descriptions the Gotti clan is now applying to Alite. But to the wives sitting over lunch that day, that wasn't the issue.

Their husbands were convicted and headed off to federal prison for the better part of the next decade. Previte, on the other hand, was a free man, moving around at will. Like Alite, he opted not to go into the Witness Security Program. To the wives, it was simple.

"He won and we lost," they said.

End of story.

Wives and daughters often have a different perspective on the gangsters who are close to them. Alite said repeatedly that he believes Vicky Gotti is sincere when she sings her father's praises, describing him as a man of honor.

Alite said he knew that was a daughter's view, clouded by love and emotion. It was not the Gotti that Alite said he knew. Emotion can distort reality.

The reality was the former Philadelphia mob wife knew too much about two murders her husband had committed. She believed he planned to kill her, so she filed for divorce and became a federal witness. While living under the feds' protection, she fell in love and married one of the agents who was assigned to guard her.

Years later she was asked what the difference was between the cops and the wiseguys.

Without missing a beat, she replied, "The cops have badges."

It's a macho world. Women have no place in it, but they very often have a better understanding of it. Alite's view from inside the Gotti home in Howard Beach underscored that point.

Around this time, Gotti was having better luck in the courtroom than he was in his living room. In several high-profile cases, he came out a winner in battles with city and federal prosecutors. Out of that was born "the Teflon Don."

First there was an assault case that ended abruptly when the victim couldn't identify his assailants. The witness, a refrigerator repairman who had allegedly been beaten and robbed by Gotti and an associate in a dispute over a parking space outside a bar in 1984, later fingered both men in testimony before a grand jury. But by the time the case went to trial early in 1986, he and the rest of New York had come to know who John Gotti was.

The high-profile publicity that Gotti used as a buffer proved to have legal benefits. Now the victim was a reluctant witness from the stand; he said he couldn't identify who had beaten him up. The judge dismissed the charges and the New York *Daily News,* in a classic headline, bannered the story the next day with a perfect description of what had happened. I FORGOTTI read the bold block print letters in the tabloid.

That form of witness intimidation was an outgrowth of Gotti's celebrity. His ability to beat two other cases, a racketeering trial in 1987 and a murder-for-hire rap in 1990, was more sinister.

"Anytime there was a trial, we tried to get to the jury," Alite said. "We did that in the first two drug trials for Genie Gotti and John Carneglia. They ended with hung juries. They were convicted at the third trial. And we did it for John's trials."

Alite played a minor but telling role. He was a spotter in an elaborate system set up to identify and tail the jurors as they left court each day.

"I'd get word that the jury was leaving or I might be in court and watch outside, looking for them," he said. "Then I'd radio someone else who was waiting in the parking lot. If they spotted someone we had identified, they would try to follow them home."

Once they had an address, it was merely a matter of determining how to make an approach. Was there a neighbor who might be connected and might be willing to make an offer to the juror? Or were intimidation, threats, and vandalism the way to go?

"You could bribe 'em or you could threaten 'em," Alite said. "The idea was to get them to realize that we knew who they were and where they lived and that we wanted them to do the right thing."

Usually, they did.

Alite saw it all for what it was. The media called Gotti "the Teflon Don" because the government couldn't make any charges stick. Like so much else surrounding the Gotti persona, it was sizzle without the steak; an image built on hype rather than reality. The charges didn't stick because Gotti and his associates were manipulating the system, not because he was innocent or because he and his lawyers had convinced a jury through evidence and testimony that the government didn't have a case. Nevertheless, the results helped solidify Gotti's image as the invincible, celebrity Mafia boss.

What's more, they came in the wake of the feds' big win in the Mafia Commission trial.

That case ended in November 1986 with convictions all around. The leaders of every other mob family in New York took a hit. Fat Tony Salerno of the Genovese crime family, Colombo boss Carmine "the Snake" Persico, and Anthony "Tony Ducks" Corallo of the Luchese organization headed the list of eight mob chiefs heading off to jail.

John Gotti, meanwhile, donned a two-thousand-dollar suit and headed off to Regine's.

CHAPTER 6

While Gotti Sr. was solidifying his hold on the crime family in the wake of the Castellano murder, the DeCicco hit, the Mafia Commission convictions, and his own acquittals, John Alite was working his way deeper into the organization.

Despite the warnings he received about Junior, he continued to develop the relationship. It was his way in. He started almost every day at Junior's clubhouse at 113th Street and Liberty Avenue and would routinely drop in to the Bergin and the Ravenite as well. In addition to working the drug business, he had convinced Junior that they could make big money taking sports bets. Alite knew the bookmaking business well. He had grown up around it. He was also a self-described "sports nut," watching any game—football, baseball, basketball—on any TV that he might be near.

Bookmaking has always been one of the economic engines that drives the finances of organized crime. While state lotteries have diminished the value of the old numbers racket, sports betting continues to thrive. It's legal in some form in only four states, Nevada being the prime location for legal sports betting parlors.

Bookies will take bets on almost any sporting event, but football is king. The Super Bowl is the pinnacle of the betting season. It is estimated that about 200 million people around the world wager about $5 billion each year on that one game. Las Vegas books take in, on average, $90 million in Super Bowl action. Another $2 billion or so finds its way to legal Internet betting services. The rest goes to illegal sports books, most tied to the mob. Do the math. There's serious money here. And it comes without all the baggage—the violence, the treachery, the informants—that is so common in the drug business.

The money is always going to be there for a smart bookmaker. Even if other jurisdictions legalize sports gambling, it's unlikely that competition will put a dent in the mob's action. Legal bookmaking parlors in casinos and online won't let you bet on credit. The mob will. A degenerate gambler who craves the action needs to know that he can place a bet even if he's got no money in his pocket and his credit cards are maxed out. He also needs to know that if he's getting buried on a Sunday afternoon in the one o'clock games, he can pick up the phone and get back in business before the four o'clock games kick off. Those are the services a mob bookmaking operation provides.

And when the hapless gambler gets in way over his head, the economics of the underworld offer an out—a shylock loan.

"There's nothing better than shark money," a former mobster, since retired, once said in explaining his loansharking business. He had connections to a mob bookmaking operation and when a gambler was swimming in debt, the bookmaker would send that gambler to the loan shark.

"Let's say the guy needs ten grand," he explained. "I give it to him at three points. He pays off the gambling debt and now he owes me the money. It's a ten-week loan. That means each week he's gotta pay me three hundred dollars in interest. That's the three points, three percent. At the end of the ten weeks, he's paid me three grand, but he still owes me the ten grand principal. At that point he either comes up with the cash, or we extend the loan for another ten weeks. What's he gonna do? We're the mob. If he don't pay, he gets hurt. Plus he gets a reputation and he can't bet no more. Sometimes that's even worse for the guy than getting his face busted up or his leg broken."

The $10,000 loan over a year's time would generate $15,600 in interest payments at $300 a week. That's the *vig* on the loan. And that $15,600—or at least a part of it—would be put back out on the street in other loans, also at three points. Not even the credit card companies, with their exorbitant interest rates, can do that well.

"There's nothing better than shark money," the ex-mobster said again.

Alite understood all of this. He saw his uncle wheel and deal in the gambling business and as a teenager he saw the action from behind the counter at Dick's Deli. He knew there was money to be made and once again he knew that if he went in business with Gotti he would be protected from the hustlers and con artists who prey on low-level bookmakers.

"The worst thing for a bookmaker," Alite said, "is the guy who bets and collects when he wins, but ducks away when he loses. That's a guy who's taking advantage. He's stealing money. That's the guy who gets hurt."

Alite and Junior set up a small book out of the clubhouse on 113th Street. They put in some phone lines and had two or three guys working them. Business was good. Small but steady profits and with each week the customer base grew. After a few weeks, Junior took Alite to see his father. This was a business—unlike the drug trade—that they could talk about openly. It was a way for Junior to show his father that he was responsible, that he could develop something on his own, that he was savvy and street-smart, two attributes that he knew his father felt he was lacking.

"One of the reasons John Gotti wanted me around his son was that I knew the streets," Alite said. "People would say later that we were best friends. And it's true, for a time we were friends. But what I really was was his babysitter. I was there to make sure he didn't get into trouble and I was there to clean up the mess if he did."

Gotti liked the idea of the bookmaking operation that Junior and Alite had set up. And to help them expand, he told them to partner with Willie Boy Johnson, one of his top associates.

John Gotti's Rules of Leadership: Whenever possible, use demeaning nicknames to describe underlings. It establishes who is in charge and who is subservient.

Willie Boy operated out of Brooklyn. Like Alite, he could never be made. He wasn't a full-blooded Italian. His mother was Italian-American, but his father was part Native American, which earned Willie Boy the nickname "Half Breed." It was a term Gotti and others used to belittle Johnson, who stood at more than six feet tall and sometimes weighed in at nearly three hundred pounds. He was nobody to mess with. He was an earner and an enforcer, someone Gotti Sr. depended on to do the work that needed to be done. But he was also someone that Gotti Sr. would mock whenever it suited him.

It was a Gotti management style, an arrogance that was probably rooted in insecurity. Both father and son were quick to make fun of those who answered to them. Nicknames were one way to establish that pecking order.

Junior had his own quirks, but no one was making fun of him. According to Alite, Vicky Gotti used to refer to her brother as "Blinkie," telling Alite that she could always tell when her brother was lying. If what he was saying wasn't true, he would blink incessantly while talking.

"He couldn't help himself," Alite said.

Some of the guys around Alite also used to refer to Junior

as Urkel, the nerd from the TV comedy series *Family Matters*. Junior, muscle-bound with a thick chest from lifting weights, had spindles for legs and a disconcerting habit of pulling his sweatpants up around his ribs.

"He'd also show up sometimes in black shoes and socks while he was wearing sweats," Alite said. "When he was dressed like that and wearing his glasses, he looked like Urkel. But of course nobody called him that to his face."

Alite understood why some of his associates made fun of Junior, but he would usually brush their comments aside. He was focused instead on business. Junior was his partner and he wasn't about to screw up a lucrative relationship.

Willie Boy Johnson told Alite and Junior that they would set up a half-sheet book. Willie Boy would be a fifty percent partner in their operation. With that they got access to the latest sports betting lines and had the financial backing to cover larger bets. The downside was that each Tuesday, Willie Boy would have to be paid fifty percent of the winnings. If a gambler was stalling, couldn't be found, or said he didn't have the money to cover his losses, that was on Alite and Junior. Willie Boy had to be paid. And since Willie Boy was Gotti's guy, Alite assumed some of that cash ended up in Gotti's pocket as well.

Johnson operated out of a clubhouse on Avenue U in Brooklyn. He had his own crew of guys and reported directly to Gotti. In many ways, he had the kind of connection that Alite saw himself developing with Junior. On the ride over to Johnson's clubhouse to discuss the bookmaking partnership for the first time, Alite learned something else about Willie Boy. He was allowing Mark Caputo to hide out at his apartment in Brooklyn.

Big Mark was the guy taking the fall for the Danny Silva murder at the Silver Fox. While Junior didn't know it, Caputo and Alite had grown up in the same neighborhood and had gone to junior high school together. During the ride over to Brooklyn, Alite said, Junior provided more details about the stabbing. He again bragged about how he had put the kid down, but also told Alite that his father had arranged to bribe a cop running the investigation and that the preliminary police reports falsely identified Mark Caputo, not John Gotti Jr., as the suspect. Caputo was hiding out until the case blew over. Willie Boy Johnson, who was a father figure to Caputo, had him under wraps.

Junior joked about it all, calling Mark a stupid fat fuck and wondering about the relationship between Willie Boy and Caputo.

"Maybe there's some fag stuff going on," he said.

Junior also had second thoughts about how the Silva case was being handled. He understood, he said, that his father was trying to protect him, but he wondered if in underworld terms that was smart.

"How am I ever going to earn respect if my father hides my actions?" Alite said Junior asked him.

Alite was struck by two things. Junior wanted to be known as a killer. Silva was dead and Junior wanted credit for it. Junior said Silva had been mouthing off to him and his friends that night at the Silver Fox and had gotten what he deserved. Junior also bragged that killing someone with a knife was a "more manly" thing to do because it was a hands-on experience.

Mark Caputo, who was one of the guys there when the fight occurred, later told Alite that there was no reason to stab Silva. Caputo said he and the others were "winning" the fight in the club that night and that no one had to die. Caputo became collateral damage in the aftermath. If anyone was going to take a fall for what happened, it would be Mark. But that's the way the Gottis operated. Everyone was expendable.

Alite recalled Junior's suscint assessment of Big Mark.

"That fat bastard couldn't kill anybody," Junior said.

Willie Boy Johnson was all business when they got to his clubhouse. He explained how the operation was going to work. Alite was told to call in three or four times a day, every day, to get the updated betting line. Smart gamblers, Johnson said, shop around and if you're late with the line and are off, even by a half point, you could get burned. This was big-time gambling, he said. Strictly business. You had to be smart and on top of your game. There was serious money out there and the idea was to get as much of it as possible.

Alite liked Johnson. He liked his approach, no nonsense, no bullshit. He also liked the fact that Johnson was looking out for Big Mark, his boyhood friend. Johnson took them up to the apartment where Mark was hiding out. The reunion took Junior off stride. Alite and Caputo hugged and laughed and started talking about the "old days" in the neighborhood. Junior hung around for a while, then got bored and asked Johnson to arrange for someone else to drive him back to Queens. Alite stayed to hang out with Big Mark.

With Johnson's backing, the bookmaking business took off.

One of their first big customers was a guy named Joe DeLuca. He was betting three or four baseball games a day and putting three or four grand on each game, significant money. Alite decided that he should get a better idea of who DeLuca was. He invited him to drop by the club on 113th Street.

DeLuca was not what Alite expected. He was a tall, thin kid, in his twenties, with a thin mustache and a quick but nervous smile. After some casual conversation, Alite got to the point. He wanted DeLuca to understand the ground rules. He told him that his business was appreciated and so far things were fine. DeLuca was paying when he lost and collecting when he won. At that point, the kid was about six or seven grand up. But Alite was curious about the source of his money.

"Do you mind if I ask you what you do for a living?" he said.

"I'm the equipment manager for the Mets," he said. "I work at Shea Stadium."

Alite, who loved the game of baseball, was impressed.

"Man, that's great," he said. Then he paused. "But how are you managing to bet this way on that kind of salary? What happens if you hit a few bad days? How are you gonna cover?"

DeLuca didn't answer at first. It looked like he was debating about whether he should say what he was thinking. Finally, he told Alite that he wasn't betting with his own money. He said the bets were for players with the Mets. They were good for the action. DeLuca made a point of telling Alite that they never bet on games in which they were involved.

Alite, who took DeLuca at his word, was delighted. He didn't care about the ethics of ballplayers betting. From his perspective, Pete Rose should be in the Hall of Fame instead of being barred from Major League Baseball for betting on games while playing for and managing the Cinncinnati Reds. It's what you did on the field that mattered according to Alite's way of thinking. If DeLuca was telling the truth, this was a money stream that might never run out. Ballplayers had all kinds of cash. He had heard of professional athletes and entertainers betting a hundred thousand dollars on a game. This really was the big leagues.

"Just be careful," Alite told DeLuca. "Make sure you come up with the cash. You're the only one we can go after if things go bad. Remember that. You're the one we'll come looking for."

And, eventually, they did.

"We used to call him 'Joe Baseball,'" Alite told a federal jury as he recounted the DeLuca story and his claim to be betting for Mets ballplayers. "Overall, the kid was a degenerate gambler. You can't win when you bet the way he did. He just bet wild."

DeLuca would later deny that he was placing bets for any ball-players. Mets standout Keith Hernandez would be mentioned in media reports that surfaced after Alite began cooperating, but DeLuca insisted that Hernandez had merely helped him out once by loaning him some money. It had nothing to do with gambling.

In fact, DeLuca took a beating from Alite when he failed to come up with cash, about fifty thousand dollars, that he owed. And Alite and Junior later had to pay a visit to DeLuca's home. He lived with his parents. His mother and father agreed to borrow money to pay off the debt. Alite said he thought they had put up their house for a loan, got a second mortgage. It was better than borrowing from a loan shark.

DeLuca was one of several customers who took beatings over gambling debts. Another was a kid named Patsy Catalano, but there was more involved in that situation. Catalano owed about six grand and wasn't paying. His father , also known as Patsy, was a made guy and big in the heroin business. Patsy would just tell anyone who tried to collect, "Go see my dad."

The debt was actually owed to "Ronnie One-Arm" Trucchio, another Gambino soldier in the Gotti crew. But there was a lot of overlap in the bookmaking business and Alite was asked to help collect. He lured Catalano to the PM Pub in Queens, telling him he was going to help work out the problem and that he could cut the debt in half.

When Catalano got to the PM, negotiations took a different turn.

"I tied him up in a chair and started squirting him with lighter fluid, telling him I was going to set him on fire," Alite said. "He was pretty scared."

But Alite wasn't going to follow through until he had the okay from Junior. So with Catalano knotted to a chair in the back of the pub, Alite headed over to the Bergin. Junior wasn't there, but Genie Gotti was. When Alite told him the situation and asked for guidance, Gene Gotti smiled. He and his partner, John Carneglia, had been having problems with the senior Catalano in the heroin business. There was a dispute over territory and money. Gene Gotti saw this as a way to handle two problems at once. Alite was told to give Patsy Catalano a beating, but not to kill him.

Back at the PM he did just that. Alite took a blackjack to the helpless Catalano, who ended up with a broken nose, a fractured eye socket, and welts and bruises over the rest of his face and upper body. He left the pub a bloody, simpering mess. And with a message to deliver to his father. "Tell him Gene Gotti is waiting to hear from him."

Two days later, Alite walked into the Bergin and was greeted with shouts of praise, hugs, and kisses. Patsy Catalano had paid off the gambling debt in full and his father had fallen in line with Gene Gotti and John Carneglia in the heroin dispute.

"Nice job, kid," Gene Gotti told Alite.

Alite was getting a reputation as someone who could be depended on. He liked it. He liked having status with the wiseguys who hung at the Bergin and the Ravenite. He liked that when he walked into those clubs now, the older guys knew who he was and made a point of acknowledging him. It was a sign of respect and in a twisted way, it was as good as or better than the money that came with the business.

He got the same sense from Willie Boy Johnson, who was impressed with the way Alite was handling the bookmaking operation. Willie Boy also appreciated the fact that Alite regularly stopped by to visit Mark Caputo. He brought food, money, and, sometimes, a hooker.

"I used to go up to Hillside Avenue in Queens," Alite said.

"There were a lot of prostitutes working there. Everybody knew me because of our cocaine business. When I would pull up in my Corvette, people would come over to talk."

Occasionally Alite would bring one of the girls with him to the apartment where Caputo was holed up.

"The first time, me and Willie Boy are in the other room and Mark can't get it going," Alite recalled with a laugh. "The hooker looked at me like, 'What kind of customer is this?' But things worked out for Big Mark and he was happy with those visits."

He said Mark couldn't thank him enough.

But not everyone was pleased with Alite's hooker connections.

For a time, he and Ronnie One-Arm were in the prostitution business for the Gambino organization. They had an apartment and a stable of hookers who would service clients by appointment.

"But we never really made a lot of money," Alite explained, "because Ronnie and the other guys were always banging the girls and I had to pay them out of our profits."

Trucchio's wife found out about one get-together that Alite had set up at an apartment on Ninety-First Street and 101st Avenue.

"We all have our cars parked along the block," Alite said. "My Corvette, Ronnie's Lincoln, several other guys' cars. Ronnie's wife comes by in her car. It's the middle of the night, or early in the morning. We had been partying all night. There was booze and cocaine and girls and people were switching off and doing all kinds of crazy stuff. We're upstairs and I hear this crashing sound over and over. I look out a window and I see Ronnie's wife. She's crashing her car into all the other cars."

Alite ran downstairs.

"I wanted to get my Corvette before she hit it," he said. "Now she's screaming, 'Where's that little motherfucker John Alite?!'" I made it to my Corvette and got out of there."

Alite shut down the brothel a short time later. It was a losing proposition. You can't sample the merchandise if you want to run a profitable business. Bookies shouldn't bet. Drug dealers shouldn't snort. And if you're going to be a pimp, you can't be a john.

Running a sports book, on the other hand, came naturally to Alite and so did his relationship with Willie Boy Johnson. They genuinely liked one another and a few months into their business relationship, while visiting the club on Avenue U in Brooklyn, Alite was asked by Johnson to take a walk. Willie Boy started out by thanking Alite for what he was doing for Mark, telling him that Caputo was "like a son to me." Then he paused, hesitated for a few seconds, and added, "I want to give you a piece of advice, the same kind of advice I'd give Mark if he were in your position.

"If you're gonna stay in this life," Johnson said, "and I really think you ought to find something else, but if you're gonna stay, keep your eyes and your ears open and your mouth shut.

"You have no real friends. None of us do. Only jealous competitors."

Willie Boy was fifty and had been running with gangsters since he was a teenager. It was too late for him to change. Too much had happened. Again, he told Alite the smart move was to walk away now. But then Willie Boy told Alite that if he decided to stay, he could always come to Willie Boy for help or advice.

Johnson said he had come up under Fat Andy Ruggiano, the same capo who had helped Alite in the Patsy Antiques dispute. Ruggiano was a "gentleman," he said. Then, laughing, he showed Alite a scar on the back of his head. Fat Andy had shot him when they were kids running with different street gangs, Willie Boy said. But that was all forgotten when they lined up together in the Gambino organization. After Fat Andy went to jail, Johnson said, John Gotti Sr. took over the crew.

"Johnny's a different type of guy," Johnson said of Gotti Sr., whom he also had run with as a teenager. "He wants what he wants when he wants it. Nothing else matters. He's just a classic case of pure greed.

"I know Junior is your partner and I hope you don't take this the wrong way, but your partner is pure garbage. We all tolerate him because he's Johnny's son. That's the way this life works."

Johnson went on to describe John Gotti Sr. as a degenerate and deadbeat gambler who was disliked by most members of the other crime families in the city. This was even before the Castellano murder, he said.

"Learn to keep your own counsel," he said. "It'll keep you alive. The glamour, money, and loyalty are all smoke and mirrors. In the end you wind up paying more than you get and you pay with things more valuable than money."

They had walked around the block and were back in front of the clubhouse on Avenue U. Willie Boy Johnson smiled at Alite.

"We never had this conversation," he said.

Although Alite didn't know it at the time, Johnson had been a government informant for years. That information first surfaced during a pretrial hearing in the 1987 racketeering case that Gotti beat. Willie Boy was one of his codefendants. An overzealous and inexperienced federal prosecutor, Diane Giacalone, had exposed Johnson in an attempt to get him to cooperate. Giacalone was clashing with the FBI agents who had worked the case and was trying to show the world that she had more balls than the agents. They had pleaded with her not to go public with the information about Willie Boy, but she didn't listen.

You could make the argument that Giacalone, in her quest for glory, had gotten Willie Boy killed.

Johnson had been promised by the FBI that he would remain a confidential informant and would never be asked to take the stand. The arrangement had been in place for nearly twenty years. Giacalone, desperate to win a conviction, threw that agreement to the curb. Johnson, however, didn't budge. Publicly, he insisted that he was not an informant. He went on trial with Gotti and the others and after they all were acquitted, he drifted away from the crime family.

Alite was told that Johnson was promised by Gotti that no harm would come to him, but that he was being put on the shelf. The fact that Johnson remained in Brooklyn and went to work every day at a construction site would seem to indicate that Willie Boy took his boss at his word.

Shortly after six in the morning on August 29, 1988, Willie Boy Johnson left his apartment and headed off to work. Two men were waiting for him as he approached his car. They opened fire, chasing him across the street as he ran.

Johnson was hit at least six times in the head, according to news accounts. He also took two bullets to the back and one in each thigh. Eighteen shell casings were found at the crime scene on Royce Street near Avenue N, less than a block from the apartment house where Johnson was living with his wife.

There was little doubt that the hit—despite the assurance that Gotti had given Willie Boy—was in response to the disclosure that he had been a cooperator. The first shot to the head, a federal source told the *New York Times,* was enough to kill him.

"The rest were for effect," the *Times* quoted the source as saying.

Thomas "Tommy Karate" Pitera, a member of the Bonanno crime family, was later identified as one of the shooters that day. The hit was done as a "favor" to John Gotti Sr.

Alite was in the dark when most of this went down. Later, he said, Junior boasted that he had been on the scene that morning driving one of the crash cars. When he learned Johnson had been killed, Alite thought back on the talk they had had as they walked along Avenue U.

He still could replay the whole conversation in his head. He remembered every word. But one thing stood out more than anything else. "You have no real friends," Johnson said. "None of us do."

CHAPTER 7

D rugs were the big moneymaker for the Gotti organization, despite what Gotti Sr. said. And today, after it has all come undone, Alite still finds it ironic that neither Gotti nor his son was ever convicted of drug trafficking. Though, if the federal government's evidence and witnesses are to be believed, they both made a fortune from the drug business but went to great lengths to put a buffer between themselves and those doing the actual work.

Gotti Sr. abandoned friends and longtime associates who got jammed up, even though he had made millions with them. Alite, and others who testified against him at his trial in Manhattan, said Junior was the same way. Like his father, he would berate the "scumbag, punk drug dealer" who was indicted even though he was receiving a steady stream of cash from that "scumbag."

The treatment that Angelo Ruggiero received at the hands of Gotti Sr. was a prime example. Mark Reiter was another. Both kicked up hundreds of thousands of dollars to the mob boss, yet he turned his back on both of them.

John Gotti's Rules of Leadership: Drug dealing is prohibited and punishable by death. (Any member or associate dealing drugs must share his profits with the boss.)

Reiter was called "Mark the Jew" by Gotti and those around him. It was another one of those nicknames meant to belittle and mock. But Reiter let it roll off his back. He played at another level. He moved multiple kilos of heroin in New York City for years and lived life to the fullest. He had a wife and two sons on Long Island. He kept a penthouse on the Upper East Side. He had a condo in Israel. He drove a Jaguar, rode a Harley, and had a cigarette boat.

One of his partners was Thelma Grant, who the feds believed had taken over the Harlem-based drug business of the notorious Leroy "Nicky" Barnes after Barnes was jailed in 1977. Barnes, one of the biggest black drug dealers in the city, eventually testified against Reiter in a 1988 drug case.

"I was friends with Greg Reiter, Mark's son," Alite said. "But I got to know his father. A couple of times I was with John Gotti Sr. when he went up to Reiter's penthouse. He had a beautiful place around Fifty-Eighth Street and Second Avenue. We're there and he pulls out a suitcase full of cash. He gave Gotti about one hundred thousand dollars. And that was just fluff money, like a tip. It wasn't even Gotti's end from a deal. That's the way Mark Reiter was. He knew how to live."

Reiter told Alite to enjoy life. He said if you make money, don't be afraid to spend it. Travel. See the world. Don't be myopic. He didn't say it outright, but Alite knew the point he was making. John Gotti thought traveling to Florida was a big deal. Mark Reiter would rather take a jet to Paris. He looked like the actor Ray Liotta and he lived like a character in a movie—the best clothes, fancy cars, and dinners at fine restaurants.

"He used to say, 'Don't be like these other guys, hanging in a clubhouse all day playing cards. Get out there and make something of yourself.'"

It was twisted advice, coming from someone who dealt heroin big-time, but it was a lesson in the life that Alite wanted to live.

"He was the real deal," Alite said. "He taught us, me and his son Greg, how to dress, where to buy our clothes, how to act. He was a gentleman, or at least he gave the impression of being a gentleman. The broads loved him. He dated models, actresses, one more beautiful than the other. I think he knew Gotti and his son were full of shit, but he couldn't do anything about it. He had no choice. He was in too deep and couldn't get out."

Reiter could never be a made guy, but his situation was better than most made guys that Alite knew. If Alite had a role model in the underworld, it was Mark the Jew, not Junior or the Teflon Don.

But in 1987, it all came crashing down. Reiter was named in the same case that targeted Gene Gotti, Angelo Ruggiero, and John Carneglia. He was free on bail in June 1987 when that trial started, and after learning that an associate had flipped and was cooperating, he took off. He would eventually be indicted in two other drug cases.

"Me and his son met him down in Florida, at Disney World," Alite said. "We took him some money. Greg, his son, went back to New York but I stayed with him awhile and then went with him to California. We were in Beverly Hills, staying at a hotel. I would go back and forth to New York. Mark was making some contacts, trying to figure out how bad the case was, to get the pulse and determine what his options were."

Alite said he cautioned Reiter to lie low, but that just wasn't in his nature.

"He's still going out at night with beautiful women, going to restaurants, living his life," Alite said, shaking his head in amazement. "He's on the run, but he's not changing who he is."

Reiter was toying with the idea of leaving the country, but he had to find a way out. Before he could set anything up, he was arrested in the Los Angeles area and brought back to New York.

"He had been calling guys back in New York, guys he trusted," Alite said. "One of them gave him up."

Mark Reiter was eventually convicted and sentenced to eighty years in prison. He was in his late forties at the time. The sentence was tantamount to life. Alite was with Gotti Sr. when he went on a rant about his heroin-dealing associate, calling him a low-life drug dealer. After Reiter was convicted, Gotti berated him again, calling him "that Jew bastard, that fuckin' heroin dealer." And when Reiter's wife, Delores, was quoted in the newspaper during one of her husband's trials, complaining about abusive government tactics, the Gottis, father and son, lambasted her for speaking out.

She was a "whore" and a "cunt," they said. She should keep her mouth shut. Alite quietly shook his head as he thought about the abrasive, flamboyant, and outspoken Victoria Gotti and her equally arrogant daughter, Vicky. But what bothered him the most was the way Gotti Sr. so readily and easily tossed Mark Reiter aside.

"This was a guy who probably made him millions," Alite said. "After he got arrested, he didn't cut a deal and cooperate. He went to jail. He could have buried Gotti, but he didn't."

Alite believes Gotti's rants were by design. He recalled how Gotti used to holler and scream about Sammy Gravano and different acts of violence that Gravano had carried out, usually on Gotti's orders.

"He was always worried about listening devices," Alite said. "So when he berated Mark Reiter or Gravano, it was like he was implicating them in crimes in case the FBI was listening. It was like he was saying, 'It's not me. It's those guys.' He was like a dry snitch."

Loyalty was a one-way street in the Gambino crime family

that Gotti was running. His son operated the same way with the crew that he headed.

The first murder Alite committed for the Gambino crime family was tied to the drug business. The victim was Georgie Grosso, the brother-in-law of Johnny Gebert. Alite had grown up with both of them and had done business with them in the drug underworld. After the incident with the Jamaicans and the drive-by shooting, Alite never trusted Gebert. Grosso was no better. They both flaunted the rules of the street. And neither knew enough to keep his mouth shut. Both would end up dead. Grosso was the first to go.

Word got back to Junior that Grosso was using the Gotti name to enhance his standing. He was letting everyone know he was "with" Gotti, in fact letting everyone know that the Gottis were benefiting from his drug dealing. Alite knew that was true. Grosso and Gebert had to kick up to the Gottis in order to stay in business. Everybody did. But Alite also knew that talking about that arrangement, bragging about it, was going to create problems.

"He was telling people, 'I work for John Gotti,'" Alite said. "You don't do that. We heard about it and confronted him. He denied it. He said the only thing he ever said was that he was a friend of Junior Gotti's. I didn't believe that and I don't think Junior did, but Junior told him don't let it happen again."

Grosso apparently didn't listen. Word kept coming back to Junior and Alite that he was still using the Gotti name. He also was apparently using some of his product, smoking angel dust, snorting cocaine, and shooting heroin.

"Junior started worrying that he might become a rat," Alite said. "There was nothing concrete, but that was always a worry. You hear about guys using drugs and the first thing you think is, 'He's weak. He's getting' high. He can't hold up.'"

Alite was running his own crew at that time and was anxious

to prove himself. He had been on the fringe of an earlier mob hit. Frank "Geeky" Boccia was shot and killed in a club in Queens by Anthony Ruggiano and Dominick "Skinny Dom" Pizzonia. Alite had been part of the conspiracy but wasn't there when the hit went down.

The conventional wisdom was that Boccia, a hothead, had been killed because he had slapped around his wife, Francine Ruggiano, Anthony's sister and the daughter of Fat Andy Ruggiano. And then, when Francine's mother intervened, Boccia had slapped her as well. Alite was close to the Ruggianos and was happy to get involved. But he later learned that the real reason Boccia got killed was that he had gotten mouthy and arrogant with JoJo Corozzo, a made guy with the Gambinos.

"That's why the hit got approved," Alite said. "Slapping the women around was an excuse to kill him, but the Corozzos, JoJo and his brother Nicky, wanted him dead for their own reasons."

Alite was moving in higher circles within the organization at this time and was able to develop a better perspective on the plays and the players. Things were not always as they seemed. And sometimes that was by design. Junior had established a new pecking order. At a meeting late in 1987 at the Our Friends Social Club, Junior told everyone that from that point on they had to go through Alite, that whatever they wanted to say to him, they should say to Alite. That's the way it was going to be.

"He was moving up and he wanted to put a buffer between himself and some of the neighborhood guys," Alite recalled. "His father always used to tell him, 'You got too many of these jerkoffs around you.' So at this meeting he says, 'Everything goes through Johnny from now on,' meaning me."

Alite liked the power and the status. He would later tell a jury that at that point he was running a crew of several dozen mob associates who were working in the drug underworld and that he controlled cocaine distribution in Queens, parts of Brooklyn, and also in sections of Long Island.

Junior would occasionally tell Alite that while he couldn't be made, he could become someone with status, someone like Jimmy "the Gent" Burke or Joe "the German" Watts. They were major players in the underworld, had their own crews and their own operations. They were like capos, maybe even better. But they weren't made guys. Burke was with the Luchese crime family. Watts was with Gotti and the Gambino organization.

Jimmy the Gent was portrayed by Robert De Niro in the classic movie *Goodfellas*. He was the mastermind behind the infamous Lufthansa airline heist in 1978.

Alite saw himself on that career path. That Burke ended up dying in prison in 1996 and that Watts is currently serving a thirteen-year sentence after pleading guilty in 2011 to federal murder and assault charges was not part of the equation. Alite focused instead on the status, wealth, power, and influence that both Burke and Watts had on the streets. That's what he wanted. And he very nearly got it.

Jimmy the Gent also played a behind-the-scenes role in the first homicide that Alite was directly involved in. Alite was a friend of Frankie Burke, Jimmy the Gent's son. The Gottis wanted nothing to do with the Burkes, but Alite ignored Junior when he told him to stay away from Frankie.

It was the same old song. "They're scumbag drug dealers. Don't bother with them."

Alite would hang out with Frankie Burke at different bars and clubs when Junior wasn't around. One night Frankie told him that from prison his father was trying to collect an old debt and that he, Frankie, was supposed to meet with two guys over in Brooklyn to settle up. He asked Alite to go along.

"Frankie told me they owed his father a couple of hundred

grand," Alite said in retelling the story years later. "I took a ride with him to meet with these guys. It was over on Linden Boulevard in Brooklyn. It was nighttime. We pull up and these two guys get out of another car and come toward us. We get out of our car. There's a guy behind the wheel of the other car, but he just sits there."

Alite said the two guys were Hispanic. He didn't know many more details about them or the debt. He just knew that instead of settling up, they got confrontational. There were shouts and threats. Alite said he did what he was there for.

"I pulled out a gun and started shooting," he said. "Frankie did the same. The two guys went down. The guy behind the wheel of their car never moved. I think he might have been there to set them up. Frankie might have wanted to kill them all along. I don't know. We just got back in our car and drove back to Queens. I never heard any more about it after that."

A few months later, Frankie Burke got involved in a fight in a bar with a guy named Tito from the neighborhood. Tito shot and killed him.

"This guy Tito owned a barbershop on 101st Street, near the clubhouse," Alite said. "He and his brother were around a lot of people. The brother ran back to Italy after being involved in a murder."

After he heard what happened to Frankie Burke, Alite went to see Tito.

"I told him, 'Look, you better get out of here.' I said, 'I might be one of the guys they send to kill you,'" Alite said. "I knew Jimmy Burke would reach out to the Lucheses and they'd arrange for someone to take Tito out."

The barber told Alite he wasn't going anywhere.

"He just sat in his barber chair with his hands behind his head," Alite recalled. "It was like he was waiting to die."

A few days later, two gunmen walked into the shop and fired nine shots into Tito's head and body. He died where he sat.

Death had simply become a part of Alite's underworld. Over the years, so many guys he knew ended up dead that he and his friends started to refer to Woodhaven, the section of Queens where they had grown up, as Death Haven. Years later, while he was sitting in prison, Alite made a list of those he knew who had either been killed or died from a drug overdose. There were more than a hundred names on that list.

Alite knows he could easily have been one of them.

But in the late 1980s he was still young and brash and thought himself invincible. He was also very rich. Together he and Junior were grossing more than a million dollars a month in the coke business, he alleged on the witness stand. His top lieutenants were earning twenty or thirty grand a month. Lower-level guys were taking home five to ten grand. Alite estimated for the jury that he and Junior were each pocketing about a hundred grand a month, although his take was usually somewhat higher because he would play with the numbers. Junior didn't pay that much attention, especially if you were flashing a big wad of cash in his face and telling him it was his cut.

But not everyone was happy with the new arrangements.

One afternoon Alite was walking along Jamaica Avenue not far from an apartment he was sharing with a few other guys. Out of the corner of his eye he saw a Lincoln slowly moving alongside him. The car jumped the curb. He looked up just in time to see John Gebert point a gun and open fire.

Alite took off running as three shots rang out. He made his way back to his apartment, where he got his own gun. Then he went to see Junior. This was still a turbulent time in the Gotti underworld. The feds had uncovered yet another plot by the Genovese crime family to kill Gotti Sr.

Louis "Bobby" Manna, a capo with the New Jersey branch of the Genovese organization, had been caught on tape plotting another assassination attempt. The FBI had planted bugs in Casella's, a restaurant in Hoboken, New Jersey, where Manna hung out. The feds had wired a private back room that Manna used as an office. They also had a bug in the women's bathroom because they heard Manna would slip in there sometimes to discuss business. Gotti and his brother Gene were the targets of the Manna plot. As they were required to do, FBI agents working the case warned Gotti. He laughed it off, but the entire crime family was again put on alert: Be careful who you're dealing with and report in on a regular basis. Let your boss know about any unusual activity.

Alite was doing just that when he went to see Junior, who was still living at home with his father and mother on Eighty-Fifth Street and 160th Avenue in Howard Beach. He told Junior about the ambush and said he wanted permission to kill Gebert.

According to Alite, Junior said he wanted to talk to Gebert first. He told Alite to get in the car and take a ride. They headed over to Gebert's apartment.

"I was steaming," Alite said. "I didn't want to go. He was making me look weak, like I had run to Junior and now Junior was going to protect me. It was bullshit."

Alite sat in the car while Junior spoke with Gebert. When he came out, he told Alite that everything was taken care of, that it wouldn't happen again.

"John, what's the matter with you?" Alite asked. "He tried to kill me. I gotta kill him."

Junior said not now. Alite would later testify that Junior told him that they would "rock him to sleep," let him relax. Then, according to Alite's testimony, they would kill him.

Gebert tried to stay out of Alite's way, but the two of them crossed paths on Jamaica Avenue a few weeks later and got into a shouting and shoving match. No guns this time, but clearly the bad blood was still there. Junior again met with Gebert and, according to Alite, again refused permission for a hit. Shortly after that, Gebert went on the lam.

He was a suspect in a rape and took off. He was hiding out in Brooklyn and wasn't around Queens anymore. That made it easier for Junior to ignore Alite's plea for permission to kill him. Alite also believed that Gebert was still kicking up regularly to Junior from his drug business and Junior didn't want to eliminate a source of income. Alite would testify that Junior told him Gebert was on a hit list, that he would be killed, but the murder was temporarily on hold.

Georgie Grosso, on the other hand, wasn't as big a source of money for Junior. Killing him would set an example. It was a way to let everyone know that using the Gotti name in the drug underworld was a capital offense.

The rules were simple, Alite said.

"Everyone knew if you got caught dealing drugs, you would be killed," he said. "One time when I met with John Gotti, he told me, 'I know what you're doing, but I don't know. And if you get caught, you're dead.'"

What wasn't said, but what Alite clearly understood, was that Junior had better not be implicated in any drug case. If Alite got caught dealing, Alite was going to take the fall. For some reason, Grosso never understood. He continued to throw the Gotti name around. Alite testified that this was the reason Junior wanted him dead. According to Alite, the fact that Grosso was there when Gebert ambushed Alite was used by Junior to enhance his order that Grosso had to go.

Alite told the court that he got the okay and set a plan in motion.

As with Gebert, the idea was to set Grosso up, make him comfortable, "rock him to sleep." Alite testified that he recruited several guys who were part of his crew to help out. There was Phil Baroni, an ex–New York City police detective; another kid named Joey Dee; and two other guys who liked to hang out with wiseguys. They were basically along for the ride.

The first thing they did was "clock" Grosso, establish his routine. He was in the habit of showing up at the White Horse Tavern late each night. One Monday night, about a week before Christmas in 1988, Alite and the others were there drinking when Grosso walked in. The Monday night football game was on every big TV screen around the bar. Alite waved and called Grosso over.

"He was leery at first, but everybody made him feel comfortable," Alite said. "I was buying drinks. Shots. I had told the bartender beforehand to just pour me water. Everyone else was getting shots of vodka. We're drinking, laughing, joking. Kiddin' around about how things were when we were kids. Everybody's gettin' a little drunk and I can see Grosso is starting to relax."

With the football game winding down, Alite suggested they all head out to an after-hours club out by LaGuardia Airport called the Executive Suite. At first Grosso said he wanted to go home, but the others convinced him to come along.

Alite, Baroni, and Grosso got into a Chevy Blazer that Joey Dee was driving.

When Grosso started to get into the backseat, Alite told him with a smile, "No. You ride up front." Alite and Baroni piled into the backseat, Alite sitting directly behind Grosso. Alite testified that the other two guys followed in another car.

"That was the crash car," Alite said as he detailed the murder from the witness stand. "Originally the plan was to pull over near a park off Eighty-Eighth Street and Atlantic Avenue. I was gonna say I had to take a piss. When the car stopped, I would shoot him and we'd dump his body."

But Alite said he worried that kids playing in the park the next day would come across the corpse. It wasn't that he was concerned about the body being discovered—in fact Alite told a jury that Junior had made a point of telling him that the body should be left out in the open so that the murder could serve as an example for anyone else who misused or abused the Gotti name.

"Don't bury him," Alite said Junior told him. "Don't put him in water. Don't hide him. Put him out in the street so people know what you did."

Alite just didn't want a bunch of kids exposed to that kind of violence. It was a strange moral code, one that Alite was constantly wrestling with as he dealt with the Gotti organization. Alite understood that even in this life there was a right way and a wrong way to do something. You didn't need to expose innocent people.

So instead of pulling off near the park, they continued to drive out toward LaGuardia on the Grand Central Parkway. They slowed off an exit at Jewel Avenue and that's where Alite pulled out his gun and pumped three bullets into the back of Grosso's head.

Then he spit on him, calling him a son of a bitch and a cocksucker.

The others took Grosso's body and dumped it in some brush near the guardrail that ran along the Jewel Avenue exit. Alite threw the gun in a nearby lake. Then they all drove to the Esquire Diner in Queens and had something to eat. Alite still remembers what he ordered that night.

"A cheeseburger with extra cheese," he said. "That's what I always got. And a Coke."

Before they headed home, Alite told Joey Dee to make sure he cleaned out the Blazer really well. He told him he ought to get rid of it after that.

"I told him he probably ought to sell it," Alite said.

The next morning Alite headed over to the Bergin, where he met Junior and told him everything had been taken care of. The two walked next door to a salon, where Alite says they got manicures. It was a routine for both of them, who liked to look sharp and always got their nails done.

It was another point that the defense would use to portray Alite as a ruthless and heartless killer. Within minutes of killing Georgie Grosso, Alite was sitting in a booth at a diner having a cheeseburger. Less than five hours later, with Grosso's remains still warm, he was in a salon getting a manicure.

While they were there, Gene Gotti walked in. Junior started to tell him what had happen. His uncle flipped out and pushed Junior outside.

"He told him, 'Are you fuckin' crazy talkin' about something like that?'" Alite recalled. "The Gottis figured the feds had bugs everywhere. We all used to go to the nail salon next to the Bergin, so Genie figured there were bugs in there too."

When Junior came back to Alite, he told him what his uncle had said. He also said Gene Gotti wanted him to make sure everything had gone down the way Alite described it.

"Junior said he wanted me to drive him back to the Jewel Avenue exit where the body was," Alite said. "I've watched a lot of movies. I know you're not supposed to go back to the scene of the crime, but that's what Junior wanted."

They jumped into Alite's Corvette and headed out on the Grand Central Parkway, pulling off at the Jewel Avenue exit. The area was swarming with police. There were several patrol cars, a coroner's van, all kinds of cops. As they drove by, Junior looked over. They were carrying Grosso's body out.

"He don't look good," Alite recalled Junior saying with a laugh. Alite just kept driving.

The murder enhanced Alite's underworld resume. Now he was someone who had done some work, someone whom others would describe as "capable." But it did even more for Junior Gotti.

Four days after Grosso's body was discovered, Junior Gotti was formally initiated into the Gambino crime family. It was the first step in what a federal prosecutor would later describe as the "rise of a vicious and violent street criminal to a savvy and money-hungry business criminal and leader of the Gambino family."

Savvy might have been a bit of an overstatement, but the point was clear. Junior had been anointed.

The ceremony took place on Christmas Eve in an apartment on Mulberry Street near the Ravenite. Sammy the Bull Gravano, who had been elevated to the position of underboss, officiated. Gotti Sr. didn't attend, but held court later at a party at the club.

"They figured it wouldn't look right if Gotti initiated his own son," Alite said.

Michael "Mikey Scars" DiLeonardo and two others guys were also made that night. DiLeonardo, like Alite, would later become a government witness and provide details about the inner workings of the Gotti crime family. But that would be years later. That Christmas Eve the Gottis, father and son, were sitting on top of their world.

Image and perception were what they were all about. Junior's rise up the ladder was the essence of underworld nepotism. While Alite may have thought that he was using Junior to get ahead in the crime family, it was actually Junior who was using him. In Italian-American communities all over America that night, the sons and daughters of immigrants were celebrating the Feast of the Seven Fishes before heading off to Midnight Mass. The Gottis, on the other hand, were pledging their allegiance to an institution they considered even more sacred than the Catholic Church.

Vicky Gotti would later write about her brother's formal initiation into the mob in her book *This Family of Mine*. She said her brother likened the ceremony to something out of the Knights of the Roundtable. She herself compared her father, brother, and the men who worked for them to Robin Hood and his band of merry men, robbing from the rich and giving to the poor. The author conceded, however, that some of the money ended up in the pockets of her father and brother.

CHAPTER 8

The Robin Hood image was partially correct. The Gottis had robbed a lot of people. Gotti Sr. started out robbing trucks and brought the mind-set of a hijacker to everything that he did. It was a quick and easy way to make money. You just took from anyone who had what you wanted. That was the approach that he followed when he became boss.

Junior, on the other hand, didn't start out targeting trucks. He went where he knew the payoff would be even bigger.

"I would say we robbed a couple dozen drug dealers while we were in the drug business," Alite said. "Some of it was penny ante, like the time we pistol-whipped that kid. But there were also some pretty big scores."

One of the biggest was on the Upper East Side, where a drug supplier named Hunter Adams had a posh apartment in a high-rise that included a twenty-four-hour doorman and lots of surveillance cameras. Alite would later testify that Michael Reiter, one of Mark Reiter's sons, came to Alite with the idea. Alite said he took it to Junior and then set the robbery in motion.

Reiter knew that Adams was going to Florida on vacation. Alite waited a few days, then called the apartment complex, posing as Adams. He told one of the security personnel that while he was away, he was having a new carpet installed. He said two workmen would be coming by and that they should be let into the apartment. He said he trusted the workers and there was no need to stay with them while they took up the old rug and installed the new one.

"I'll make sure they take care of you," Alite, as Adams, told the apartment guard, holding out the prospect of a nice tip. "I think we gave him a nickel [five hundred dollars], which right away let him know something was wrong. But he took the money and let them in."

Alite tapped Mike Finnerty and Patty DiPippa to carry out the heist. Both were friends of his from the neighborhood. DiPippa was the brother of a woman who would eventually become Alite's common-law wife and the mother of two of his kids.

"They wore hats and hoodies and used the service elevator," he said. "They had an old rug that they had rolled up and a dolly and a tool box. They got right in."

They spent a few hours in the apartment so it would seem as if they were, in fact, replacing a rug. What they actually did was locate a safe that Adams had in his apartment, take it out of the wall, and put it on the dolly. They then covered the safe with the old rug and exited the apartment building. They told Alite there was $160,000 in the safe when they broke it open.

"Probably was more than that," Alite said, repeating a story that he had also told a federal jury during Junior's 2009 racketeering trial. "It's part of the business of the street. . . . Everybody is robbing everybody. They probably took thirty, forty, fifty thousand out before they told me it was a hundred and sixty thousand."

Knowing the way Junior operated, Finnerty and DiPippa wanted to make sure they got a good cut, Alite said. Junior was notorious for leaving himself the lion's share whenever he racked up a score.

In this case, Alite said, he and Junior split one hundred

thousand and Finnerty and DiPippa, who did all the work and took the biggest risk, split sixty thousand with Mike Reiter, who had come up with the scam to begin with. That was the economic reality of the Gotti underworld. Everyone knew it. Privately, guys would complain to him, Alite said, but publicly there was nothing they could do.

"It was a complete dictatorship," he said.

John Gotti's Rules of Leadership: Always keep underlings waiting. It reminds them who's in control without saying a word.

Junior was running his crew the same way his father ran the crime family. He'd call a meeting and then show up an hour later, just to keep everyone waiting. He'd go to a card game and the guys with him would have wait for hours until he was ready to leave. And he demanded a piece of everyone's action.

Money flowed up, never down. There were a few times when Alite was able to challenge that situation, but not very often. The only way to ensure a fair split, he and the others knew, was to cook the books, to lie about the actual number before turning the take in to Junior.

There was more than one occasion, however, when that wasn't possible. Junior seldom got directly involved in a heist after he was initiated as a mob soldier, but, according to Alite, he still liked to be on hand when things went down. Alite would recall him being off to the side, sitting in a car a block away, maybe using a police scanner and serving as a lookout. Alite believes this was Junior's way of being sure the robbery went down. It also put him in a position to get away as quickly as possible if something went wrong.

The robbery of John Kelly, another big-time drug supplier, went down as planned, but Alite ended up doing jail time in the aftermath. Kelly, according to Alite's testimony, was the brother of Tony Kelly, the guy from whom Alite, Junior, and Kevin Bonner were buying after Bonner was "persuaded" to change suppliers.

In fact, Alite told a jury, it was John Kelly who was the source of the cocaine they were buying.

"This guy was moving fifty to a hundred kilos a month," Alite said. "Junior wanted him to kick up some cash, like two thousand a kilo."

It was the typical mob street tax that Junior imposed on anyone he could get this hooks into. But John Kelly figured he was playing at a higher level and ignored the request for a tribute payment. In fact, Alite said, the message he sent back was "Fuck you."

"I went to see him," Alite said. "I didn't want to rob the guy. I said, 'John, just give him some money. Keep the peace.' But he didn't want to pay."

A lesser player, like Georgie Grosso, was killed for that kind of attitude, but Kelly was such a big moneymaker that it made more sense to go after his cash.

"At this point, in the late 1980s, I'm not even touching cocaine anymore," Alite said. "I have other guys who are making the deliveries, collecting the cash, cutting the product, whatever. We're still big in the business, but we're not in the business, if you know what I mean."

The idea was to set up a buy from John Kelly and then rob him. Keith Pellegrino, who was one of Alite's major operators in the cocaine business, put in a request for five kilos of coke.

"This was Junior's idea," said Alite. "I know Kelly is not going to show up with five kilos. He's too smart and too paranoid for that. He'll sell us the five, but it'll be two kilos now and two kilos next week and another kilo after that. That's what happened here."

Kelly showed up at Pellegrino's mother's house, around Eighty-Seventh Street and 103rd Avenue, Alite said. He brought two kilos of cocaine. Pellegrino paid eighty thousand in cash. Kelly put the money in a satchel and dropped the satchel in the trunk of his car as he left the house. There were six sets of eyes on him as he pulled away. Alite and Junior sat in one car watching. Phil Baroni, the former New York City police detective, and a kid named Frankie were in a second car. Two other associates were in a third. Depending on which way Kelly turned, one of those three cars would pull him over. Baroni had gotten badges for everyone. They were going to pose as cops and rip him off. Kelly turned Baroni's way and within a minute, he was pulled over.

Baroni and the kid Frankie flashed their badges. Kelly and his young girlfriend, who was in the passenger seat, were asked to step out of the car. The "cops" searched the inside of the vehicle and then the trunk, taking the satchel with them as they left Kelly and the girl on the sidewalk. Alite told the jury that the money was returned to Junior and after Pellegrino cut and sold the two stolen kilos of coke, the crew split what amounted to 100 percent profit.

Alite said he and Junior each got about thirty grand from the score while the others split another sixty thousand. A few years later, after that money was long gone, Alite, Junior, Frankie, and a few others guys were on Fire Island one summer afternoon when John Kelly walked by. Everyone said hello, but Kelly recognized Frankie as one of the "cops" who had rousted him. He had originally written the heist off as the work of a couple of rogue detectives. Now he knew better.

"He couldn't do anything to Junior," Alite said. "He knew that, but he called me up and threatened me and Keith Pellegrino." A few years later, Kelly would follow up on that threat and Alite would end up in jail as a result.

Not every robbery, of course, went off as planned or brought back the cash that was expected.

Alite testified that Junior sent him to Florida late in 1987 to follow up on a tip that came from one of Junior's cousins, a kid named John DiGiorgio, the brother of Sonny DiGiorgio. These were cousins on Junior's mother's side. Junior said his cousin was trying to help out a woman who was caught in a bad marriage. Her husband was some kind of doctor or surgeon and he was abusing her. The doctor, said his wife, had a million dollars stashed in his house. DiGiorgio, through Junior, wanted Alite to rob the doctor and rough him up in the process.

"Bobby Boriello had two tough Spanish kids who were with him at the time," Alite said. "He told them to go down to Florida with me for this job."

Boriello was a big, six-foot-two, 250-pound mob soldier and one of Junior's best friends. He would be Junior's best man at his wedding a few years later.

"I always liked Bobby," Alite said. "He was a tough kid, but a genuine nice guy. Funny. But he didn't know how to make money. He had a nephew who was a jockey and one time the three of us, Bobby, Junior, and me, went down to Delaware, Dover Downs, I think it was, to watch the kid race."

The kid was giving his uncle Bobby tips on what horses to bet. Boriello told Alite and Junior and they placed their bets accordingly.

"We're watching the races with the kid's wife, who was pregnant at the time," Alite said. "We bet a few races, but we're not doing too well. I was beginning to wonder about how good the info was."

But on the fifth race that day, the kid had given them three horses and said to bet a trifecta. These were the horses that were going to come in.

"We bet them," Alite said. "They were all long shots, the four, the six, and the eight. I think we put a couple of thousand on the trifecta, which would have paid off big-time, maybe a hundred grand, maybe more. We're watching and those three horses are out front coming into the stretch. We're screaming. Bobby especially 'cause he doesn't have a lot of money."

But out of the corner of his eye, Alite saw another horse coming up on the outside. It was the horse that Bobby's nephew was riding.

"I can't believe it," he said. "The kid's horse breaks up the trifecta. We lose. Now Bobby's screaming. He's running after his nephew. We lost a couple of grand, but Junior and I both start laughing. Bobby's hollering, 'I'm gonna kill you!' He's running after the jockey. The kid took off. The other people just think it's a disgruntled gambler who lost, which was true. But they don't know the whole story. The kid's wife is crying. I think we laughed all the way back to the city, although Bobby didn't think it was so funny. He never caught up with his nephew, which was probably a good thing. I never knew what happened that day. The kid must have panicked or something. We would have won big money if he had just held his horse back."

The Florida robbery was another bust.

"When we get there, DiGiorgio picks me up at the airport," Alite said. "Bobby's guys had come in on another flight. DiGiorgio was supposed to have all kinds of intel for me, whether there was a security system in the house, where the money was. He was also supposed to get us a car and some guns. All he had was a fake gun. Nothing else."

He drove them to the doctor's house in Fort Lauderdale.

It was across the street from a police station.

"Bobby's guys don't want to do it, but I said, 'We came this far. We're going in,'" Alite said while recounting the story to a federal jury in Manhattan.

He said he knocked on the door and when the doctor answered, he coldcocked him, knocking him out. He and the two Spanish kids went into the house, rolled the doctor up in a rug, covered his mouth with duct tape, and began searching the premises.

There was supposed to be a safe with a million dollars in cash.

They found about three grand in a drawer in one of the bedrooms. There was no safe.

"We poured some water on the doctor to wake him up," Alite said, "and I pulled the duct tape off his mouth. We asked him where the cash was."

The doctor, lying on the floor with just his head sticking out of a rolled-up carpet, went on a rant about his wife. She had taken up with this drug dealer, he told Alite. This was her way of punishing him. He had no cash. It was all bullshit.

Alite, who knew a little about vindictive women, thought the doctor's story had the ring of truth. And knowing the way the Gottis operated—he considered the DiGiorgio branch of the family part of the same bloodline—he accepted the story. Junior's cousin, Alite thought, was probably having an affair with the woman and this was his way of showing her how tough and connected he was. Once again it was more perception than reality. Alite was carrying the ball for another branch of the family.

Alite and Boriello's two guys left the doctor where he was, wrapped in a rug, lying on the floor just off the foyer of the house. They headed for the airport and a flight back to New York City. Alite told Boriello's two guys to split the three grand they had found in the home.

The take didn't even cover expenses.

Paul Silvers was a more lucrative score. Alite robbed him twice. The story, which Alite would also recount for the federal jury in Manhattan, offers a glimpse at the petty, everyday deceit that is so much a part of the mob underworld. Men of honor may show up in mob movies, but Alite ran into very few in Queens or Manhattan.

Silvers was a drug dealer whom Junior had grown up with. They were friends of sorts. But when Silvers went into the drug business, he hooked up with Tommy Stabile, who was tied to the Luchese organization. Silvers was kicking up to him every week. Stabile was Silvers's insurance policy. Junior didn't care. According to Alite's testimony, he sent Alite to rob Silvers.

Silvers had an apartment on Queens Boulevard. Alite arranged for a drug purchase but showed up with a gun instead of cash.

"Come on, John," Silvers said when he realized what was going down.

"Talk to the other guy," said Alite as he walked out with a kilo of coke and several thousand dollars. They both knew Alite was referring to Junior. Silvers did what would be expected. He went to Stabile. Stabile, in turn, asked to meet with Junior.

This was mobster-to-mobster, the typical way disputes of this kind were settled. Junior brought Alite along for the meeting at a car lot Stabile owned on Atlantic Avenue near Eighty-Sixth Street. The negotiations were short and sweet. Paul Silvers got screwed.

Stabile said Silvers was paying him between two hundred and three hundred dollars a week. Alite watched and listened as Gotti negotiated. According to Alite's recollection, Junior offered Stabile five thousand dollars, part of the take from the first robbery, and said they intended to rob Silvers again. Stabile would be in for a piece of that as well. All he had to do was tell Silvers that everything had been straightened out and that it wouldn't happen again.

A few weeks later, Alite said he was back at Silvers's apartment for another drug buy. When Alite got off the elevator, Silvers had his girlfriend waiting.

"I'm sorry," she told Alite, "but he wants me to frisk you."

Alite held out his arms as the attractive young woman began patting him down. She moved her hands over his sides and along his thighs. She lifted his pant legs to see if he had an ankle holster.

Alite smiled, looked at his crotch, and said, "Do you want to check my balls?"

She laughed and said, "That won't be necessary."

Turns out it was.

Once inside the apartment, Alite reached into his pants where he had a gun stashed in a jock strap. Again Silvers said, "Come on, John." Alite just rolled his eyes and walked out with cash and coke that was worth about $75,000. Stabile got 10 percent. Alite says he and Junior split the rest.

"With Junior, it was always about money," Alite said. "Friendship didn't matter. You could have been his friend for a dozen years and he'd still rip you off. He didn't care. That's just the way he was. Him and his father, both the same."

Silvers figured in another, more lucrative heist that Alite pulled off several years later, although Junior wasn't thrilled with the outcome. Posing as cops, Alite, Baroni, and Pellegrino hit an apartment owned by Dennis Harrigan, another major drug dealer.

They had badges, but that wasn't enough.

"After we busted in, Harrigan's girlfriend, who was in the shower, came out with just a towel wrapped around her," Alite recalled. "Her name was Claudine. I didn't recognize her, but she recognized me. She owned a beauty parlor where my girlfriend Claudia was working. She was also dating Louie Dome [Louis Pacella], who was one of the leaders of the Luchese crime family."

Alite stared at the woman. He had a gun in one hand and a badge in the other.

"John, I know it's you," she said. "I know you're not a cop."

There was nothing that Harrigan could do, however. Alite and his partners walked out of the apartment with more than $120,000 in cash. But before taking the money to Junior, Alite took $65,000 and gave it to Greg Reiter. Reiter, in turn, gave the cash to his mother, Delores, the wife of Mark the Jew, the jailed drug dealer. Greg, who was a good friend of Alite, had gotten involved in a drug deal with Harrigan and Silvers in Mexico a few months earlier. The deal went bad. Someone had set them all up and all their cash was stolen. Greg Reiter's end was sixty-five grand, money he had taken from his mother without her knowing about it. The son figured he would turn a profit and give his mom back more than he had "borrowed." Instead, he had lost it all.

Alite used the Harrigan robbery to make Delores Reiter whole again. The rest of the cash he took to Junior.

"He was screaming," Alite said, "but I didn't care."

It was the first time Alite had openly defied Junior Gotti. They still were partners and he still was Junior's go-to guy on the streets, but the relationship was beginning to change. Alite began to recognize his role in the organization, the place he held in Junior's world and, to a lesser extent, in John Gotti Sr.'s world. He was someone they both found useful. And as long as he was able to deliver, things would be all right. But if he wasn't able to meet their needs, then he was expendable. It was a way of life in the underworld. It was, he told a federal jury, like walking a tightrope.

"Everything we do, one step and you could be killed; one step and you could get a life sentence. We all think we're smarter than everybody else. All we do is lie. And all we do is kill and hurt."

By this point Alite's reputation on the street, coupled with his connection with the Gottis, had given him power and status. He was fearless, "crazy" in the eyes of some of the people he dealt with. It was a persona that he knew kept him alive. It was an outgrowth of the lessons his father had taught him about not backing down.

"I was never a bully, but I was always the guy that friends would call when they had a problem," he said. "They knew I would come."

Joe O'Kane, who had stood with him during the White Castle brawl, called one night from a club in Brooklyn where he had gone with his girlfriend. Three guys in the club, the Bulkhead Bar, were hassling him.

"I'll be right there," Alite said.

There was a bar in the front and a dance floor with a disc jockey in the back. Alite headed for the dance floor, which was jammed with people. He spotted O'Kane and asked him to point out the guys who were creating a problem. One of them was on the dance floor with a girl.

Alite walked up to him and over the noise and the music, asked, "You got a problem with my friend?"

The guy told Alite to fuck off. Alite pulled out a gun and shot him in the hip. When he went down, Alite kicked him in the face. His girl screamed and people all around finally started to realize what was happening. Alite calmly walked out of the bar and headed toward his car. Then he heard footsteps, turned around, and saw two other guys coming for him. He couldn't believe it.

"I said to the one kid, what are you, fuckin' crazy? Then I shot him. He went down and the other kid took off."

Alite kept walking, past his car and toward a corner store. From there he called Keith Pellegrino and told him to pick him up.

"I didn't want to get in my car because somebody might get a tag number," he said. "I left it there till the next day. Nobody in the bar identified me. That was the end of it. In those days, I just didn't care. I thought of myself as a nice guy. I would always be a gentleman. I wouldn't start no fights. But if something happened, or if one of my friends was in trouble, then I would take it to the extreme. My attitude was, if you were gonna hurt somebody, you hurt them real good. If not, they'd come back after you."

It really didn't matter who. Alite was just five foot eight, and even when he was boxing and in top shape, he never weighed more than 180 pounds. Size wasn't the issue.

"I'm home asleep one night," he said. "I'm still living in the basement of my parents' home at the time. The phone rings and it's my friend Joey Mathis. He's just a straight kid. He was at the Old Brother Inn on Jamaica Avenue, a few blocks from where I live."

Three bikers had come to the bar that night and were causing trouble. The bartender threatened to call the police. The bikers had gotten into it with Mathis and now they were outside with chains and baseball bats waiting for him to leave at closing time.

Alite got dressed, grabbed a bat, and headed up Jamaica Avenue.

"I go in the bar and tell Joey Mathis, 'Come on, we're goin' home,'" Alite said. "When we walk out the bikers are there. One of them tells me, 'Mind your business. This has got nuthin' to do with you.'"

Alite hit him in the head with the bat, knocking him out cold. Then he turned on a second biker as Mathis and another guy from the bar, Kenny Nicole, grabbed the third. In the melee, Alite accidentally hit Nicole in the head and ended up taking him to a hospital out on Long Island.

"I didn't want to go to a local hospital in case there were any police," he said.

A few days later, Alite got word that nearly a dozen bikers were back at the bar looking for him. Alite had friends who were Hells Angels and went to see them at their clubhouse. He asked about the bikers and was told they were part of a ragtag outfit out of Kew Gardens.

"What the fuck kind of biker gang comes out of Kew Gardens?" he asked. He got the name of one of the leaders and was told the name of the bar where they hung out. He took a gun and a knife and Mike Finnerty.

"I told Mike just to stay by the door and be ready with the car," he said. "But he came in anyway."

Alite had been told to look for a guy named Brian, who was one of the leaders of the renegade biker group. Brian was sitting by the pool table. He was in a chair and had his thighs straddling a girl who was with him.

"I heard you got a problem with me," Alite said.

"Who are you?" asked the biker.

"John Alite. I heard you were looking for me."

As the girl moved away, Alite pulled out his knife and jammed it into the biker's thigh.

"Now you found me," he said. "Look for me again and I'll kill ya."

With that, he and Finnerty left the bar.

Violence was a part of who Alite was. Looking back on it now, and aided by weekly sessions with a therapist, he says he was like an alcoholic. He was drawn toward it. Sometimes he didn't even know why. Part of it was survival. Part of it was to establish a reputation in the world in which he was operating. And part of it was a crazy, antisocial streak that even today he struggles to control.

There was an incident at another bar in the neighborhood that captures exactly who Alite was when he was running wild on the streets. The bar was owned by two New York City cops who were allowing Alite's crew to deal drugs from the establishment. One night Alite walked into the bar wearing a suit and tie and a scarf. Two patrons started making fun of the way he was dressed, referring to him as a "pretty boy." One reached over and flicked the scarf up in Alite's face. Alite didn't even think. He just reacted. He punched the first guy in the jaw, knocking him out, and then turned on the other guy, pummeling him to the ground. A friend of theirs whom Alite also knew tried to intervene and calm him down.

"What are you doing, John?" the guy screamed.

Alite pulled out a gun and shot him in the chest.

It was senseless. Totally unreasonable. He was out of control.

He knows that now. But what he also remembers while re-counting the incident was the reaction of the two cops who owned the joint. They were concerned that a shooting would bring a law enforcement investigation that might result in the bar being closed for a period of time. As the victim lay bleeding and moaning on the floor, the two cops berated Alite for creating a situation that might result in a loss of business.

"I told two other guys to drag the body out onto the sidewalk," he said. "This way it would look like the shooting occurred on the street. That made the cops happy."

The shooting victim survived, but the incident reinforced the local perception that John Alite was not someone you wanted to fool with.

"People knew that about me," he said. "I even shot my own cousin."

That incident also stemmed from a bar fight. This time it was in an after-hours club that Alite had in South Ozone Park. Two of his associates had gotten into an altercation with a guy who turned out to be an off-duty transit cop. One of them shot the cop. They were arrested and charged with assault. The cop survived.

Alite had a cousin who was running the club and also happened to be the cop's neighbor. They lived next door to one another. Alite gave his cousin sixty thousand dollars to bribe the officer, who, a few days later, said he was unable to identify his assailants when they were paraded before him at a police lineup. The case went away.

But a few years later, the cop, through some connections he had with the Genovese family, complained that he had never gotten paid. Both Junior and Charles Carneglia asked Alite to look into the problem. Alite went to see his cousin Nicky, who everyone suspected had pocketed the sixty grand.

"He got fresh with me," Alite said. "His wife was telling him to watch how he spoke, but he kept getting in my face. I had a gun and I pistol-whipped him, hit him in the head a few times. But he wouldn't stop."

So Alite shot his cousin in the hip and in the leg, which later had to be amputated.

Junior Gotti's defense attorney would bring out that shooting and the fight and shooting involving the scarf when he cross-examined Alite during the 2009 trial. Alite didn't try to sugarcoat any of it. That was who he was, he told the jury. And that was why the Gottis had him around.

CHAPTER 9

While he was on the run in 2003, Alite popped in and out of Albania three times. Each visit gave him a chance to catch his breath and to feel his roots. He had an uncle who operated a hotel in Tirana, the capital, and he had aunts, uncles, and cousins living in the countryside.

The trip was an easy one. He made his way to Bari, an Italian port city on the Adriatic, and then took the ferry over to Albania. His relatives treated him royally. Most were unaware of his notoriety. He was Johnny from America, an athlete of sorts, although past his prime.

"I trained a little with the Albanian Olympic boxing team while I was there," he said. "I was still in shape and told them I had fought in America. One thing about boxing, you can't hide. You get in the ring and you have to produce. They saw I knew how to handle myself."

Alite also made some connections with Albanian mobsters, a violent group of gangsters who, unlike many of his relatives, knew or quickly learned about his criminal history.

"These guys all lived in mansions," he said. "Forts really, houses with gates all around for their own protection because they all kill like crazy."

Clannish and secretive, Albanian mobsters are major players

in drug trafficking, gun running, and white slavery, supplying heroin, weapons, and young women from Eastern Europe to underworld buyers in Italy, France, and Spain.

"I took a couple of these guys to my uncle's restaurant one night," Alite said. "He was really angry. Afterwards he told me, 'Don't ever bring those kinds of people to my place again.'

"It's different over there. A lot like Cuba, really. There's not enough to do and there are all kinds of problems. The electricity doesn't always work. The lights are always going out. But the women were beautiful. They dress nice, really sexy. But you have to be careful. Their fathers or brothers will kill you. It's very hard to get laid. . . . I had to get out of there."

Alite never had a problem connecting with women. While he was on the run he managed to hook up with a beauty in every city where he spent time: Paris, Amsterdam, Barcelona, Havana, and Rio. In fact, when he finally settled in the Copacabana section of Rio, he started dating a young schoolteacher who introduced him to her circle of friends and helped him blend in.

Back in the States he had an ex-wife with whom he had had two children, a common-law wife with whom he had two others, and several girlfriends with whom he kept in contact. John Alite liked women. And for the most part, they liked him.

There were times, as he looks back on it now, when he realizes his macho, Mafia arrogance destroyed or undermined what could have been a good relationship. It also took a toll on his kids. Today he's still battling, and not always successfully, to reestablish a relationship with his son Jimmy and his daughter Chelsea, the two children he had with his wife Carol. It's easy, in retrospect, to say that he was often a jerk, that he took advantage of situations, and that, like the Gottis, he used people. Saying he was wrong and that if given a second chance he might do things differently doesn't change the reality. Alite doesn't kid himself about what he was or what he has done. But he's trying to make his children, now grown and beginning lives of their own, understand that he was wrong and that there are other, better ways to deal with problems.

But while he was on the streets and riding high in the Gambino organization, Alite lived in the moment. The violence and the sex and the arrogance were all part of the world in which he did business. He readily admits that he was "a wild man."

Sexual promiscuity was also a part of that image. Getting laid was part of the lifestyle. Being faithful was rare in the underworld. In the testosterone-laden, boys' locker room setting in which Alite moved, being committed to just one woman was often interpreted as a sign of weakness. Guys routinely cheated on their wives with a steady girlfriend. And then they would cheat on that girlfriend with another girlfriend.

"It's typical in the mob," he would later tell a federal jury. "We all do it. We have wives and we have girlfriends and we have girlfriends after the girlfriends. It's just the way it is."

John Gotti's Rules of Leadership: No member or associate is to fool around with the wife, girlfriend, or daughter of another member of the organization.

Alite's introduction to the dos and don'ts of Mafia dating began shortly after he began doing business with Junior in 1983, or to be more precise, after he met Junior's sister, Vicky. She was the second daughter in the family. Her older sister was named Angel. Smart, sassy, and good-looking, Vicky Gotti, then twenty-two, was a stylish and spoiled Mafia princess. Alite said he knew she was not someone with whom he should get involved. But a series of events revolving around both Vicky Gotti and her boyfriend and later husband, Carmine Agnello, created a set of problems for him and ultimately contributed to his falling-out with Junior and his father.

When he testified against Junior in the 2009 racketeering trial, the tabloids had a field day with the he-said, she-said story of Alite's relationship with Vicky Gotti. She denied ever having sex with Alite. He testified that they had "feelings" for each other both before and after she married Agnello. Today he says he "softened" the story while testifying. The reality, he says, is that Vicky Gotti was a fatal attraction that he was continually trying to avoid.

Responding in the media, Vicky Gotti said nothing ever happened between her and Alite. She called him an "out-and-out liar," claiming that he had a crush on her, but that she never responded. She also said she took a lie-detector test that proved she never had sexual intercourse with him.

Alite's version differs but he says there's no point in providing chapter and verse. His life inside the Gotti organization was complicated and dangerous. Vicky Gotti was just a small part of a much larger problem. He admits that he found Vicky Gotti attractive. But he says that he knew she was the boss's daughter and that fooling around with her could have amounted to a death sentence.

Never mind that Gotti Sr. always had a girl, a *commare,* on the side and that at one point was said to be running around with Neil Dellacroce's niece. Never mind that Junior, even after he was married, seemed to lust after every woman who crossed his path. The rules were always bent in the Gottis' favor.

Alite said he was hanging at the clubhouse on 113th Street and Liberty Avenue back in 1984 when Vicky Gotti showed up looking for her brother. Junior wasn't there. Alite asked her if he could do anything. At first she said no.

"Her lip was swollen," he recalled. "She had big sunglasses on and she had a bit of a shiner on her eye."

It didn't take long for Alite to figure out what had happened or to get Vicky to provide the details. Agnello, her boyfriend, had slapped her around . . . again. This was a few months before they were to be married. Alite told Vicky that he would tell her brother or her father. She panicked.

"Don't," she pleaded. "They'll kill him."

Vicky Gotti had been dating Agnello since high school. Agnello owned a tow truck company and liked to talk tough. But Alite said he was a punk. Vicky had spent some time in college, but dropped out. Now they were engaged. When she stopped by the club that afternoon, Alite already knew the backstory, knew that Agnello had a history of abusing her. In fact, Gotti had had Agnello beaten up once before for assaulting his daughter. It was a warning. That's why Vicky knew Agnello would be killed if Alite told her father what was going on.

While Vicky Gotti has denied the story, mob informant Peter Zuccaro, a convicted murderer, testified as a government witness at two trials and said he took part in the beating of Agnello on the orders of John Gotti Sr. Vicky Gotti, in a piece she wrote for the New York *Daily News* in 2009, said Zuccaro and Alite were both lying "stooges." She added that her father despised Alite and his "disgusting and despicable ways."

Alite said that after Vicky came to him, he went to see Agnello himself and told him that "if I got to Junior or the father, 'you're gonna be butchered.' Then I told him not to touch her again."

"Mind your own business," Agnello replied.

It was a difficult position for Alite to be in and one that got more complicated as plans for the wedding moved forward. Alite says that Vicky would come by the clubhouse and spend time with him and would ask her father to have Alite drive her places as she made preparations for the wedding.

There was an underworld code that was in place at the time.

Everyone had a beeper. If you got a numerical message that read "911-98," it meant there was an emergency and you were to go to the clubhouse on 101 Street and 98th Avenue. If the message read "911-98-38" it meant bring a gun. Alite got one of those "911-98" messages and rushed to the clubhouse. Gotti was there and when Alite arrived, he didn't say anything. Finally, Alite asked what was up.

Gotti looked perplexed.

"I got a 911 call," Alite said.

"Oh, yeah," said Gotti. "My daughter has to pick up her wedding dress and I want you to drive her."

"That's the emergency?" Alite asked.

"She asked for you," Gotti said. "Just go with her."

It was one of several trips he would have to make as Vicky planned her nuptials. On these trips, Alite says, she would touch his arms, rub his shoulder, smile, and flirt. When he resisted, she would taunt him, he said, saying things like "What's the matter? You scared of my brother? You scared of Carmine?"

The only person Alite was afraid of at that time was her father, but he wasn't going to tell Vicky that. So he tried to bob and weave, like a boxer, avoiding her when he could, trying to make sure someone else was with them whenever possible. Alite said he felt constant pressure. He was trying to maintain his position within the crime family and observe all the protocols. He could deal with the risks that came with life on the streets, but not with the boss's daughter.

Alite told himself it was nuts. He knew that he could wind up dead. There were rules to the game he was playing but they were often broken. He was aware of the treachery and deceit within the crime family. All it would have taken was for somebody to tell Gotti that Alite was fooling with his daughter. Whether it was true or not didn't matter. If Gotti believed it, Alite would be summoned to the club one day and he'd never come back. He knew how volatile the mob boss could be.

It was a nightmare senario and there was a time when he thought it was coming true.

One afternoon, Alite was called to the Ravenite by Gotti. He wondered if someone had seen Vicky and him together and had tipped off her father. In a way, it was almost as bad.

"My daughter would like you to be in her wedding," Gotti said.

Alite was taken aback. He wasn't sure he had a choice, but tried to bow out, claiming that while he was honored, he was not really family and not particularly close to the bride or the groom. He said he would feel awkward.

"I'm not asking you," Gotti said. "I'm telling you."

The wedding was a lavish affair. Alite was one of nearly two dozen groomsmen. There was Vicky dressed in white. Her sister Angel, dressed in red, was the maid of honor. There were three young flower girls, also in red. The rest of the wedding party was made up of men, all in black tuxedoes, all there to pay homage to the Mafia princess.

"No other women in the wedding," Alite said. "She didn't want anyone to take the spotlight away from her."

Vicky arrived at St. Mary Gate of Heaven Church in Ozone Park in a white Bentley. Her father wore a custom-made tux. In her book she would claim that her father told her she could still call it off, even with the church packed and with a thousand people scheduled to attend the reception that night at a posh resort out on Long Island.

"We'll just make it a big Christmas party," she said her father told her. She declined the offer and went forward with the marriage, which took place on December 9, 1984.

Alite claims that she tried to come on to him during the reception after he helped her collect some of her gifts and was storing them in a room set aside for that purpose. She has said that it was Alite who came on to her and that she rebuffed his advances. In the greater scheme of things, whether they had any kind of relationship before, during, or after the wedding is really a secondary story. But in the soap opera world of the Gottis, it was another chapter that underscored the family's dysfunction.

Vicky and her husband went to Las Vegas for their honeymoon. They stayed at the Mirage. A day after the wedding reception, Alite got a call from Junior.

"Pack a bag," he said. "We're going to Vegas."

Gotti wanted his son and Alite out there. He said it was for security, that they would be bodyguards for the couple. Alite was told that Vicky had asked for him specifically. Apparently, she was bored and homesick. Her father was only too happy to fulfill her request. Alite thought the real reason that he and Junior were dispatched was that Gotti wanted to make sure Agnello didn't abuse his daughter. The trip was uneventful, but costly.

"We were out there gambling," Alite said. "Junior was a big Dallas Cowboys fans. They were playing Miami. We each bet ten thousand on Dallas and lost. Then I think we dropped another thirty thousand playing blackjack and craps."

Before their flight back to the city, they were reduced to gambling at the nickel slot machines, he said.

Alite said his relationship with Vicky continued after her marriage and eventually led to a confrontation with Agnello. But in the mid-1980s, there was so much else going on, so much money being made, so much maneuvering on the streets and in the underworld, that no one paid much attention.

"During the trial I said we had feelings for each other. I'm not sure that's true. She was just playing, seeing what she could get away with. The same way her father and brother used me, she was using me, but for different reasons. I was just trying to stay alive."

That's when Alite said he decided to put some distance between himself and the madness that was life with the Gottis. He used some of the cash that was coming in from the drugs and the sports book and the robberies to invest in real estate. His money wasn't sitting in a bank, but he had ready access to it. It was standard for him and Junior to let their drug-dealing partners hold their money, he said.

"We knew they wouldn't cheat us," he said. "They knew they'd be killed if they did."

There were times when he might have a half million to a million dollars on call, so to speak. If he needed the cash, he would go to one of his dealers and ask for it. But he also decided that it would be smart to put some of that money in property. He bought two condos in Queens as investments and two more in Princeton, New Jersey. He bought another condo in South Brunswick, near Princeton, and bought an apartment in lower Manhattan, not far from the World Trade Center.

But he also wanted to have someplace where he could get away from the day-in and day-out hustle of the neighborhood. There was a woman he was seeing off and on in South Jersey. She and her husband were divorcing and selling their property, a sprawling, fifteen-acre site off Route 73 in Voorhees Township. The property came with three houses. Alite paid about $600,000 for the estate and eventually moved his fiancée and other family members there. His parents moved into one of the houses, his grandmother into another. He and his soon-to-be wife settled in the third and largest. A few years later, in 1994, he would buy another home, this one on Brick Road in a residential neighborhood in Cherry Hill.

The South Jersey properties were less than a two-hour drive down the Jersey Turnpike from the city. For a kid who grew up in a Queens neighborhood with relatives living upstairs and across the street, owning property in Voorhees and Cherry Hill was suburbia writ large. It was a different kind of status, a sign of wealth that might not have meant much to the Gottis but was a demonstration to Alite's own family—his father and mother, his grandmother, his brother and sisters—that he was making something of himself, that he was successful.

Alite still bristles at the notion that he was "chased" out of Queens by Junior. Their falling-out and the death threats that would follow were still several years away when he bought the first property in 1987. He was looking for a place to put some of his cash, and real estate seemed like a smart move. "Nobody chased me out of the neighborhood," he said. "I still was there almost every day. It just was good to have someplace else where I could go."

On Valentine's Day of 1989, before a justice of the peace in the Queens County courthouse, John Alite married his longtime girlfriend Carol Defgard. Junior was his best man. Johnny Ruggiero was the other witness. It was a no-nonsense civil ceremony, the total opposite of Vicky Gotti's lavish affair. The only similarity was that neither marriage would last.

"We had known each other since we were kids," he said of his wife Carol. "I cheated on her before and after we got married."

They chose Valentine's Day not because of the romance surrounding the date, but because February 14 was Junior's birthday. He had suggested it as a way of showing respect and Alite went along. It really didn't matter to him. He and Carol were living in the property in Voorhees and a few weeks later they left for Hawaii on a belated honeymoon. While they were gone, Alite had arranged with a local contractor to have some work done. He wanted a hot tub installed on the porch, a satellite dish on the roof, and a high-tech electronic security system in place so that alarms and beeps would go off inside the main house whenever anyone entered the property off Route 73, the main highway. The house was set nearly a half mile off the highway and access was along a dirt road. Alite figured it would be good to know in advance if he was getting company. Alite gave the contractor twelve thousand dollars in cash and expected that the work would be done by the time he returned.

While he was in Hawaii he checked his phone messages from home daily. One day a friend left a confusing message telling him that he had stopped by the house to see him and didn't mean to intrude. He had looked in the bedroom window and saw who he thought was Alite making love to a woman.

Alite called his friend up to find out what he was talking about.

"He thought it was me and my wife," said Alite. "It was the contractor and this girl he was fooling around with. This guy was married, but he brought his girlfriend to my house and they're having sex in my bed."

When Alite and Carol returned, none of the work had been done. He told his wife to call the contractor and tell him that he had left a couple more thousand dollars for him and that he, Alite, was going to Florida. He wanted the work done before he got back in a week.

The contractor came the next day looking for the additional cash. Instead, he got a beating.

"I told him, 'You think you're gonna make an asshole out of me. I'm gonna make an asshole out of you.'"

With that, Alite stripped the contractor, beat him with a pipe—"I broke his ribs, his jaw, and an arm, I think"—and then threw him in a small lake that was on the property.

"I had a gun and kept shooting at him," Alite said. "I wouldn't let him out of the water. It was like thirty degrees out."

Finally, he took the contractor, tied him up naked, and put him in his garage. Outside several Rottweilers that Alite kept as watch dogs prowled back and forth.

"I went out to dinner," Alite said. "I left him there. But I forgot about a back window. He apparently got loose, climbed out the window, and ran naked through the woods. The cops found him on Route 73."

Police took a complaint from the contractor, but before moving in to arrest Alite they contacted organized crime investigators, who tried to set up a sting. They wanted the contractor to call Alite and get him to admit what he had done and, hopefully, to brag about his mob connections.

"But before they could do that, the guy's girlfriend called and warned me," Alite said. "She said they were gonna try to tape me. She said she was telling me because he had screwed her. He kept telling her he was going to leave his wife, but he never did. This was her way of getting back at him."

The taped phone conversation went nowhere but the complaint from the clearly beaten, bruised, and terrorized contractor led to aggravated assault, kidnapping, and related charges that would hang over Alite's head for more than a year before he worked out a plea deal and headed for prison.

While his permanent residence was now Voorhees, New Jersey, Alite still spent almost every day and most nights in Queens. Shortly after returning from Hawaii, he was feted at a big party hosted by Junior at Altadonna, a restaurant on Cross Bay Boulevard. It was a bachelor party in reverse, held after the wedding and the honeymoon, a couple of dozen guys laughing and drinking while their wives and/or girlfriends sat at home.

By this point, Alite was hanging out regularly at the PM Pub on 101st Avenue and Eighty-Fourth Street. He was growing closer to Ronnie Trucchio, the crime family soldier who had been part of the brothel business and whose wife had gone on the automobile rampage. Alite and Trucchio would still laugh about the incident when they shared drinks at the pub, which was one of Trucchio's joints.

As a child growing up in Ozone Park, Trucchio had been the victim of an automobile accident that left him with a paralyzed right arm. It earned him the nickname "Ronnie One-Arm," but that didn't stop him from moving up the mob ladder. A boyhood friend of John Gotti Sr., Trucchio was formally initiated into the crime family in 1990 and would later become a capo.

Trucchio also became a partner with Alite in some businesses that he and Junior set up in Tampa. While on his honeymoon, Alite had, through an acquaintance, reconnected with an old friend from his brief stay in college, a kid named Tim Donovan, who had remained in the Tampa area and was now in the valet parking business. Alite said Donovan was fascinated with the mob life and invited him to come down when he was back on the East Coast. Alite visited Donovan and liked what he saw. He and Junior, along with Trucchio, established a base in Tampa. Alite insists that the businesses there—a valet parking service, a glass shop, and a restaurant and nightclub—were all legitimate even though they were funded by drug and gambling money.

"For a while my sister and her husband lived down there and kept an eye on things," Alite said. "But they eventually came back north."

The businesses in Tampa flourished and provided more income. But the presence of New York wiseguys in the Florida city, especially wiseguys linked to the infamous Gotti name, did not go unnoticed in law enforcement circles. The U.S. Attorney's Office for the Middle District of Florida and the FBI there began building a case against Junior, Alite, Trucchio, and several of their known associates. Donovan would testify for the prosecutin in Tampa, alleging from the witness stand that Alite, Trucchio, and others threatened him and ran him out of the valet business.

At first, Alite was unaware that he had any problems in Florida. His more immediate concerns were much closer to home. As he later would tell a jury, Alite said he was sitting in the PM Pub one afternoon when Carmine Agnello and four others guys, all of them armed, showed up. Agnello's entourage included his brother Mikey, a mob associate named Angelo Castelli, another kid Alite knew only as Anthony, and a guy named Ricky Red.

"They weren't tough guys, they were stone junkies," Alite said. "Those were the kind of guys Carmine used to hang out with. They were always getting high. Later, a couple of them told me they had no idea what Carmine was planning."

They knew Alite by reputation. They had heard the stories. A few weeks earlier he had shot up a street corner after learning that a couple of guys who hung there had been robbing his drug dealers at the Flight 116 Bar.

"I got a call that there was a problem," Alite said. "I was going out. I'm dressed in a suit and tie. Me, Tony Kelly, and another guy were going out to Metro 700, this really nice club. They picked me up. I had a trash bag with me and inside I had a gun with one of those banana clips, fifty rounds. They don't know it. I say to them, 'We gotta make a stop first.'"

They pulled up about a block from the Flight 116 Bar. Guys were hanging out all over the street in front of the bar. Alite said he got out of the car, took out the gun, and started to spray the corner. Everyone scattered. Alite said he chased down a guy who he suspected was robbing his dealers.

"I grabbed him," Alite said. "I knew his brother. I said, 'The only reason I ain't gonna kill you is I know your brother. I'm giving you a pass this time, but if you or your friends keep bothering my people, I'll come back and then I will kill ya.'"

With that, Alite put the gun in the trash bag and headed back for the car, where Kelly was waiting.

"You all right?" Kelly asked.

"Sure," said Alite. "Let's go."

"Go where?" asked Kelly.

"Metro 700," said Alite. "But let's swing back by my apartment first so I can drop this off," he added, pointing to the trash bag and the still-warm gun.

"I never picked fights," Alite said, returning to a theme that he repeated again and again as he told his story. "I wasn't a bully. But if there was a problem, I would act. I guess you might say I would overreact. I just believed that if you start something you take it all the way. I was a little extreme."

The guys with Carmine Agnello knew of Alite's reputation for violence when they walked into the PM Pub that afternoon. Agnello was a made guy by then, another example of nepotism in the Gotti organization. The rank gave him status and in the pecking order, it put him above Alite.

The confrontation was a typical Agnello move, Alite said, a lot of noise and posturing, but not much action.

"Carmine wasn't a tough guy, but he tried to act tough," Alite said while testifying about the incident. "He fronted. If somebody wanted to kill me, if five guys come in just shooting, there is no talking. I'm dead."

Instead, Alite stared at Agnello and reached behind his own back, pretending to have a gun. Ronnie Trucchio, sitting at the bar nearby, also pretended to have a gun. Seeing it all going down, a kid named Mondo, a friend of Alite, took off out a back door to retrieve a pistol that Alite had stashed in a nearby apartment.

Agnello moved in close to Alite and in a whisper said, "You and me have a problem."

"Yeah, we do," Alite replied.

The bad blood between Alite and Agnello stretched back to before the burly tow-truck operator had become a Gotti son-in-law. They genuinely didn't like each other and that dislike had continued to build as each moved up the mob ladder. Agnello, Alite knew, had a leg up on him but that was no reason for Alite to back down.

"Carmine and I walked out together," Alite said. "By this point, I've got the gun that Mondo brought me, a nine millimeter. When we get outside, Carmine takes a swing at me, hits me in the head with his gun."

Alite wanted to strike back, but he hesitated. He was still playing by the rules of the underworld and in that underworld, if you strike a made guy you could be sentenced to death.

"It was frustrating," he said. "I knew about the rules, but I think I would have shot him anyway. At that point I'm not afraid of him or of Junior. But what's in the back of my mind is Gotti. He's the boss and this is his son-in-law. That's the reason I don't strike back. Me and Carmine are screaming at each other and I see Junior pulling up in a car. Vicky's sitting next to him. He parks down the block and gets out. She stays behind."

It appeared they already knew a little of what had happened, but Alite filled in the missing details. He also told Junior that he wanted to kill Agnello.

"You ain't touching him," Junior replied, stepping between the two.

It was the Johnny Gebert scene played out with even more drama. This time it was about blood. Agnello, even though he was a punk and even though he was abusing Junior's sister, was family. John Alite was not.

"At that point I found out I was an outsider," Alite said. "That's when I really understood. He allowed this Carmine to put a gun to me, to come with four other guys to kill me, and he wouldn't let me get retribution because it was his brother-in-law. . . . I understood. It's blood. I'm not blood. I was just another guy he used to hurt people and to make money. And that was it."

It was the way the Gottis operated. They always came first.

Later that year, Angelo Ruggiero died of cancer. He had remained on the shelf, persona non grata, for nearly four years, banished from the underworld by his former good friend John Gotti. Gotti, in fact, didn't even want to attend Ruggiero's funeral but Sammy Gravano convinced him that he should go.

Gotti appeared somber and subdued at the wake, but everyone knew he was just playing a role. He was the boss and this was an underling whose passing he would acknowledge. That was the extent of it. What Ruggiero had done for him wasn't part of the equation. Alite was beginning to see how things really were. In fact, he was experiencing it. But he wasn't ready to break away.

Early in 1990 Greg Reiter disappeared. The word on the street was that he had been killed in a drug dispute, but his body was never found. No one was ever charged with his suspected homicide. Alite and those around him were convinced that Tommy "Karate" Pitera, the shooter in the Willie Boy Johnson hit, had taken Reiter out.

"He had a reputation for chopping up bodies," Alite said. "He would kill people and they would just disappear. We all figured it was him."

Reiter and Pitera had been sometimes partners in the drug business and had made—and occasionally lost—money together. There was an ongoing dispute over twenty thousand dollars when Reiter disappeared. Alite never learned the motive for the murder but suspected that the Dennis Harrigan robbery also might have been part of the problem. Harrigan worked with Pitera in the drug business. Greg's brother Mike had helped set up the heist. If you robbed Harrigan, you were by extension robbing Pitera.

Tommy Karate is currently serving a series of life sentences after being convicted in 1992 of six homicides. Pitera was with the Bonanno family, but often contracted out to other families who had some work that needed to be done. Whether the Reiter murder was a sanctioned mob hit or simply a drug underworld killing has never been determined. For Alite it didn't really matter.

Greg Reiter was his friend. Pitera had killed him. And now the word on the street was that Tommy Karate was looking for Alite.

A few months after they moved into the property in South Jersey, Alite got a call from his wife. Carol was panicked. She said there were armed men moving around in the woods outside the house. Alite rushed home, driving in by way of a back road on the property. Once inside the house, he grabbed an Uzi machine gun and a revolver and in the dark began stalking those who were stalking him.

"They were Spanish guys," he said in retelling the story of a shootout that sounded like something out of a *Die Hard* film. "I could hear them talking. I think they were Mexican."

Alite said they had inadvertently tripped two alarms as they made their way up a dirt road that led to the house where he and Carol lived. Their presence had also set off the dogs.

"They were chained, but they were barking like crazy," he said of the Rottweilers.

Alite slipped out a back door, moved into the woods, and knelt down, letting his eyes adjust to the dark. Then he moved.

"I knew the grounds better than they did, which helped me," he said. "And at first, they didn't know I was there. They thought we were all in the house. I think they were either waiting to ambush me if I came out or were planning to storm in and open fire. I decided to go after them instead."

Shooting as he ran, rolling in the brush for cover and coming up firing again, he engaged in a brief firefight, Alite said. He is certain that he hit two of the intruders before they ran from the property.

The next morning he and a friend went out to look around.

"There were no bodies, but lots of blood," he said. "I was sure Pitera had sent them. He dealt with drug dealers from Mexico. It made sense."

Alite said his suspicions were more than confirmed when a few days later he got word that Gotti wanted to see him at the Ravenite. Tommy Pitera had asked for the meeting.

"I go there not knowing what to expect," Alite said. "This guy has killed Greg Reiter, whose father had made Gotti millions and who had taken a pinch and not given Gotti up. For that reason alone, Pitera should have been killed. But Gotti didn't see it that way. He tells us that whatever happened happened and that now it's over. Settled. We both have to agree."

But outside the club, as they walked toward their cars, Alite said he told Pitera nothing had changed.

"Whaddaya mean?" Pitera asked. "The man said it was settled."

"Nothin's settled," Alite said. "I'm still gonna kill ya."

Pitera was arrested and jailed before Alite could make good on his threat.

CHAPTER 10

I n any business, the guy in charge sets the tone. Some guys are good leaders. Others don't know how to lead but love being boss. John J. Gotti was part of that second group. He had taken control of the biggest crime family in New York, but he ran it like a street gang out of Howard Beach.

He demanded respect but never worried about earning it. He required those around him to acknowledge his position through everything they said and did. He called it protocol. It was something that Junior emphasized from the very first time he met Alite. And it was something that Alite watched play out again and again as the Gottis interacted with those around them.

John Gotti's Rules of Leadership: Always acknowledge the presence of the boss first in any public or social setting. In any social setting with members of other crime families, make them come to you to pay their respects. Going to them first is a sign of weakness.

"If you went into a room where there were a bunch of guys, you had to go up to the highest-ranking guy first," Alite said. "You kiss him on both cheeks. Then you acknowledge the other guys. If Gotti's in the room, he's the one you go to.

"Whenever we were going out, you were supposed to dress nice. But you were never supposed to dress better than the boss. I remember one time I had to change my jacket because it was like the one Gotti was wearing. I thought to myself, 'What are we, girls?' But that's the way he and Junior were.

"When they called, you had to come. Drop everything and come. If you weren't at the club on the night everyone was supposed to meet, you'd get in trouble. At first, I didn't think I had to be there. I'm home and here's Genie Gotti at the door. 'What the fuck's the matter with you? Why ain't you where you're supposed to be?'"

Saturday night Gotti Sr. would hold court at a dinner at the Bergin Hunt and Fish Club. Everyone had to be there. A few guys would cook in the kitchen in the back of the club. Then everyone would sit down, twenty to twenty-five guys, made members and associates, for a meal. But even then there were rules.

"Nobody ate or put a fork in their food until he [Gotti] put a fork in his first," Alite said. The same scene played out on a smaller scale on Tuesday nights at the Our Friends Social Club down the street. That's where Junior would hold court and Alite and the rest of the crew were required to gather.

"You hadda be there," Alite said. "It wasn't like, 'I'm busy. I gotta go to dinner with my wife. My son has a cold.' That doesn't fly."

The meals at the Tuesday gatherings were supplied by the owner of La Villa, a restaurant in the Lindenwood section of Howard Beach, Alite said. The owner "would pay tribute to [Junior Gotti] by sending meals over to us for free."

Some guys could ignore the protocols, but they were the rare exceptions. Charles Carneglia, with whom Alite would eventually form a shaky alliance, was one who never showed up. But he was considered a little crazy, off balance to say the least, so he got a pass.

"He had a screw loose," Alite said of Charles Carneglia, whose brother John was a made guy and a member of the Gene Gotti–Angelo Ruggiero heroin ring. Carneglia—no one ever called him "Charlie"—eventually became a made member as well, but that was really just an attempt to keep him close. He was a stone killer, but completely unstable.

"He kind of enjoyed his work," Alite said of the murders that Carneglia carried out. "Some guys do it and just do it because we gotta do it. He liked doing it."

Carneglia didn't read much, but he had books in his apartment dealing with dissecting bodies. He once asked Alite if he wanted to borrow one. Alite politely declined. Alite would testify against Carneglia in 2009, linking him to several mob hits, including the murder of Louis DiBono.

DiBono had been marked for death by Gotti for the simplest of reasons: he didn't come when he was called.

The sixty-three-year-old construction contractor was a long-time soldier in the Gambino family and a major moneymaker. When Castellano was alive, DiBono had clashed with Gravano over a construction job dispute and had survived. But now Big Paul was gone and Gravano still held a grudge. DiBono had a multimillion-dollar fire insulation contract at the World Trade Center at the time and was supposedly pocketing a couple of million in a scam that involved shoddy work. Gravano was stirring the pot with Gotti, whose hackles always were aroused when he thought someone wasn't kicking up a piece of his action. He called DiBono to a meeting, but DiBono made an excuse. He was called a second time, and again he was a no-show.

At that point, Gotti ordered him killed.

According to federal prosecutors, Junior got the contract. It was a coming-out assignment of sorts.

In April 1990, Junior had married Kim Albanese in a big

wedding that was part high society, part underworld royalty. The reception at the Helmsley Palace Hotel was an even more lavish affair than Vicky Gotti's wedding six years earlier.

Later, authorities would discover a list Junior kept of the guests and the amount of cash each had given him. The list was on a bookkeeper's ledger with names and amounts neatly written. The total from 173 guests—made members or associates of one of the five New York crime families—was $348,700.

"That is more money than most people can save in a lifetime," a prosecutor would later tell the jury at Junior's trial in 2009. Gotti Sr. gave his son an even more impressive gift. He promoted him to the rank of capo, much to the chagrin of many veteran members of the organization.

"John wasn't well liked to begin with," Alite said of Junior. "This just pissed a lot of people off. They felt he hadn't earned it, but was made a skipper because of his father."

Two months after the wedding, Alite and Bobby Boriello, who had been Junior's best man, were outside the Our Friends Social Club when Junior asked them to take a walk with him. The so-called walk-talk was another device developed by his father to avoid FBI listening devices. During the walk, Alite would testify, Junior said he had gotten the DiBono contract. He didn't say why, but he told Alite and Boriello that DiBono had to be killed. Both were to be part of the hit team. It was his first job as a capo and he wanted it to go off without a hitch.

"Bobby was concerned at that time about a guy named Preston Geritano," Alite said. "They had this dispute over money and Geritano had threatened to kill Bobby. This Preston had connections with the Genovese family. Bobby wanted Junior to assign me to kill Geritano, but Junior blew it off.

" 'We don't have time for that now,' he said. 'We'll deal with it later. For now it's DiBono.' They heard Louie DiBono was spending a lot of time in Atlantic City. I had my place in South Jersey then and was spending time at the casinos. Junior asked me to check around and see if we could locate DiBono and set him up."

The planning continued through the summer. Charles Carneglia and Boriello were going to be the shooters. Alite had no luck in Atlantic City and sometime in September Junior told him to forget about it.

"He said they had located him and it was being taken care of," Alite told a federal jury.

On October 3, 1990, Louis DiBono's body was discovered in his own 1987 Cadillac DeVille parked in an underground garage at the World Trade Center. He had been shot three times.

Alite was unaware of the murder when he ran into Junior that day.

"He told me I should congratulate him," he said. "I kissed him on both cheeks, then asked him, 'What am I congratulating you for?' He said, 'Because my first job as a skipper was successful.' Then he told me to read the papers. That's when I learned DiBono was dead."

Louis DiBono didn't come when he was called. It was a simple breach of protocol and it cost him his life.

Junior told Alite the murder would serve as an example for everyone else. When you're called, you come, he said. When you're ordered to do something, you do it. You don't ask any questions.

Alite understood the concept, but said Junior often abused the protocol.

"One time we were out drinking," he said. "Five or six of us and some girls. In those kinds of situations, John would also have to show everyone he was the boss. We're sitting at a table, smoking cigars. He looks at me and says, 'Get me an ashtray.' I don't move. He starts to get mad. One of the other guys reaches over to another table and gets an ashtray and puts it in front of him."

The tension was obvious to everyone. But one of the women at the table cut to the heart of it.

"John," she said to Gotti, "stop trying to show everyone how important you are. Nobody here needs to be impressed."

Alite said the girl had more balls than most of the guys around Junior.

"She was a tough girl, wasn't afraid of anything," he said. "But it shows you that people knew him for what he was, not for what he thought he was."

Later that night, when they were alone, Junior confronted Alite.

"What's your problem?" Junior asked.

"I got no problem," Alite replied.

The issue remained unresolved. Alite knew what Junior was getting at, but wasn't about to have a discussion about it. He wasn't ready to put it all out in the open, to tell Junior he was acting like a jerk and an asshole. More and more people were beginning to think that way, but ironically it was a woman who had the guts to say it.

"If he had asked me, 'Hey, John, could you get me an ashtray?' then there's no problem," Alite said. "Everybody understood what the protocols were. It's just that the Gottis used them to bully people. And I wasn't gonna be bullied."

A similar situation occurred one night when Alite was out to dinner with Junior and Richie Gotti, Junior's uncle. They were at a table when Alite's young cousin Patsy Andriano walked in. At the time Patsy was dating Richie Gotti's daughter Danielle.

Patsy came up to the table, kissed Alite on both cheeks, then kissed Richie Gotti, then kissed Junior. Junior went nuts.

"He started screaming at him about proper protocol and respect," Alite said. "We just stood there."

Later, Alite said, his cousin Patsy laughed it off.

Junior Gotti and John Alite surrounded by some of the crew. *(U.S. Justice Department exhibit)*

Junior Gotti and John Alite during their early years. *(U.S. Justice Department exhibit)*

Junior with Alite after the birth of Alite's son Jimmy. *(U.S. Justice Department exhibit)*

GOVERNMENT
EXHIBIT
216

GOVERNMENT
EXHIBIT
301D

Junior Gotti and Alite outside a Manhattan federal courthouse during a proceeding for Gotti Sr. *(U.S. Justice Department exhibit)*

John and Claudia at their home in Cherry Hill, New Jersey. *(Photograph courtesy of John Alite)*

Working out with his sons at the gym on his Voorhees, New Jersey, property. *(Photograph courtesy of John Alite)*

John with visitors Claudia, Matt, Johnny, Jimmy, and Chelsea at the federal prison in McKean, Pennsylvania. *(Photograph courtesy of John Alite)*

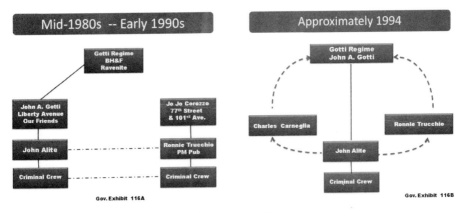

Mid-1980s -- Early 1990s

Gotti Regime
BH&F
Ravenite

John A. Gotti
Liberty Avenue
Our Friends

Jo Jo Corozzo
77th Street
& 101st Ave.

John Alite

Ronnie Trucchio
PM Pub

Criminal Crew

Criminal Crew

Gov. Exhibit 116A

Approximately 1994

Gotti Regime
John A. Gotti

Charles Carneglia

Ronnie Trucchio

John Alite

Criminal Crew

Gov. Exhibit 116B

Flowcharts of the Alite-Gotti-Gambino connections.
(U.S. Justice Department exhibit)

John J. Gotti. *(U.S. Justice Department exhibit)*

The Dapper Don.
(U.S. Justice Department exhibit)

John A. "Junior" Gotti.
(U.S. Justice Department exhibit)

Ronnie "One-Arm" Trucchio.
(U.S. Justice Department exhibit)

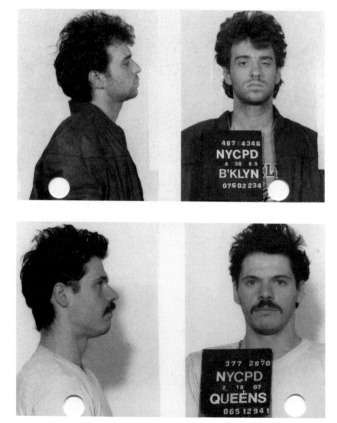

Johnny Gebert,
murder victim.
*(U.S. Justice
Department exhibit)*

Bruce Gotterup,
murder victim.
*(U.S. Justice
Department exhibit)*

Relaxing with "friends" in Colombia.
(Photograph courtesy of John Alite)

With Claudia in Paris.
(Photograph courtesy of John Alite)

A camel ride in Senegal while waiting for fake passports.
(Photograph courtesy of John Alite)

Girlfriend Rose in Copacabana.
(Photograph courtesy of John Alite)

At his apartment in Copacabana.
(Photograph courtesy of John Alite)

On the street in his Rio neighborhood.
(Photograph courtesy of John Alite)

An inmate "showers" in Ary Franco.
(Photograph courtesy of John Alite)

The Ary Franco chow line, bug- and mice-infested rice and beans.
(Photograph courtesy of John Alite)

Alite and cellmates feasting on food smuggled in by bribed prison guards. *(Photograph courtesy of John Alite)*

Alite and Klaus in Ary Franco. *(Photograph courtesy of John Alite)*

FD-302 (Rev. 10-6-95)

FEDERAL BUREAU OF INVESTIGATION

Date of transcription 01/16/2006

JOHN A. GOTTI, also known as (aka) JUNIOR (GOTTI, JR.) (Protect Identity) was present at the United States Attorney's Office, Southern District of New York (SDNY), 500 Pearl Street, New York, New York on January 18, 2005 for a proffer session. This meeting was arranged at GOTTI, JR.'S request. Also present were GOTTI JR.'S attorneys, JEFFREY LICHTMAN, Esq., and MARC FERNICH, Esq., as well as Assistant United States Attorneys (AUSAS) Robert Buehler, Joon Kim and Jennifer Rodgers, SDNY.

After GOTTI, JR. and his attorneys read the proffer agreement and the terms of that agreement were explained to them by the AUSAS, GOTTI, JR. signed the agreement. GOTTI, JR. thereafter provided the following information:

The Murder of Danny Silva

In the early morning hours of either March 11th or 12th, 1983, GOTTI, JR., along with his friends, MARK CAPUTO and ANTHONY AMOROSO, were present at the SLIVER FOX bar located on 101st Street and Liberty Avenue in Queens, New York. At some point, TOMMY Last Name Unknown (LNU) aka "ELFIE" approached GOTTI, JR. who was seated at the bar with a female friend, DONNA LNU. According to GOTTI, JR., "ELFIE" repeatedly bumped into him. Words were exchanged, one thing led to another and GOTTI, JR. ultimately hit "ELFIE" with a broken glass bottle. GOTTI, JR. then stabbed "ELFIE" with a knife that GOTTI, JR. had obtained from AMOROSO.

According to GOTTI, JR, a melee ensued involving approximately 30 to 40 of the bar's patrons. GOTTI, JR. recalled that among those involved in the melee were: DANNY SILVA, JOHN and GREG MASSA, ANGELO CASTELLI, JOEY CURIO, First Name Unknown (FNU) RILEY and JOHN CENNAMO. GOTTI, JR. stated that DANNY SILVA was stabbed and killed during the melee.

GOTTI, JR. described a meeting, which occurred a short time after the incident at the SLIVER FOX, between ANGELO RUGGIERO, SR. and a New York City Police Department (NYPD) Detective, JOHN DALY. GOTTI, JR. drove RUGGIERO to the meeting, which took place at the Sherwood Diner located near the Five Towns, on the Queens-Nassau County border. Before the meeting GOTTI, JR. and RUGGIERO discussed the purpose of the meeting. According to GOTTI, JR.

Investigation on 1/18/2005 at New York, New York

File # 281A-NY-281763 Date dictated

by SA Cindy A. Peil

First page of Junior Gotti's 302 proffer memo.
(Photograph courtesy of John Alite)

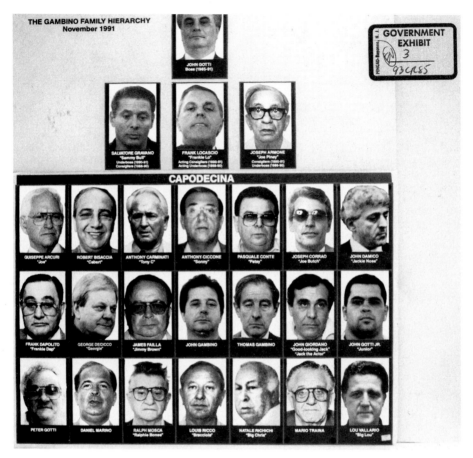

Gambino crime family organizational chart from 1991.
(U.S. Justice Department exhibit)

It was just one example of Junior's standing in the New York underworld. His status was built on nepotism and even though most of his associates didn't know the meaning of that word, they grasped the concept.

Junior had the title, but he never had the respect of the rank and file. And it would get worse. Depending on your perspective, the DiBono murder was either the last hurrah or the final nail in the coffin for Gotti Sr. Time was running out for the Dapper Don. There was some indication that he might have been aware of the situation. But as always, his arrogance got in the way.

Gotti had beaten another case in February 1990, tap-dancing from charges that he had hired members of the Westies, an Irish street gang, to assault a union official. He emerged from the courthouse in an expensive topcoat over a tailored suit and tie, his fist raised in triumph. He had won again. No one knew at the time that a juror had been bribed. In the media, he was "the Teflon Don." None of the charges thrown at him would stick.

But as a wise federal prosecutor once pointed out in a discussion about mob cases, "They have to win every time. We only have to win once."

The feds just kept on coming.

A few months after the Castellano murder, early in 1986, Gotti was picked up on an FBI listening device laying out the future for his organization.

"The law's gonna be tough with us, okay," he said on the now-infamous tape. "If they don't put us away . . . if they don't put us away for one year or two. That's all we need. But if I can get a year run without being interrupted, get a year, gonna put this thing together where they could never break it, never destroy it. Even if we die. Be a good thing."

"It's a hell of a legacy to leave," said the associate to whom Gotti was talking as the FBI listened in.

In fact, Gotti got a five-year run at the top. But the organization he left was considerably more disorganized than the one he took over after Castellano was blown away.

Making his son a capo was seen as part of the Gotti management style that destroyed the organization. In Gotti Sr.'s mind, this might have been an attempt to maintain control of the crime family in anticipation of what was coming. But to the rank and file, it was just another example of Junior being spoiled and coddled, of being given, rather than earning, a spot in the family hierarchy.

Junior tried to keep Alite happy despite the growing tension between them. Still seething over the Agnello confrontation, Alite was told he could go after Ricky Red, one of Agnello's guys and part of the entourage that Agnello brought with him the day he confronted Alite in the PM Pub.

"Since he wouldn't let me kill his brother-in-law, he coughed up Ricky Red," Alite would later tell a federal jury. "He didn't care about Ricky Red. It's his way of satisfying my problem and it's also his way to show other guys you don't go after anybody, I don't care if you're with my brother-in-law or not, that's around me."

A few days later, Alite told the jury, he and Junior took Ricky Red for a ride.

"The Gottis had a connection with the owner of the limo company," Alite said. "He was with them. So we're in this limo driving around Ozone Park and we spot Ricky Red walking along Liberty Avenue."

The limo pulled over to the curb and Junior Gotti signaled for Ricky Red to get in.

"I guess he thought Junior wanted to talk to him about something," Alite said.

Ricky Red climbed into the back of the limo where Gotti and Alite were already sitting. After a few minutes of small talk, Alite pushed a button, locking the back doors. With that, Ricky Red was assaulted by Gotti and Alite. According to Alite's testimony, they punched and kicked him repeatedly. All he could do was hide his face in his arms, trying to ward off the blows. The limo driver either didn't know or didn't care what was going on. He just kept driving.

"Back then they had car phones that were attached to long cords," Alite said. "Junior took the phone cord and wrapped it around [Ricky Red's] neck several times. I was gonna choke him to death. We're pounding on him. I pushed the button to unlock the doors. The limo's going about sixty miles an hour. We're on Woodhaven Boulevard in Howard Beach by this time and we're gonna throw him out of the car. He's fighting to stay in, but we kept punching and pushing."

With the phone cord still around his neck, Ricky Red bounced out of the limo and onto the highway. He was dragged along for about a hundred feet before the cord snapped and he rolled away.

Ricky Red survived, but the incident further enhanced Alite's reputation as a violent maniac who wasn't someone you wanted to cross. It was a reputation, he believes, that helped keep him alive.

On December 11, 1990, just five days short of the fifth anniversary of the Castellano murder, John J. Gotti was arrested on federal murder and racketeering charges. The case included the allegation that he had ordered the hit on Paul Castellano in a bloody coup and had taken control of the crime family as a result. Frank Locascio, Salvatore Gravano, and Tommy Gambino, who would later be severed from the case, were also named in the indictment. Racketeering, extortion, and jury tampering—the bribing of a juror in the Westies case—were also part of the eleven-count indictment.

The murders detailed in the indictment included the hits on Castellano and Tommy Bilotti outside Sparks Steak House in December 1985; the murder of mob capo Robert DiBernardo, often described as the porno king of America, in June 1986; the killing of mob soldier Liborio Milito in March 1988; and the hit on DiBono in October 1990.

The case also included a murder conspiracy charge tied to a plot to kill Gaetano "Corky" Vastola, a capo in New Jersey's DeCavalcante crime family. Gotti had spent some time in jail with Vastola in 1987. Vastola was awaiting trial in an extortion case tied to a record company scam that linked back to MCA Records in Los Angeles. For some reason, Gotti believed Vastola would never hold up in prison and figured he would eventually become a rat.

The plot to kill Vastola was never carried out, but if Gotti was concerned about cooperators, he probably should have been looking closer to home. He, Gravano, and Locascio were picked up by a team of more than a dozen FBI agents at the Ravenite. The arrests made headlines across the country the next day.

TEFLON DON GOTTI INDICTED IN SLAYING OF MOB BOSS was the headline on a *Washington Post* article that went on to describe Gotti's "silky elegance and apparent invincibility," noting that he had beaten four other cases in the past five years. The piece included an angry comment from Andrew Maloney, the U.S. attorney for the Eastern District of New York, who said of Gotti, "He's a murderer, not a folk hero."

Gotti, Gravano, and Locascio were all denied bail as the government laid out part of its case. There were, prosecutors said, dozens of secretly recorded conversations as well as testimony from informants that would tie the defendants to the crimes charged.

Among other things, the FBI had bugged an apartment above the Ravenite where Gotti and others would often hold conversations that they believed were outside the FBI's listening range. The informants included Philip "Crazy Phil" Leonetti, the onetime underboss of the Philadelphia mob.

Leonetti was the nephew of Philadelphia mob boss Nicodemo "Little Nicky" Scarfo, who, from his perch in Atlantic City, launched one of the most violent eras in the history of the Philadelphia–South Jersey underworld. Taking over after the murders of mob bosses Angelo Bruno and Philip "Chicken Man" Testa (whose murder was noted in the song "Atlantic City" by Bruce Springsteen), Scarfo ruled from 1981 through 1988. During that period at least twenty-five mob members or associates were killed and two dozen more were indicted. In a crime family whose membership topped out at about seventy made members, the result was devastation.

Scarfo and Gotti were in many ways Mafia bookends, mob bosses who rose to power through violence and whose management style was based on treachery, greed, and deceit. Convicted along with his nephew and thirteen other codefendants in a 1988 racketeering trial, Scarfo is still serving a fifty-five-year sentence. His parole date is 2033, when he will be 103 years old.

His handsome nephew was sentenced to forty-five years but decided that cooperating with the feds would be a smarter move. Leonetti testified in a series of mob trials up and down the East Coast and appeared as a witness before the grand jury that handed up the indictment against Gotti, Gravano, and Locascio.

Among other things, Leonetti testified that at a meeting he and Scarfo attended, Gotti had boasted about having Castellano killed. Leonetti himself admitted to his own involvement in ten murders but offered this classic comment when a defense attorney, pointing to that bloody history, sarcastically asked if he knew what it meant to be ruthless.

"I know what it means to be ruthless," he said as he sat on the witness stand dressed like a fraternity rush chairman in a blue blazer, tan slacks, and a crewneck sweater over a blue button-down shirt. "But I don't remember ever doing anything, as a matter of fact I know for sure, I never did nothing ruthless besides, well, I would kill people. But that's our life. That's what we do."

Described as one of the best witnesses in a long line of cooperators who came from the Philadelphia mob, Leonetti eventually had his jail sentence reduced to five years, five months, and five days. The lesson was not lost on any of Gotti's codefendants as they sat in a federal lockup, denied bail as the case moved slowly toward trial.

The arrests caused a stir in the Gambino family, but given Gotti's track record of beating cases, no one was yet ready to concede that his reign was over. In the interim, Gotti issued orders from prison and set up a committee to handle day-to-day operations. His brother Peter and his son were part of the new hierarchy.

Alite didn't have much time to digest what the arrest meant because in March he himself headed off to jail. The assault and kidnapping of the contractor back in South Jersey had finally been resolved. Originally Alite had been offered a plea deal that would have brought a maximum seven-year sentence in state prison. He figured he'd have to do about two or three years.

"That was the deal they offered," Alite said. "We took it, then rejected it. My lawyer got word that Bobby Cabert had a connection and could work out something better for us."

Bobby "Cabert" Bisaccia was a ruthless and well-connected Gambino crime family capo who operated out of North Jersey. He had been around for years and had connections in both law enforcement and justice circles, according to Alite, who said he was never told the hows and whys of what was negotiated.

"The windup was I pleaded guilty and got a one-year sentence," he said. "I ended up doing three or four months."

He surrendered to New Jersey prison authorities in March 1991, a day after Junior and a dozen other mobsters held a "going-away party" for him at the Our Friends Social Club. The party included a sheet cake decorated with caricatures of two prison inmates. Another Junior associate was also headed off to state prison. ALCATRAZ OR BUST was printed in big red letters across the top of the cake.

It was a rite of passage for Alite. He was doing time, keeping his mouth shut, and going off to prison. Never mind that the crime was something of his own making; he was a stand-up guy who was doing the right thing.

It was all part of the life.

A few days after Alite was jailed, Charles Carneglia was formally initiated into the crime family. Alite had been asked to set up the ceremony, which was held in the basement apartment of the home he was then living in with Claudia DiPippa, who would become his common-law wife and with whom he had two children. The house belonged to DiPippa's parents.

Carneglia was made that day because of his role as a shooter in the DiBono hit. Three others were also initiated at the ceremony overseen by Junior Gotti and other members of the ruling hierarchy. Alite was supposed to attend, but instead was being processed as an inmate in the Camden County Jail in Camden, New Jersey.

He had, however, set the whole thing up, arranging for the basement to be cleaned and rearranged for the ceremony and posting different members of the crew in a four-block radius around the home in Howard Beach to ensure that there was no police or FBI presence.

Carneglia's brother John was already a made guy and by that time was doing time for his conviction with Genie Gotti in the heroin case. Charles Carneglia wasn't as sharp or sophisticated as his brother. He wasn't an "earner;" in fact, Alite said he knew very little about how to make money.

But he was a killer and that had its own value in the organization. Alite took pride in the fact that even though he could never be made, he was entrusted with setting up a making ceremony. At that point, he was still enthralled by "the life," even if he was becoming more disenchanted with the leadership.

That disenchantment would grow as he sat in an orange jump-suit and white sneakers without laces as a guest of New Jersey authorities in downtown Camden, one of the poorest and most violent cities in America.

Alite would often joke that the Woodhaven neighborhood in Queens where he had grown up was one of the most violent sections of New York City. But that area of Queens had nothing on Camden, where drug dealers controlled dozens of corners and literally held the city's population of eighty thousand hostage.

Alite got to see some of the violence from his prison cell in the form of the inmates who were constantly coming through the jail. Drugs, guns, and money were what the Camden underworld was all about.

He and his associates—Gotti was a prime offender—would often berate and belittle African Americans, referring to them as lowlifes. A common insult was to tell someone he was "acting like a nigger." The cast of characters who passed through the Camden County Jail while Alite was housed there reinforced that stereotype in his mind. But the reality was that the guys Alite worked with in Queens weren't any different. They operated behind the patina of organized crime, using the myth of the Mafia to justify what they did, but their actions and their arrogance were the same as those of the drug gangs that ripped Camden apart. It wasn't about color. It was about greed, stupidity, and senseless violence.

A month after Alite was jailed, Bobby Boriello was killed.

Boriello, who had celebrated his forty-seventh birthday two weeks earlier, was shot seven times outside his home in Benson-hurst, Brooklyn. He was gunned down as he walked toward his brand-new Lincoln Town Car. Boriello's wife and two young children were inside the family home when the hit went down.

The immediate reaction in the underworld—and from Gotti Sr. in prison—was that Preston Geritano had settled his beef with Boriello. Mikey "Scars" DiLeonardo would later testify that Junior met with the Genovese crime family leaders demanding that Geritano be killed. He was told it would be taken care of. It never was.

When Alite got out of prison three months later, he confronted Junior.

This was in July 1991. Alite remembers the date because he was at the hospital with Claudia, who had given birth to their son, John. Junior and several others visited the hospital in South Jersey, "but she wouldn't let them in the room," Alite told a jury.

Claudia DiPippa, wiser than Alite, didn't want Junior Gotti or his people around her common-law husband. She saw them for what they were and knew that things could only end badly for John.

At the hospital, Alite confronted Junior about the Boriello murder and asked what was being done about it.

"This guy was the best man at his wedding," Alite said. "I told him we had to do something about it. I wanted to kill Geritano. He put me off. He said it was being taken care of. I thought that was bullshit, another typical Junior Gotti move."

The Boriello murder, on April 13, 1991, was an act of revenge but it had nothing to do with Geritano. Boriello had been one of the suspected shooters in the Castellano hit. Frank DeCicco, also part of the Castellano assassination team, had died in the car bomb blast five years earlier. It was no coincident that Borriello's murder occurred on the anniversary of DiCicco's death, April 13, 1986.

Informant testimony from Anthony "Gaspipe" Casso provided the details several years after the fact. The Lucheses had taken out

Boriello. Casso, then the Luchese underboss, had ordered the hit. It was, like the DeCicco murder, a message to Gotti Sr. that the Castellano murder would not go unavenged.

Someone would have to be accountable; if not Gotti himself, then those around him. A few months earlier, in November 1990, Edward Lino, another Gambino soldier tied to the Sparks shooting, had been killed. Lino was shot nine times. His body was found behind the wheel of his 1990 Mercedes, which had rolled into some bushes off a service road leading to the Belt Parkway in Brooklyn's Brighton Beach. Casso also took credit for ordering that hit, which he told authorities was carried out by corrupt New York City police detectives Louis Eppolito and Stephen Caracappa, the two so-called Mafia cops who were later convicted for their roles in a series of mob-related murders.

Gotti was out of the line of fire as he sat in the Metropolitan Correctional Center awaiting trial. But he had bigger problems. As the case moved forward, the defense was given access to the FBI tapes around which the charges were built. Gravano got to hear Gotti berate and belittle him and link him to several murders. It was all Sammy the Bull needed. Early in November 1991, he fired his lawyer, hired a different attorney, and cut a deal with the government, agreeing to cooperate.

The move created even more tension within the Gambino crime family. Now Gravano was described as a thug and murderer who used violence to line his pockets. He was no good, a creep, a degenerate. The Gottis were in media spin mode. The potential impact of Gravano's decision could undermine everything John J. Gotti had been trying to do.

In a broader sense, Gravano's decision was part of a pattern that was spreading throughout the underworld. It was something for the sociologists and, urban anthropologists to ponder. It was the death of omertà and with it, the death of the American Mafia.

If you were paying attention, you would have seen it coming.

You could make a legitimate argument that mobsters from the 1920s and 1930s, at least some of them, bought into the concept of the Mafia as a secret society populated by men of honor. *Omertà,* in a literal translation, means "to be a man." And a man, in that world, took care of his own problems, never went to the authorities for help, and never sought the protection of the police. The Mafia, for someone like Carlo Gambino in New York or Angelo Bruno in Philadelphia, was truly a way of life. That was the real protocol to be followed.

Two generations later, those in power had lost touch with the old ways and, more important, those who had been recruited by them were in it simply to get rich. The Mafia was no longer a way of life, but a way to make money. And when those individuals found themselves jammed up, found themselves facing RICO prosecutions built around informant testimony and devastating tape recordings, they made a business decision.

The question they asked themselves was How do I cut my losses?

It wasn't about omertà, it was about survival.

Sammy Gravano was simply following in the footsteps of Phil Leonetti and dozens of others who had turned government witness. A lighter prison sentence and life with a new identity in the Witness Security Program—a really secret society—were the inducements.

John Alite would grapple with those same issues fifteen years later. But when Gravano flipped, Alite was still very much a part of the organization. He had soured on Junior Gotti and had come to see John Gotti Sr. for what he was, but Alite was still very much a part of the life, still making lots of money, and still willing to kill in order to stay ahead of the game.

CHAPTER 11

There's a great but often overlooked line in *The Godfather* when Michael first meets Apollonia while strolling the Sicilian countryside. His bodyguards, two hit men who have sawed-off shotguns slung over their shoulders as they walk beside him, realize the jeopardy Michael has unknowingly placed himself in by inquiring about the beautiful young girl, more Greek than Italian, whom he had encountered while out walking that day.

One of the bodyguards comes to realize that the bar owner to whom they have made the inquiry is, in fact, the father of the beautiful young woman in question. The bodyguard urges Michael to quickly finish his drink and leave the bar. Michael, of course, refuses, and ends up putting himself at the mercy of the bar owner, who soon becomes his father-in-law.

The incident is underscored in a piece of Sicilian wisdom uttered by one of the bodyguards when he first notices that Michael has been smitten. "In Sicily," he says, "women are more dangerous than shotguns."

While not as romantically expressed, the role of women in the world of John Alite and Junior Gotti was just as dangerous and potentially as deadly. Alite's situation with Vicky Gotti was just one example. He also found himself in the middle of another marital rift when John Gotti Sr., a few years earlier, asked him to take care of a problem Gotti's oldest daughter, Angel, was having with her then husband, Louis Albano. In reality, it was Gotti who had the problem, not his daughter. She just wanted a divorce.

Albano and Angel Gotti had a young son they named Frankie, after her brother who had died in the accident that cost John Favara his life. But Alite said Albano also had a girlfriend on the side, that he was an unfaithful husband.

Gotti Sr.'s initial reaction when he learned about this was to have Albano killed. He said as much to Alite. But his daughter interceded. She told her father the marriage was over. They were divorcing. And, according to Alite, she didn't want Albano hurt.

There were, of course, other ways to inflict pain. Alite said he was first ordered to go to Albano's father, who had cornered the illegal fireworks business in Queens and Brooklyn. Gotti Sr. had a piece of that action and was the reason that Albano had no competition. Alite was told to let Albano Sr. know that he was now out of the fireworks business. What's more, he was told that a fifty-thousand-dollar loan, money that he owed to Gotti Sr., was now due in full.

Alite said he was also ordered to read Angel's husband the riot act. While he wasn't going to be hurt, Albano was told that he was on the shelf, no longer welcome in mob clubhouses, restaurants, or bars. He was also was told that he'd be wise to take his girl-friend and move to Florida. Alite said he delivered the messages, telling Albano that Gotti "never wanted to see him again."

Albano had been guilty of something that was commonplace in this world, according to Alite. Gotti Sr. himself had a girlfriend on the side, Alite said. Being married was never an issue.

But Gotti Sr. cautioned Alite that he didn't want anything about his daughter Angel's situation to "get out." Alite said every-one was aware of what was going on, but no one spoke of it pub-licly. He also said Gotti Sr.'s concern did not appear to be based on a desire to protect his daughter from any ridicule, but rather to save himself from being humiliated and made to look the fool.

Alite, who readily conceded that he was never the model husband, acknowledged that a double standard was in play. Wiseguys had girlfriends and wives, but wives were to abide by the marriage vows. It was almost like the Taliban. Philosophically some guys would have been comfortable with their wives in a hijab, or the even more extreme burka.

There was one mobster, Alite said, who would not let his wife address a male waiter when they were dining in a restaurant. Another refused to let his wife be treated by a male doctor. No matter what the issue, she had to find a female physician. And he knew of several wiseguys who would be upset if their wives wore the kind of revealing or tight-fitting clothes that were part of their girlfriends' wardrobes. In a more extreme example of the double standard, authorities in New Jersey are still searching for the body of a mobster who disappeared after he began an affair with another wiseguy's wife. That the offended mobster had been cheating on his wife with the young niece of the murder victim was of no matter.

Guys who were serial philanderers would hold their wives to a strict standard of conduct, calling them at home during the day to ask what they were doing, who they had seen or talked with, and what they were wearing. But wives weren't supposed to ask those same kinds of questions of their husbands. It was the way of the underworld.

Alite and those around him were very conscious of the issue and acted accordingly. Once, he said, Junior ordered an associate to pick up some things—diapers and other supplies—that his wife needed for their baby. The mob associate got the goods but was nervous about the delivery.

"He rang the bell, left them on the stoop, and ran away before Kim answered the door so that she wouldn't have any contact with him," said Alite, who twenty years later still shook his head over the twisted and paranoid relationship.

The Gottis, in any public statement they have made about Alite, insist that he has fabricated or exaggerated details in order to make them look bad and make himself look better than he was. Junior, in particular, has denied ever cheating on his wife. Alite, who has told many of his stories under oath and in front of juries, says he had no reason to lie.

Alite admits that in terms of being faithful, he was no better than Junior. It was more a question of style than it was a matter of conduct. As he said several times, most of the mobsters and mob associates he knew cheated on their wives with a girlfriend. Alite said many others, himself included, cheated on their girlfriends with yet another woman. It was part of that macho lifestyle that defined a wiseguy. It was sophomoric, like a neighborhood lothario bragging about his conquests. But most of the guys Alite hung around never outgrew the street corner mentality.

They were the grown-up version of the junior high bad boy. They knew intuitively that that image was attractive to a certain kind of woman and they used it.

At the time, Junior Gotti had access to one of the biggest sex markets then operating in New York City. Members of the Gambino organization, one crew from Westchester County and another from Arthur Avenue in the Bronx, had gotten their hooks into a "gentleman's club" that became one of the hottest spots in the city.

It was called Scores and it generated millions of dollars for the mob and millions more for its corrupt owners. The name was perfect. A brilliant marketing device. Scores is about sports and celebrity and, of course, sex. Did you score last night? The name is a wink and a nod and a sly smile.

The club attracted wiseguys and wannabes, Wall Street titans and downtown hustlers, guys and dolls, freaks and geeks, cross-dressing celebrities and buttoned-down nine-to-fivers who'd spend thousands of dollars a week chasing a fantasy that appeared onstage in a G-string. The girls were beautiful. All shapes and sizes and colors.

On a certain level, Scores was a candy story for little boys with bulging pants and wallets to match. It was not a complicated business. By the mid-1990s, Scores, which started out as a sports bar, was the number-one gentleman's club in Manhattan. It was located on the Upper East Side, just a block, in fact, from the posh penthouse that Mark Reiter owned. You could look down from Reiter's windows, Alite said, and see the club.

Scores became the prototype for a multimillion-dollar industry built around the glitz and glitter of tits and ass. There was an economic bonanza that took place within the gentleman's club business in the 1990s, a bonanza fueled by the high-flying wheeling and dealing on Wall Street that eventually brought the country to the economic brink.

The same guys putting together hedge fund deals and bundled derivatives (does *anyone* know what a bundled derivative is?) during the day were using their black AmEx corporate expense account cards to wine and dine customers with two-thousand-dollar bottles of champagne and two-hundred-dollar lap dances at night. Scores was always packed. Never any downtime. But the weekends, usually Thursday through Saturday, were nuts. There'd be six to seven hundred customers jam-packed around the bar, in the main room, and in the more exclusive President's Club and Crow's Nest.

Everyone had money.

And everyone was willing to spend it.

Professional athletes, celebrities, politicians, Wall Street power brokers, they all were attracted to what the *New York Post* used to refer to as the East Sixtieth Street "mammary mecca." Howard

Stern, then riding high on the popularity of his radio show, was a frequent visitor and would routinely tout the club during his broadcasts. Scores set the bar for what a gentleman's club was supposed to be. Tom Wolfe's "masters of the universe," the real-life versions of the financial wheelers and dealers who populated *The Bonfire of the Vanities,* would come in with clients, negotiate deals over drinks, and seal the agreements with handshakes and lap dances. Dozens and dozens of dances. On any given night, they would drop thousands of dollars in cash. But who cared? It was expense account money. A cost of doing business.

They reaped millions each day creating fictions in the financial world and at night they spent tens of thousands chasing girls with silicon breasts. Nothing was real. But it didn't matter.

It was about the moment.

It was about feeling good and looking good and playing the part.

Scores was the perfect backdrop. It was like a casino. Once you were inside, time stood still. You could be whoever you wanted to be. As long as you had the cash.

So the CEO from a communications company based in St. Louis shows up one night with his AmEx card and, after several hours of exclusive dances in the President's Club, runs up a tab of $241,000.

Lawsuits quickly follow and the *Daily News,* jumping on the story with the headline GOIN' BUST FOR LUST, reports, "In the mirrored room, popular with high rollers and celebrities, the stripper enthusiast demanded 10 dancers lavish him with attention at the eye-popping cost of $4,000 an hour."

That apparently did not include tips and other gratuities.

A Bangledeshi businessman filed a similar suit after claiming he was billed $129,626 in credit card expenses. Again, the story made tabloid headlines.

But for every complaint, there were dozens of guys who dropped astronomical amounts of cash and never said a word. Making it with beautiful women, that's what Scores was about for the guys who could afford it. Maybe it was easier than trying to hustle a broad at a bar. You never had to worry about pickup lines or women who weren't interested. You also didn't have to worry about women who wanted you to call the next day or take them to dinner or talk about their feelings.

Scores was "dating" without the hassles.

It was a Mafia version of *Animal House*.

Mob guys would "front" themselves as the owners of Scores but the real owner was Michael Blutrich. He and a partner would eventually get jammed up in a multimillion-dollar fraud case involving the Heritage Fund down in Florida. Squeezed by the feds in that case, Blutrich would agree to cooperate with authorities, giving up the mob's role in his club.

Alite was a friend of Blutrich's and had helped out with a problem the bar owner had up in Westchester County even before Scores had become famous. Alite also knew and liked Steve Sergio, a mob associate who ran the club. Coincidentally, Blutrich and Alite ended up serving time together years later after they had both cut their deals with the government.

The funny thing was, Blutrich was making so much money at Scores he didn't care that the mob was ripping him off. He and his partner were taking in $10 million to $15 million a year. And that was just the money they were showing on the books.

It didn't include whatever they might have been skimming and whatever they had to kick back to the wiseguys who owned the parking valet concession, supplied the bouncers, controlled the coat-check room, and routinely shook down the dancers and the DJs. Junior Gotti would plead guilty to taking a hundred thousand dollars out of the club as his end of the mob scam.

Alite said he never had a piece of the action at Scores, but went there on occasion as a customer. What's more, he said, "I always paid my own way. A lot of guys just went in, ran up a tab, and never paid. I was always a gentleman."

That wasn't the case in Queens, however, where Alite had hit upon another moneymaking scheme built around fear and intimidation. He later explained it all to a federal jury. The idea, he said, was to "unionize," in an organized crime sense, the bouncers at bars and clubs throughout the neighborhood. The unionizing eventually spread out to Manhattan and Long Island as well.

"There was a lot of money in that," he said.

It started, Alite said from the witness stand, when Junior took over the Harbor Club, a bar and restaurant in Middle Village, Queens. The owner was in debt to Junior and gave up the place to make up for what he owed.

"We put two bouncers in there," Alite said, "and then we put the word out that we were gonna be the ones to place bouncers in other places. And we told the bouncers, if you want to work, you have to go through us. . . .

"You don't have to have too much intelligence to really run it," he told a federal jury at Junior's trial in 2009. "All you have to do is come in and bully it. That's what we were good at."

The math, he added, told the story. A head bouncer who was making $100 a night would now be getting $85, with Junior and Alite taking $15 off the top. A second bouncer, who might be making $75, would now be making $65, with the $10 off the top going to Junior and Alite.

"It sounds like pennies," he told the jury, "but when you add it up, when there's a hundred bouncers working a night, it starts adding up to serious money each month, each year. So we were unionizing, basically, the bouncer service."

Most clubs and most bouncers went along.

"They had no choice," he said. "We let them know we were taking over. If you want to work, you go through us." Most bar and restaurant owners also went along. But one balked and the result was what anyone around Alite and Junior Gotti at that time would come to expect.

There was a club called Stingers on Metropolitan Avenue in Middle Village, Alite said. It was connected to a guy named Vito Guzzo, who was with the Colombo crime family. He didn't want bouncers sent by Alite and Gotti.

At a meeting at the Our Friends Social Club he adamantly refused. Junior told Alite to "get a little forceful" and Alite said he offered Guzzo a chance. "I told him I'd fight him right out in the street, me and him, a fair fight," Alite recalled. "If I won, the bouncers are ours. If he wins, we leave him alone."

Guzzo turned down the offer to tangle with Alite, but continued to refuse to do business with him and Gotti.

"Some of the bouncers he was using also worked for us at a club called Avanti," Alite said. "They were told not to go to work on this Friday. That anyone who did would be shot."

That night, Alite said, he, Junior, and several others were hanging out at the Our Friends. Alite sent an associate out to Stingers to see what was going on and the word came back that the bouncers were there.

"I'll be right back," Alite told Junior as he headed for the door. "I'm going to take care of this."

Alite and an associate got into his Corvette. Mike Finnerty followed in another car. They pulled up to Stingers. Alite got out of the Corvette and told his associate to get behind the wheel and drive the car to a gas station across the street.

"I didn't want anyone to see the license tag," he said.

Alite, brandishing a .32-caliber pistol, walked up to a bouncer who was standing at the door and asked, "Didn't you get the word not to come to work today?" Before the bouncer could reply, Alite shot him in the leg.

Three other bouncers came running out of the club. Alite shot all three. Then he walked into Stingers looking for Guzzo.

"They told me he had gone out the back," said Alite, who turned and walked out of the club. On the way out, he grabbed the manager by the hair, held the gun to his head, and said, "The next time I'm coming back and I'm gonna shoot you and Guzzo in the head."

And that's how Alite said he and Junior Gotti "unionized" the bouncers in dozens of clubs in and around New York. The list, he told a jury, included places like "Bedrocks, Decisions, Attitudes, Avanti, the Swim Club, Northern Lights, the Harbor Club, Café Iguana, Limelight. Just off the top of my head. If I sit here and think, I could probably come up with some more."

He also said that after the shootings at Stingers that night, he went back to the Our Friends Social Club. Junior, in typical fashion, wanted to drive back out to the scene to see what was going on. Junior liked to feel the rush, but wasn't that anxious to take part in the action. It was like the Grosso murder all over again.

"We used to call him Peewee Herman," Alite said of Junior's obsession with returning to crime scenes. "He was like the guy who got caught jerking off in the porno movie house. That's the way Junior was with the shootings. He liked to watch."

They drove back to Stingers in Junior's car. As they passed the club on Metropolitan Avenue, they saw the place awash in law enforcement.

"There were seven or eight police cars and two ambulances," Alite said. "People were all over the place."

All four bouncers survived the shooting. Alite was never charged. But no one else balked when he moved in to "unionize" the bouncer service. The move, however, had created a permanent problem for him with Guzzo, who Alite knew was a "serious" individual. Guzzo might have declined to fight Alite with his fists, but that didn't mean he was afraid of a fight. He was the leader of a loosely affiliated mob crew out of the Ridgewood section of Queens that terrorized the area. They were into bank robberies, extortions, and murders. The feds, who launched an investigation into Guzzo's organization in the late 1990s, referred to them as the Giannini Crew because they operated out of the Caffe Giannini in Ridgewood.

Despite their business success on the streets, Alite frankly admits that he was feeling "conflicted" about his relationship with Junior in the early 1990s. From the witness stand, he said he continued to commit acts of violence for Gotti, even though he was growing tired of Junior's attitude and arrogance and felt that some of the things he was being asked to do made no sense and served no underworld purpose.

The kidnapping of a kid who apparently had been mouthing off about Junior's wife, Kim, was a case in point. The issue came to a head when Junior and the mouthy twenty-year-old drove past one another in the neighborhood. Junior returned to the clubhouse on 113th Street that day ranting and raving about "the fat motherfucker." He told Alite he wanted him to kill the kid.

The fact that the kid was then dating Jodi Albanese, Junior's sister-in-law, might have been another motivation, Alite believes. "Junior always wanted to look tough in front of members of his wife's family," he said.

The order to kill Jodi Albanese's boyfriend further eroded the relationship between Alite and Junior Gotti. It was a typical Gotti move, Alite said, a senseless show of bravado that served no underworld purpose.

It wasn't business; it was clearly personal. What's more, Alite said, "It was stupid."

About a year earlier, Alite said, Gotti sent another associate to avenge some other perceived personal slight. The particulars are not important, but the bottom line was the guy didn't get the job done. Instead, he took a beating and ended up in an emergency room.

That may have been why Junior tapped Alite for this particular assignment. He wanted to be sure it was carried out.

The kid Alite said Junior wanted killed hung out at a bowling alley on Rockaway Boulevard. Alite, who recounted the incident in detail from the witness stand, said he was told to grab him and bring him to a mob clubhouse in Staten Island, where Junior would be playing cards. From there they would figure out how to kill him and where to dump the body.

Alite quickly found the kid outside the bowling alley and told him to get in the car. Mike Finnerty was along to help, Alite said. When the kid balked, Alite spoke quietly but forcefully.

"Either you get in the car or I'm gonna shoot you and put you in the car," he said. "One way or the other, you're getting in. You decide."

The kid opted to go along for the ride. First they headed over to Staten Island, but plans quickly changed and Alite was told to bring the kid to a building on 104th Street that Junior maintained. It wasn't a clubhouse, although he kept some weights and training equipment in the basement. He also stashed guns, ammunition, and cash there, sometimes upward of four hundred thousand dollars, Alite said.

He was told to put the kid in the basement. He sat him in a

chair and tied him up with duct tape. A few minutes later, Junior showed up with Jodi, Alite said. Recounting the story to a jury, he said Junior said to Jodi, "You see your boyfriend. He's going to die."

At that point, Alite said, he was beating the kid, who sat helplessly tied to the chair.

Jodi, according to Alite's testimony, acted "defiant . . . but if you saw her face, she was petrified." She left as the beating continued. Alite said he and Pat DiPippa, who had been ordered to show up, took turns hitting the kid.

According to Alite, Junior kept insisting that he wanted him dead. Alite said Junior handed him a gun and said, "Kill him."

Alite handed the gun back to Junior.

"You kill him," he said.

Alite said murdering the kid made no sense and he tried to convince Junior of that. Among other things, there were "too many people" who knew they had snatched the kid from the bowling alley. He also argued that the offense didn't warrant murder; that there "were so many other guys that did stuff to us that we need to kill," and that murdering this kid "for something stupid" served no purpose. He also appealed to Junior's conscience, telling him that the kid was the same age as Junior's brother Frankie would have been and asking why he wanted to inflict the same hurt on this kid's family that Junior and his family had suffered after Frankie had been killed.

During a break in one of these beating and arguing sessions, Alite drew close to the kid, who sat whimpering and bleeding in the chair. He whispered, "Just keep your mouth shut. Whatever he says, keep quiet. I'm gonna hurt you and send you to the hospital, but I promise I won't kill you. . . . You're going to get a beating, but you won't die tonight."

The kid, whose name Alite never learned, did take a beating that night, but Junior finally agreed that he would not be killed. DiPippa and Finnerty were told to drive him to an emergency room and drop him at the door.

Alite never saw the kid again, but he believes he saved his life.

The next person, Alite would tell a federal jury, that Junior wanted him to kill was Bruce Gotterup. Alite said he had no second thoughts about carrying out that order.

CHAPTER 12

Alite and Junior had been getting reports that Gotterup was causing problems at Jagermeister's, a bar on Jamaica Avenue where several of Alite's associates were dealing cocaine. Gotterup was the late George Grosso's brother-in-law and also an associate of Johnny Gebert. They and the guys around them, Alite would tell the jury, were "like a clan of wild junkies, drug dealers, and thieves." They often got high on their own product. But at the same time, he said, they were killers, known in the underworld as "serious guys."

Gotterup was robbing drug dealers and shaking down the owner of Jagermeister's even though he knew the dealers were working for Alite and the bar owner was linked to Junior Gotti. But Gotterup told everyone and anyone that he didn't care. He showed up with a gun one night and shot up the place. He was demanding a weekly extortion payment from the owner.

Unlike his late brother-in-law, Gotterup made no attempt to hide his disdain for the crime family. "Fuck Gotti," he said. "I'm not afraid of him or John Alite."

Alite was living at one of his condos in Whispering Woods, a development in South Brunswick, New Jersey, about a thirty-minute ride down the New Jersey Turnpike from the city. His "legal residence" was the fifteen-acre complex in Voorhees where his estranged wife, Carol, was living with their son Jimmy. Alite was also spending time with Claudia, his common-law wife and the mother of his infant son John. It was a complicated situation, he says. He had finished his sentence for assaulting the contractor but was on probation for that Camden County case.

"Because I was on probation, I had to show a residence in Camden County," he said. "I wasn't really living with my wife, but I would have to spend some time there."

One thing led to another and shortly after his release from prison in the summer of 1991, Carol was pregnant again. She would give birth to Alite's only daughter, Chelsea. The pregnancy caused all kinds of problems for Alite with Claudia, with whom he was trying to start a new life.

"She wouldn't talk to me, didn't want to know anything," said Alite. "I slept with Carol one time and she got pregnant. It just complicated everything. It became one more thing I had to deal with. I'm living in Jersey, staying mostly at the condo, and I'm in the city every day taking care of business.

"Junior is getting more and more arrogant and more and more paranoid. It was a strange time."

Sammy the Bull Gravano's decision to cooperate was having a ripple effect throughout the Gambino organization. While everyone talked tough and belittled Gravano, the reality was that they all realized his decision to cooperate could cripple the crime family. Everyone knew that Gravano had been one of John J. Gotti's closest associates, that he had had a dozen people killed on Gotti's orders, and that he was there with Gotti watching when Castellano was murdered. Those were the things he was now telling the feds, sometimes in dramatic fashion. When he finally got on the witness stand, Gravano seemed to enjoy the limelight. No longer in Gotti's shadow, but rather center stage, he took the opportunity to enhance his own role as a cold-blooded enforcer while insisting that he was doing it all at Gotti's behest.

"When he barked, I bit," Gravano told the jury.

Alite says Gravano was mostly talk.

"Did he have a lot of people killed?" Alite asked. "Yes. Did he do it himself? Not very often."

Over the course of his twenty years as Junior Gotti's muscle, Alite has estimated that he shot between thirty and forty guys, that he piped or baseball-batted a hundred more. How many of those people died? He says he doesn't know but admitted his own involvement in six homicides. There were probably more.

The Gotterup murder was one of the few in which he did not pull the trigger.

Working on Junior's orders, Alite would tell the jury at Junior's 2009 trial, he said he put a crew together. He got some of the guys he hung out with at Ronnie Trucchio's PM Pub and set the hit in motion. A tough kid named Johnny Burke (no relation to Frankie Burke, another Alite associate) was going to be the shooter along with Burke's brother-in-law, a guy Alite knew only as "King" because he was a member of the Latin Kings gang. Once again, the idea was to make the target comfortable and then kill him.

"He continued to shake down the bar and we told the owner to make the payments, make Gotterup think everybody was okay with what was going on," Alite explained.

The extortion payment, a couple of hundred a week, was peanuts in relation to the drug operation that was being run out of the bar. That was generating thousands of dollars for Alite and Gotti. Jagermeister's was one of "forty or fifty" spots out of which Alite and Junior were selling drugs, Alite told the jury. It was a good spot, but it wasn't their best spot, he said. O'Brother's and the White Horse were the top-earning locations for a cocaine network that in the late 1980s and early 1990s was generating millions in income each year. At the time of the Gotterup hit, Alite estimated they were moving four kilos of cocaine "in pieces" and four more kilos "in weight" each month from Jagermeister's.

"Pieces" meant the coke had been broken down into small quantities, usually about a gram, and sold in individual packets that went for about twenty dollars. The "retail" deals sometimes included slightly larger quantities known as "eight balls." An eight ball is one-eighth of an ounce, or 3.5 grams of coke.

"It was like a Stop 'n Shop," Alite said of the drug operation. "We had all kinds of customers."

"Weight" on the other hand, meant the coke was being sold in quarter, half, or full kilo amounts. The cash from those sales totaled in excess of $250,000 a month, Alite said, again emphasizing that Jagermeister's was not the largest moneymaker, but a substantial one in the drug network he said he and Junior had set up.

Gotterup was just bad for business. In addition to showing disrespect to the Gotti name, he was scaring regular customers away. No one wanted to be in the bar if a juiced-up Gotterup showed up waving a gun and got off a couple of shots. There also was the issue of protection that Alite told a jury he and Junior had promised the owner in exchange for allowing them to move drugs through the bar. Finally, Alite said, there was the very real concern that Gotterup might decide to turn his gun on a member of the crew, somebody like Ronnie One-Arm or Alite.

Alite, who had already had the go-round with Gebert and Grosso that resulted in Grosso's murder, didn't want to be looking over his shoulder every time he went into Jagermeister's. Neither did Trucchio.

On November 20, 1991, Bruce Gotterup showed up to make what had become his normal shakedown collection at Jagermeister's. Then he started drinking at the bar. Frankie Burke and

King, who were already there by design, started drinking with him. It was not unlike the Grosso setup. The three became good friends that night and decided to go clubbing. While they were driving toward Rockaway Beach, Gotterup said he had to take a piss. They pulled the car over and let him out along the side of the road. While he was urinating, King pumped two bullets into the back of his head.

No one disrespects the Gottis. That was the message when Gotterup's body was found the next day. The murder fed into Junior's growing ego. With his father in jail, he was now sitting atop the crime family, albeit as part of a ruling committee, but nevertheless a leader of the biggest Cosa Nostra organization in New York. It was the biggest, but not nearly as sophisticated or circumspect as the more powerful Genovese organization.

Like his father, Junior never understood the subtleties involved in making a crime family work. Vincent "the Chin" Gigante, on the other hand, was a master at it. The Genovese crime family boss, who by then had perfected his crazy routine, was spotted regularly walking around Sullivan Street in Greenwich Village in a bathrobe and slippers. By day, he was the "crazy" old Mafioso who mumbled and stumbled. But, as an FBI affidavit would later note, at night he would shower, shave, and be secretly driven to his mistress's condo on the Upper East Side. Gigante was a master criminal who knew how to play the system and manipulate the mob. There was a standing order within the organization that no one was to utter his name. Wiseguys who wanted to refer to him during a conversation might say "this guy" while they were rubbing their chin. It was a clear reference to Gigante and the mobsters in the conversation knew that. But if there was a listening device in the room, the result would be a transcript with the words "this guy" and no way to determine who it was that was being referred to.

The Genovese also had a habit of putting someone else up to "front" as the boss. It was another misdirection play aimed at both the feds and at the other crime families in the city whom the Genoveses never completely trusted. Gigante, said investigators at the time, was crazy all right. Crazy like a fox. He would eventually be brought to justice, but his run was longer and more lucrative than the Teflon Don's. The only thing the two organizations shared was a penchant for violence. But even at that, the Genovese crime family was more circumspect. They knew how to do it.

Junior Gotti, on the other hand, didn't have a clue.

Shortly before Gotti Sr.'s trial began in federal court in Brooklyn in the winter of 1992, Curtis Sliwa, the founder of the Guardian Angels and a radio talk show host in the city, went on a rant about the Gottis. It was a regular theme on his broadcasts. And it drove Junior nuts.

"He was bad-mouthing Senior every day," Alite said. "One day I'm taking a walk with Junior and he says to me. 'I wanna hit this Sliwa.'"

Alite said he couldn't believe what he heard.

"What are you, fuckin' nuts?" he asked Junior. "Are you out of your fuckin' mind?"

"No one bad-mouths the chief," Junior replied, referring to his father by the nickname that Senior had adopted after Joe Watts gave him a wooden sculpted head of an Indian warrior as a present. Gotti loved it and kept in his clubhouse. From that point on everyone referred to him as "the chief." Unlike the physical reference to "the chin" for Gigante, there was never any question about who was being discussed when "the chief" was mentioned on an FBI tape.

Alite said he tried to talk Junior out of hitting Sliwa. It wasn't a smart move. It was around that time, Alite said, that Junior started to develop an even more arrogant attitude. It was clear

Junior liked being the boss of the entire family and realized he would benefit from his father being convicted and sent to prison for the rest of his life, Alite said.

"He thought he was gonna be in charge and I think he was looking forward to it," Alite said. "I don't think he really cared what happened to his father, but hitting Sliwa was a way to make people think he did."

Perception over reality. That was the Gotti way.

"I told him even if Sliwa wasn't that well liked by others in the media, we would get attacked by everyone," Alite said. "I told him killing a reporter would be like killing a prosecutor."

Junior settled on a beating. But like so much else during his brief reign as part of the Gambino family's ruling committee, things didn't go as planned.

Neither did the trial of John J. Gotti. The Teflon was coming off the Don. The proceeding in federal court in Brooklyn was a major media event, with newspaper and television coverage nearly every day. The Gotti organization launched its own publicity counter-offensive, convincing celebrities to show up at the trial in support.

"Mikey Scars" DiLeonardo later testified that he helped arrange for some of those supporters—including actors Mickey Rourke, John Amos, and Anthony Quinn—to attend trial sessions. Gotti Sr. came up with the idea, DiLeonardo said.

"He wanted to have some famous people in the gallery to smile at the jury," DiLeonardo said from the witness stand.

There also was another strange ritual that played out almost every morning even before the jury was seated in federal court in Brooklyn. Each day about a half dozen Gotti associates, usually led by Jackie D'Amico, would show up early and take seats in the closest row to the defense table to which the public had access. Gotti, who was in custody, would be brought in by federal marshals before the judge or jury. He'd be dressed in one of his tailor-made, $1,500 suits, his hair still neatly coiffed, his skin tone not yet showing the signs of prison confinement. When Gotti entered the courtroom, D'Amico and the others stood and remained standing while he smiled and nodded hello. Once he was seated, the group of Mafia sycophants would sit down until the judge entered the courtroom. At that point, everyone in the room stood.

Standing was a sign of respect. Everyone was required to show it to the judge. Only a chosen few had to do it for "the chief."

John Gotti's Rules of Leadership: Never talk business indoors. The government has "ears." If you are talking business in a car, be sure the radio is turned up loud. Best to talk on the street while walking.

Gotti, of course, went down in flames along with Locascio. Gravano proved to be a highly effective witness. But just as damaging were the tapes, the secretly recorded conversations that proved beyond any doubt that Gotti was the leader of the crime family and the man who directed the racketeering operation at the heart of the case. Defense attorneys could rant and rave and attack Gravano's credibility and his motives for testifying, claiming as they do with all mob witnesses that the government has made a deal with the devil. The same arguments would surface in 2009 when Alite testified. But what the defense lawyers couldn't challenge were the tapes. Gotti's own words buried him. And in that respect, it was fitting. The celebrity gangster who dominated the New York underworld for nearly a decade, the mob boss who basked in the limelight and who had perfected the thirty-second sound bite that the media loved and that old time gangsters detested, was hung out to dry by his own words.

The tapes included Gotti talking about "whacking" a business

associate who had crossed him; about severing the head of another gangster suspected of horning in on a Gambino gambling
operation; and about how, if he got the time, he would ensure the
continuation of Cosa Nostra for another thirty years.

The jury also heard Gotti acknowledge to an associate that he
was the target of a major federal investigation.

"Don't I know they ain't gonna rest until they put me in jail?"
he said. "So I fight it tooth and nail to the end." But if he ended
up "in the can," Gotti said on the tape, he had already designated
a top associate to look out for the interests of the crime family.

"I love him," Gotti said of his designee. "I'm gonna go to jail
and leave him in charge."

The man Gotti was talking about was Salvatore "Sammy the
Bull" Gravano.

Gotti's conviction on April 2, 1992, brought the same kind of
screaming headlines that his indictment and arrest had generated
nearly two years earlier. JOHN GOTTI, GUILTY AT LAST was the
headline on a *New York Times* editorial the next day praising the
prosecution for "a major achievement, a community and national
service."

Sliwa was one of the many other commentators who jumped
on the story. He had been blasting all the Gottis in his radio ha-
rangues, including Vicky. Junior decided enough was enough.
The tipping point was apparently a postconviction broadcast on
WABC-AM in which Sliwa appeared to be popping a bottle of
champagne in celebration.

A month after the conviction, three thugs attacked Sliwa with
baseball bats. He fought them off and was back on the air continuing his harangue. A few weeks later, according to the testimony of
DiLeonardo, Junior met with him and several other mobsters at the
Carousel, a diner on Cross Bay Boulevard in Queens. During that
meeting, DiLeonardo said, Junior ordered a "hospital beating."

"Put him in the hospital," a frustrated Junior said of Sliwa, ordering DiLeonardo and the others to beat Sliwa "as bad as you can without killing him." Like Alite earlier, DiLeonardo said he questioned attacking a member of the media, even someone like Sliwa, whom other reporters and commentators considered a self-promoting blowhard.

"If you attack a member of the press," DiLeonardo said he told Junior, "whether they're in good standing with other press members, is one thing. [Sliwa's] still a member of the press. You'll get destroyed. We'll be destroyed."

Sliwa, who lived in the East Village at the time, routinely went to the radio station each morning in a taxi. On the morning of June 19, the taxi he hailed was being driven by mobster Joey D'Angelo. Scrunched down in the front passenger seat was mob associate Michael Yannotti. The taxi had been rigged and as soon as Sliwa got in the backseat, the doors locked. Yannotti popped up from the front seat, pulled a gun, and shot Sliwa in the thigh and groin. D'Angelo later testified that he was as shocked as Sliwa. They were supposed to beat the radio talker, D'Angelo said, not shoot him.

Sliwa, who would testify about the incident at three different trials, said he desperately fought his way out of the rogue taxi, flailing away and climbing over the armed Yannotti and jumping out the front passenger window.

D'Angelo later pleaded guilty to the assault. Yannotti was acquitted, but convicted of several other charges and sentenced to prison. Junior beat the Sliwa charge three times. Like his father, he had some judicial Teflon when it came to the radio host's assault. To Alite the attacks on Sliwa were confirmation of what he had been anticipating. Junior Gotti didn't know how to run a crime family and if he remained in charge, they would all end up dead or in jail.

Five days after the Sliwa shooting, John J. Gotti was sentenced to life in prison. The hearing, in the same federal courthouse in Brooklyn where he had been convicted, drew several hundred supporters. Denied access to the jammed courtroom, they rallied in the streets outside the federal building, chanting, waving signs, and singing the praises of John J. Gotti. It was a great show and it attracted lots of media.

But it was a meaningless gesture, another Gotti flashpoint that the media jumped all over.

"Junior and some other guys set that whole thing up," Alite said. "I didn't want any part of that nonsense. They had kids from the neighborhood and guys from some of the unions that we controlled."

The so-called rally went on for two or three hours. Several cars were overturned and traffic disrupted. The sentencing hearings for Gotti and Locascio, on the other hand, were over in about fifteen minutes. Judge Leo Glasser imposed life without parole on both defendants.

Gotti declined to comment.

Locascio, loyal to the end, told the judge that he was "innocent." Then he added, "I am guilty, though. I'm guilty of being a good friend of John Gotti. And if there were more men like John Gotti on this earth, we would have a better country."

U.S. Attorney Andrew Maloney, whose office prosecuted the case, tried to provide the proper perspective for the Gotti conviction, describing the trial as "just one more battle" in the war against organized crime in New York. He also said "media buildup" had helped create the myth of John J. Gotti and "media hype" had fueled the demonstration that was taking place out in the streets.

Gotti's lawyers promised an appeal.

Within the Gambino organization, however, no one expected Senior to return. The only question was who would be in charge. Junior clearly thought he had the mantle. But there were several others who wanted to go in another direction. They wanted Junior to step down. And if he balked, they wanted him dead.

John Alite was asked to handle the problem.

CHAPTER 13

John J. Gotti thought he could run his crime family from prison. While it had been done before by other bosses with varying degrees of success, it was not a very good idea.

"Little Nicky" Scarfo had tried to do it down in Philadelphia. Convicted of racketeering and murder in 1988, he set his son up as his proxy. Nicodemo S. Scarfo was known as Scarfo Jr. even though he and his father (like the Gottis) had different middle names. Like Junior Gotti, the younger Scarfo wasn't that well liked by other members of the Philadelphia crime family. They saw his father as a bloody psychopath who had used murder to establish his control. The violence had destabilized what had once been a quietly efficient organization. About two dozen mob members and associates were killed during Scarfo's bloody reign, which had begun in 1981. What's more, bullets and dead bodies attracted law enforcement. Do the math. A crime family that at best had boasted seventy members had lost nearly half that number to murders or prosecutions. The Philadelphia mob was in shambles when Scarfo Sr. was convicted.

On Halloween night in 1989, Scarfo's attempt to run the organization through his son came to an end. The younger Scarfo was dining at Dante & Luigi's, a popular eatery in the heart of

South Philadelphia. He was enjoying a plate of clams and spaghetti, sharing a meal with his cousin and another mob associate.

At first no one noticed the masked trick-or-treater who walked into the restaurant carrying a Halloween bag, the kind that kids all over the neighborhood were using to collect their candy that night.

Candy wasn't the issue, however.

The guy wearing the mask walked up to Scarfo's table, pulled a 9 mm machine pistol out of his bag, and opened fire. Scarfo was hit six times. The gunman turned and walked briskly out of the restaurant and onto Tenth Street, where a car was waiting for him. Other customers were stunned. It happened in seconds. The shooter, as he stumbled down the restaurant steps, dropped his gun. Was it an accident or by design?

Years later, a mob informant told authorities that the gunman deliberately left the gun. The reason? He knew the elder Scarfo was a big fan of *The Godfather,* especially the scene where Michael Corleone avenges the shooting of his father by gunning down a rival mobster and his police protector in an Italian restaurant in the Bronx. As he leaves, Michael flips the gun onto the floor as he had been instructed to do by the veteran mobsters who set up the hit.

The shooting of Nicky Scarfo Jr. (he survived) was a bloody homage of sorts to a classic mob movie and was also a way for the shooter—no one has ever been charged with the attempted murder—to thumb his nose at the jailed Philadelphia mob boss.

The shooting effectively ended any attempt by Scarfo Sr. to control the crime family from prison. The Gottis, according to Alite's accounts of his firsthand involvement, appeared to be headed in the same direction. But then, Alite said, greed got in the way. In the Gambino crime family that the Gottis had created, that was all too often the case.

The plot to kill Junior, his uncle Pete, and Carmine Agnello began to percolate within months of Gotti Sr.'s conviction. Alite knew some of the players and heard about others. John Carneglia, who was convicted with Gene Gotti in the big heroin case, was one of the instigators. Nicky Corozzo, a mob capo, was also in on it, Alite said. Danny Marino, another capo, may have been involved, or at least given his tacit approval, Alite believes. Charles Carneglia, John's psycho brother, also played a role.

"John Carneglia was in jail and the Gottis, first the father, then the son, were taking advantage of him," Alite said. "He still had guys out on the street who owed him money and the Gottis just took it. They told anyone who owed Carneglia that they should pay the money to them instead. It was the same old story, 'Fuck John Carneglia. He's a scumbag drug dealer.' But the Gottis were happy to take the money that he was owed from dealing drugs."

From prison, Carneglia got word to his brother Charles, who in turn enlisted Alite.

"Charles told me what they wanted to do and asked me, 'Would you take care of that half Jew?'" Alite said. Anytime anyone wanted to belittle Junior they would bring up the fact that his mother was Russian Jewish on her mother's side. Consequently, they would call Junior a Jew.

Alite weighed his options. His view of the Gottis had changed.

"When I first got involved, I would have died for that family," he said. "But the longer I was around them and the more I saw, the less I believed in what they were saying and doing."

There was also a very practical underworld assessment. With Senior in jail for life, the family was splitting into factions. Whose side did Alite want to be on? Junior was a bumbler who didn't know how to run a criminal organization. The odds were he would end up dead or in jail. Did Alite want to go down with him or roll the dice with someone else?

Alite agreed to be part of the murder plot. A few weeks later, John Carneglia's mother-in-law passed away. Junior put out the word that no one was to attend the wake or funeral, but Alite went to the viewing with his own crew of four or five guys.

"There was a big snowstorm that night," Alite said. "While I'm at the funeral parlor I'm told there's a phone call for me. I pick up the phone and it's John Carneglia. Somehow he had gotten the use of a prison counselor's phone and called."

Inmate phone calls from federal prisons are monitored and recorded. But calls from a counselor's phone are not. Alite said John Carneglia asked him, "Can you take care of Junior?"

"Sure," Alite said. "No problem."

One of the great ironies was that Alite intended to use Junior Gotti's own guns to kill him. Earlier Charles Carneglia had borrowed a 9 mm handgun and an Uzi machine gun, along with ammunition, from Junior.

"Junior had bought several machine guns and Charles asking to borrow one wasn't any big deal," Alite said. "Everybody knew Charles was crazy and a killer."

Charles Carneglia gave the guns to Alite, who stashed them at a friend's tattoo parlor. The idea was to make Junior "comfortable," set him up, and then blow him away, the same routine that had been used on Grosso and Gotterup. Alite and some associates had begun to "clock" Junior's movements. They learned that he was going to the same restaurant for dinner on Friday nights. Alite's plan was to show up there and take him out. Everyone was on board. Nicky Corozzo, Alite said, hated Gotti Sr. and despised the son. That's one reason he got involved in the murder plot. But somewhere along the way, Alite said, Corozzo saw a way to cash in. He decided to trade bullets for dollars.

"Nicky Corozzo sent his nephew to visit Gotti Sr. in prison and to deliver a message," Alite said. "The word from Nicky to Senior was that 'We can't protect Junior on the streets. He's gotta slide over or he's gonna be killed.' Senior knew right away what was going on. And he worked out at deal."

Alite believes that from prison Gotti arranged to have several hundred thousand dollars funneled to Nicky Corozzo. The payoff ended Corozzo's involvement in the murder plot. Corozzo had turned the planned hit into an extortion scheme. He shook Gotti down the same way Gotti had shaken down dozens of others when he was running the crime family. Shortly after Corozzo backed out, Charles Carneglia began complaining about being "caught in the middle." Carneglia sold out for a lot less.

"He was a killer, but mentally he was very weak," Alite said. "You couldn't depend on him for anything. Not even his brother could count on him," Alite said. "Gotti arranged for Carmine Agnello to put Charles on the payroll at the auto salvage yard he owned. They were paying him seven hundred and fifty dollars a week."

Once he started collecting his weekly pay, Charles Carneglia told Alite the hit on Junior had been canceled.

"It's off," he told Alite. "Give me back the guns."

"What do you mean, it's off?" Alite asked.

"Change of plans," said Charles Carneglia.

Alite was dumbstruck. He also was adamant about the guns.

"You're not getting them back," he told Carneglia.

"But Junior wants them," he said.

"Fuck Junior," said Alite.

At this point, Alite's relationship with Junior was broken beyond repair. He was spending most of his nights in New Jersey, but he was in Queens almost every day. He and Junior were still making lots of money together, he said, but as he later told a jury, "It was like a bad marriage. We stayed together, but we weren't getting along."

Alite said he had seen the Gottis turn on too many of their top associates to believe that he was somehow going to survive. "I still believed in the life of crime, the life of the Gambino family, the mob," he said. "I just didn't have any faith in the Gottis anymore."

In fact, he had tried to get "transferred" to the Luchese organization. He had friends there and thought he could get out from under the Gottis by making that move. But Gotti and the rest of the Gambino hierarchy wouldn't approve the shift. So Alite decided to make the best of a bad situation.

He started to use Charles Carneglia and Ronnie One-Arm Trucchio as buffers. He and Junior would usually communicate through one of those two guys. Technically, Alite, an associate, would be answering to the made guys. The reality was Alite was doing whatever he wanted, still making money on the streets and still moving around with a crew whose loyalty he could depend on. They were guys he trusted. Guys he had grown up with. Guys like his young cousin Patsy. Alite didn't trust Trucchio or Charles Carneglia, but he knew he was smarter than they were and could effectively use them as a safeguard.

Alite, who had been the hunter, was very aware that he could easily become the hunted. He stopped showing up at the social clubs. He varied the way he moved around, avoiding any set pattern. He didn't come when he was called. If someone wanted to meet with him, Alite would usually use his cousin to set it up.

It was at this time that he started to pick up bits and pieces of information, indications that he had a problem. A friend of another cousin was playing handball with a several of Junior's associates and heard them joking about Alite, whom they referred to as "the sheriff."

"The sheriff had a problem," one of them said. "He was going to be killed. Junior had put out a contract on him."

Trucchio also offered what amounted to a half-assed warning.

He tried to dress it up, but said Junior and others in the administration were concerned that Alite wasn't coming when he was called. Louis DiBono had paid the ultimate price for violating that protocol. Alite knew the consequences. But he also knew that, unlike DiBono, he was feared. Everyone knew that if they went after him, there would be a fight. There were no guarantees, but Alite was willing to take his chances. He continued to live life in the underworld on his own terms. He wasn't about to run and hide. And he also continued to follow the other rule.

He had two scores, two robberies, working at this time and cleared both of them with Charles Carneglia, putting them "on the record" with the Gambino crime family. The two heists were supposed to generate serious cash. Alite, who testified about both incidents at Carneglia's trial in 2009, came away with nothing. But he was so flush at the time that he took it in stride.

The first robbery was a Sears store in Vineland, New Jersey, about forty minutes from Alite's home in Cherry Hill. A kid named Steve brought the deal to Alite.

"I knew him and his brother from the neighborhood," Alite said. "His brother was a drug dealer and I helped him out from time to time."

Alite said the kid's father, George Lopez, was the head of security at the store.

The elder Lopez had worked in the local sheriff's department and later was the warden at a jail or prison in the area, Alite said while testifying about the heist. He also was a bookmaker who edged off some work to Alite, who was in the process of establishing his presence in the South Jersey underworld.

Alite went down to Vineland and met Lopez. They mapped out a plan to rob the office where the cash proceeds were kept. The robbery was to go down on Labor Day. Alite was told there would be a lot of sales over the holiday weekend and that there might be up to a half million dollars in cash on hand. Alite still shakes his head as he talks about the robbery.

"This guy, he's an Hispanic guy, right," Alite said. "I'm in his basement making plans and I see these sheets and hats hanging in the corner. He's a member of the Klan, the KKK. An Hispanic guy! I can't believe it. He goes upstairs to get something and I put the robe and the hat on and when he comes down I'm prancing around, just busting his balls. He didn't think it was funny."

Alite was dumbfounded.

"I said to him, 'Whaddaya do, throw a rope over a branch and hang yourself?'"

Alite had recruited a few associates who came down from New York and carried out the robbery. Two guys would go in posing as Secret Service agents. Alite had given them a counterfeit hundred-dollar bill. Their story was that there were a lot of these bills circulating and they wanted to examine the cash that had come through the store that weekend. Lopez said he would send the two security guards working that day out to lunch when the heist went down. He also promised to adjust the security cameras so that no one's face would show up on video.

Alite and Kevin McMahon stayed outside in the parking lot with scanners to monitor local police activity. Lopez had said the police would not be a problem.

Things went as planned until the two "agents" started to count the money in the store's safe. One of the women working the office that day panicked or figured out what was going on. She slammed the safe shut. Alite's two guys scrambled out of the store and ran to the parking lot where their own car was waiting. They ended up with $25,000 in cash, hardly the score that Alite had been expecting.

"I set twenty-five hundred dollars aside for Charles and another twenty-five hundred for Ronnie One-Arm," Alite said.

"They were the guys I was supposedly working for and they had the right to a piece of whatever we did."

The rest he gave to the guys involved in the heist. Alite took nothing. As he later told the jury, "I didn't want pennies. I wanted big money. I had money. I was doing well for myself. It didn't mean anything to me, a couple of dollars."

The other heist was at the Papavero Funeral Home on Long Island (the funeral parlor from which, several years later, John J. Gotti would be buried). The backstory was not unlike the robbery of the doctor down in Florida. Again, Alite explained it all to the Carneglia jury.

A woman Alite knew was married to the brother of one of the owners of the funeral parlor. She said he was abusing her and to get back at him, she told Alite about cash, upward of $400,000, and jewelry, worth about $300,000, that was kept in the safe at the funeral parlor.

Alite cleared the move with Charles Carneglia. Among other things, he was concerned about a connection the funeral parlor had with Skinny Dom Pizzonia, another Gambino capo. Carneglia told Alite not to worry about it.

Alite sent Kevin McMahon to the funeral home to scope it out. McMahon's story was that his grandmother had passed away and he wanted to plan a funeral. He arranged for a second meeting on a Sunday night, when Alite figured there wouldn't be any workers around. That's when the heist was supposed to go down. That night, Alite and McMahon stayed in a car outside the funeral parlor. As they had done during the Sears heist, they were listening to police scanners.

Kevin Bonner and another guy went into the funeral parlor, accosted and tied up the owner, and demanded he open the safe.

"Somehow he got away from them and hit a fire alarm," Alite said. "They came running out of the place and we all took off."

Empty-handed.

It was a run of bad luck that had begun earlier that summer for Alite.

He had attended an engagement party in Mineola and afterward was sitting in the Caffé Bianco with a female cousin drinking champagne. He was already pretty drunk when John Kelly and two goons walked up to him, showed him their guns, and told him to come with them to the parking lot. Kelly was the drug dealer who was ripped off during the phony police stop that Junior and Alite had set up a few years earlier. Kelly had promised to get back at Alite and when he saw him drinking at the bar, he moved in.

Alite reached for the bottle of champagne, pretending that he was going to take another swig. Instead he swung the bottle at Kelly. Had he been sober, Alite figures, he would have knocked Kelly out. But in the state he was in, Alite couldn't focus. The bottle just grazed Kelly's head. Still, it was enough to catch everyone off guard and it gave Alite a chance to break away. He headed to the parking lot, got to his car, a black Nissan 300Z, and reached into the glove compartment, where he had a hammer.

"It's the only thing I had," he said as he recounted the incident years later. "They thought it was a gun. They jumped into their car. I got in mine."

Kelly was driving a fancy Excalibur with the spare tire mounted outside the trunk.

"The kind of car pimps used to drive," Alite said.

Before Kelly could get out of the parking lot, Alite rammed his Nissan into the Excalibur. Police, responding to a call for assistance from the bar, arrived within minutes. Alite, drunk and disoriented, rammed the police car, then got into a fight with two of the responding officers. He was arrested and charged with assault and related offenses.

"I took a beating that day," he said. "Those cops piped me pretty bad. I just kept fighting them. I don't know. That's just the way I was back then. I try to control it now, but it was like a button got pushed and I wasn't gonna stop."

Free on bail, Alite went right back to the streets and the violence that had become so much a part of his life. It was all that he knew. It was how he survived. A few months earlier, Guy Peden, a drug dealing associate, had been arrested in a casino in Atlantic City. Peden had set up a drug deal but ended up caught in a federal sting. Alite was supposed to be there that night but didn't show up.

"I told Guy not to go through with that deal," he said. "He didn't even know who he was selling to. Turns out it was an informant and he got pinched."

Peden was off the streets but was still owed money from several earlier deals. Steve Newell, a friend of Junior's, was on the hook for a kilo of coke, Alite said. That amounted to about forty grand. Alite was going to collect. Newell balked at paying.

"So I shot him," Alite said. "I saw him walking along Cross Bay Boulevard. I got out of my car and I shot him in the butt. When he went down, I kicked him and punched him."

Word got back to Junior, who sent word to Alite, telling him to back off.

A week later, two FBI agents showed up at the home of Alite's mother and father in Queens. They were looking for Alite. His parents told the agents they hadn't seen or heard from him in several days.

"My mother started crying," he said. "She thought I was dead."

The FBI didn't do much to calm her fears. They said they needed to talk with her son and they had information that someone wanted to kill him. When Alite was told this by his parents, he arranged to meet with the agents. But first he called Richie Rehbock, a defense attorney who was representing him in the

Mineola case. Rehbock was one of the "approved" defense law-yers that the Gotti organization wanted to represent members and associates.

"I told Rehbock the FBI wanted to talk with me," Alite said. "I wanted to let him know, and that way let Junior know, that I wasn't cooperating; that I was going to meet with them to find out what was going on and who they thought was trying to kill me."

Alite already had a pretty good idea where the threats were coming from. In a way, he was playing a mind game with Junior. I know it's you, he was saying, and you know I know. But let's play this out as if neither one of us has a clue about what's going on.

Alite met with the two agents at a rest stop near Exit 8A on the New Jersey Turnpike, not far from his condo in South Brunswick. They told him he had a problem. They said they were required by law to warn anyone who they believed had been targeted. They wouldn't say who and they wouldn't say how they knew, but they insisted that the threat was real and that Alite's life was in danger.

He took it all in and then joked with the agents. Carmine Ag-nello had recently been involved in a beef with a meter maid in New York. The meter maids all wore yellow vests.

"As long as I'm not wearing yellow," he told the agents, "I'll be safe."

They didn't think it was funny. Or they didn't get the refer-ence. They offered him protection and suggested he come in and cooperate.

"Thank you, but no thanks," Alite told the agents. "That's not for me."

At that point, Alite said, he still thought he could protect him-self. He knew that he had the street smarts and the heart to beat Junior and those around him at their own game. And he wasn't ready—yet—to stop playing.

Following the meeting with the FBI, Alite told anyone and

everyone that the agents had played a tape for him and that he heard Peter Gotti, Carmine Agnello, and a third individual who he believed was Junior Gotti, though he couldn't be certain, plotting to kill him.

It was a bogus story. There was no tape. But it was Alite's way to flush Junior out. It also offered, at least in the short term, some life insurance.

"I figured if they thought there was a tape with their voices talking about killing me then they wouldn't try anything because if I were killed, they'd be the suspects," Alite said.

A few days later, Alite's cousin Patsy was contacted by Steve Kaplan, one of Junior's associates. Junior wanted to meet. Alite agreed. He suggested the Aqueduct Racetrack, a public place with lots of people. No one was going to stage a hit in that setting.

Alite showed up at the Queens racetrack with two or three associates. Junior came with a party of six, including Carmine Agnello.

"I'm not talking to that pig," Alite said when Junior approached with Agnello.

It set the tone for the face-to-face Junior and Alite had that afternoon.

"First he denied everything," Alite said. "I mentioned the tape and he said, 'I had nothing to do with that.'"

That told Alite two things. There was a murder plot and the three individuals he had named—Peter Gotti, Agnello, and Junior—were involved.

"Stop bullshitting me," Alite said. "Nobody does anything like that without your okay."

The conversation got heated after that, Alite said, with Junior threatening Alite's brother Jim.

"My brother wasn't a street guy," Alite said. "He had nothing to do with this life. I told Junior, 'You have a brother, too.' He went nuts. He said, 'Are you out of your fuckin' mind? I have a thousand guys.'"

Alite just shook his head, looked Junior in the eye, and said, "You go near my brother, I only gotta kill two." With that, Alite made it clear that Junior and Carmine Agnello were in jeopardy if anything happened.

In typical fashion, Junior tried to turn things around. When threats didn't work, he tried to be conciliatory. He said Alite was "paranoid," that nobody was out to get him, that they all were friends. The sit-down at the racetrack ended with them shaking hands and embracing, but Alite knew it was all for show.

Then, in a move that Alite still has trouble comprehending, Gotti suggested that Alite take a trip with him and Carmine. They were heading to a house Gotti had upstate. They were going "hunting," Junior said, and asked if Alite wanted to join them.

"What a fuckin' moron," Alite said as he recounted the story. "Did he think I was stupid?"

At the time, Alite joked about the offer, telling Gotti, "'Yeah, sure. I'll put on Bugs Bunny ears and you two can shoot at me.' Everybody laughed, but I wasn't kidding. We shook hands, but I knew eventually he'd try to kill me or have someone do it."

The game of cat-and-mouse continued for the next year. Alite and Gotti communicated through proxies. Ronnie Trucchio was one of the messengers.

"I told Ronnie, whenever Junior tells you to call me, call," Alite said. "That way you don't get in trouble with him. But when you call, I ain't comin'. I'll get back to you, or you contact my cousin Patsy. I'll find you and roll up on you."

Alite said he knew the game too well. There was no way he would show up at a meeting that Junior or one of his associates had set up; no way he would get in a car with any of them. He had seen, and carried out, too many shootings to put himself in that kind of jeopardy. If they met, it would be on his terms and at a location he selected.

That's how he ended up on the Boardwalk in Atlantic City in one of his first face-to-face meetings with Junior after the confrontation at the Aqueduct. Junior was having a problem with some Albanians and wanted Alite to intercede. According to Alite, the root of the problem was a typical Gotti scam that reinforced his opinion of Junior as a petty, spineless mob boss.

"His cousin, Johnny Boy Ruggiero, had been dating this girl Janet, who was Albanian," Alite said. "Johnny Boy had 'borrowed' sixty thousand dollars from her. She wanted it back. These Albanians, friends of hers or relatives, were threatening to kill Ruggiero if he didn't return the money. A guy named George, who I knew, was one of the guys making the threats. He ended up marrying Janet."

Alite figured Junior had gotten half of the sixty grand. That's the way he operated. Ripping off a young woman was a typical predator-type move that Junior would either come up with or approve, Alite said. Junior and Johnny Boy probably figured the woman would have no recourse.

"I agreed to meet Junior on the Boardwalk in Atlantic City," Alite said. "He was down there for the fights in one of the casinos. At the meeting he tells me about the problem. First he's acting real tough, like 'Do they know who they're dealing with?' I had to tell him that they didn't care. They'd kill Johnny Boy and they'd kill him and then the next day they'd be back in Albania where no one would ever find them."

Just as he had done at the Aqueduct meeting, Junior started out with threats, telling Alite that he would kill the Albanians first.

"I told him he didn't even know who they were," Alite recalled. "Then he says to me, 'Would they take forty-five thousand instead of the sixty?'" Alite brought the request to George the Albanian, who, through Alite, sent word back to Junior Gotti.

"He told me to tell Gotti, 'Not only won't I take forty-five thousand, I won't take fifty-nine thousand.'"

Janet got her sixty grand back.

CHAPTER 14

His break with Junior Gotti didn't stop Alite from wheeling and dealing in the underworld. In fact, it opened up opportunities to expand. He already had established a presence in Tampa, where he and Ronnie Trucchio had "planted the flag" of the Gambino crime family, moving from drug dealing and extortion to legitimate interests in nightclubs and a valet parking business.

In the mid-1990s, Alite also set up shop in the Philadelphia–South Jersey area, where he already had two homes. His common-law wife, Claudia, had moved into a house he purchased in a residential neighborhood in Cherry Hill with his young son John. Another son, Matt, would be born a short time later. Alite still used the condo in South Brunswick but also spent time in one of the three homes located on the fifteen-acre tract he owned in nearby Voorhees Township. He and his wife Carol had divorced but their two children, son Jimmy and daughter Chelsea, sometimes stayed with him. Alite's parents and, for a time, his grandmother, also lived on the property. Alite had turned the grounds into an athletic facility of sorts with an outdoor gym and boxing ring equipped to train fighters. Boxing remained a big part of his life. He never hesitated to get in the ring. And as he got older he came to realize that his fascination with the sport wasn't just about winning. A good fighter not only knew how to throw a punch, but how to take one. Alite brought that same attitude to the streets. You might knock him down, but unless you knocked him out, he was getting back up. And if he did get back up, you had a problem.

Junior Gotti wasn't big enough, tough enough, or smart enough to knock him down.

A few years after establishing a base in the Philadelphia suburbs, Alite was moving easily in and around the local underworld. He knew some members and associates of the Philadelphia crime family and they, in turn, introduced him to others. He quietly went about his business, never calling attention to himself or boasting about his New York connections. Guys who needed to know found out quickly enough. For most other people, it didn't matter. Who he was was not the issue. What he was doing was what mattered.

Ironically, Junior had paved the way for Alite by making some introductions several years earlier. One of his first forays into the local underworld involved a check cashing and money laundering scheme that Gotti had set up before he and Alite had their falling-out.

"Junior had this guy who was in the kitchenware business," Alite said. "He had this warehouse in the Bronx. I went there one time and it was empty. Couldn't even get a frying pan for my wife."

But the guy was making money, big money.

"He had some deal with these Colombians," Alite said. "They were moving coke. And this guy needed to wash the money through his company. He asked Junior for help and Junior brought me in."

Over the course of a six- to eight-month period in about 1991, Alite said, he cashed several million dollars' worth of checks for the businessman. They were company checks but they weren't made out to anyone. Alite used a pawnshop and a check-cashing business in Philadelphia to clear some of the money, then made a connection with a guy he knew who owned a big construction company.

They'd take the checks, make them out to themselves or their businesses, and give Alite 80 to 90 percent of the face value in cash. Alite and Junior would take another 10 percent off the top before the businessman got his money, but even at that, he and his Colombian partners were turning a profit.

"We were just making a lot of money a lot of different ways," Alite said.

In the middle of the check-cashing operation, Junior told Alite that two of the Colombians' business associates, a husband and wife, had been busted. The drug traffickers had been using the couple's home in Brooklyn as a stash house. They were nailed and there was no way out of the case, but they asked Junior if he had any influence with the courts. The couple had pleaded guilty and were going to be sentenced.

"We said we could work something out," Alite said. "It was a lie. We had no influence. But they promised to pay us two hundred and fifty thousand dollars if we could arrange a sentence of fifteen years or less."

Alite showed up at two court hearings to make it look like he had some clout.

"At one of them I was the only person in the courtroom," he said. "We were just taking a chance, trying for a score. And at the sentencing hearing the judge, who had no idea, imposed a sentence of fifteen years on the husband and fifteen years on the wife."

The Colombians forked over the quarter of a million in cash, Alite believes, although he never saw any of it.

"Junior said to me that his businessman friend was having a tough time of it and we ought to let him keep the payoff, that we had already made a lot of money with him," Alite recalled. "I think

Junior split the money with him and cut me out. But I wasn't gonna make a big deal out of it. He was right. We had made a lot of money with the guy. This was just Junior's way of making more."

Philadelphia presented lots of other opportunities for Alite once he started to look around. In the mid-1990s, bars and restaurants were sprouting up along the Delaware Avenue riverfront from Center City to South Philadelphia. The popular nightspots attracted the young and the wealthy from both the city and the suburbs. There also were more than a few wiseguys and wannabes and the beautiful young women who chased after them. Parking was always a problem and each establishment had a valet service.

Alite, who already had a big valet business in Tampa, simply muscled his way in, using threats and beatings when necessary, to push out any competitors. In less than a year he had control of the valet parking at about two dozen spots along Delaware Avenue, a few in South Jersey, and a few more in Atlantic City. He even had a few locations in upscale shopping centers. It was like the "unionizing" of the bouncers in Queens. It was a cash business and, other than paying for insurance, there was very little overhead.

Alite charged the businesses a flat fee for the valet service, arranged off-site parking, and set up two or three kids at each site to park the cars. Their biggest income came from the tips.

Several of the clubs along Delaware Avenue, places like Rock Lobster, the Eighth Floor, Egypt, and KatManDu, also attracted local celebrities and the city's sports stars. One night Alite was checking on his businesses when he saw a Bentley parked in a VIP spot next to the entrance at one of the clubs. It was standard for whoever parked in that spot to put twenty dollars in the tip bucket. All the tips went to the guys Alite hired to park and watch the cars. This night, the tip bucket was empty. Alite asked who owned the Bentley. One of the valet workers told him it belonged to Allen Iverson, the basketball star.

Alite went in the club and found him.

"Move your car," he said.

Iverson was taken aback.

"What?"

"Either move your car or put fifty dollars in the bucket," Alite said. "Usually it's twenty dollars, but for you now it's fifty."

Alite said Iverson tried to play the celebrity card, asking him if he knew who he was.

"I know who you are," Alite said he replied. "I don't give a fuck. You're too cheap to tip. Move your car."

Iverson said he was a friend of the owner of the club and that his presence generated business. Alite said that didn't do him or the kids parking cars any good. Iverson walked away, but Alite later found out he had asked the owner who Alite was.

"He came out after that and put money in the bucket," Alite said. "He apologized. Said no hard feelings. Keyshawn Johnson [a star wide receiver for the Tampa Bay Buccaneers] was the same way down in Tampa. Never tipped. Warren Sapp [an All-Pro defensive tackle for the Buccaneers], on the other hand, was generous with everybody. Maybe that's why he ended up bankrupt."

Valet parking became a legitimate source of income. It was a way for Alite to launder some of the cash that was flowing in from his drug dealing, gambling, and loansharking operations. And it was there for the taking.

"It was wide open and I just moved in," he said. "I couldn't believe the local guys hadn't gotten into this."

At the time Alite started making his moves in the Philadelphia area, the local mob was in turmoil. Little Nicky Scarfo's bloody reign as mob boss had ended with his arrest and conviction on racketeering charges in 1988. He was succeeded by John Stanfa, a Sicilian-born Mafioso with ties to the old leadership of the Gambino family. Stanfa was banging heads with the sons, nephews, and cousins of members of the jailed Scarfo crew. The young group was headed by Joseph "Skinny Joey" Merlino, whose father had been Scarfo's underboss. The Stanfa and Merlino factions were busy cruising the streets and shooting at one another. They didn't have the time or the inclination to go after the valet parking businesses that Alite had targeted.

There was one incident involving a guy who claimed to be Stanfa's nephew. He slapped around one of the valet attendants working for Alite at a Delaware Avenue nightclub. Alite got a phone call from the panicked attendant, who said these guys were trying to take over.

"I'll be right there," Alite said.

He got a friend to drive him over to the club.

"I was wearing a leather coat and I had an Uzi slung over my shoulder under the coat," he said. "This guy who claimed to be Stanfa's nephew, I'm not even sure if he was, wasn't around, but one of his associates was still here. They were in the valet business at the time. I showed him the gun and said I was taking over their business, not the other way around."

Alite ended up with four more spots. He saw it as simply a business opportunity, part of his foray into a new and economically fertile area. He was very comfortable moving around on the fringes of the volatile Philadelphia underworld. He and Junior had met Scarfo in Atlantic City in the early 1980s before the mob boss went to jail. He knew of Merlino and some of the younger guys around him. He also had a business connection with a second group of renegade gangsters led by a kid named Louie Turra. Turra was like Merlino, a thirty-something high-profile gangster, a John Gotti wannabe, a celebrity wiseguy but without the New York stage to play on. Turra was in the drug business. One of his suppliers was Keith Pellegrino, who worked for Alite.

"I tried to stay low-key," Alite said. "I didn't need a PA system to let people know who I was. But word got around. I'd say hello to guys, but not much more. I didn't really need to get involved with any of them. I was making plenty of money on my own."

But that didn't stop Louie Turra from trying to hire him as a hit man.

"I hardly know these guys, right?" Alite said. "They've got this Christmas tree lot on Oregon Avenue and Pellegrino takes me there one day to meet with Louie Turra."

Turra's father, Anthony, and uncle Rocco, a legendary South Philadelphia tough guy, were in the produce business and during the holiday season they also had a lot from which they sold trees. It was there that Turra asked Alite if he would be willing to kill Joey Merlino.

"First, I don't want to get involved in their problems," he said. "Second, they hardly know me and they're asking me to kill somebody. I figure I'm not the first one they've asked. I tell them, look, you got a problem with this guy, don't go after him right away. Make up, get him to relax, set him up. That's the way we do it in New York. They didn't want to hear that. They were crazy. I stayed away from them for that reason. If something happened to Merlino, everybody would know it was them. Louie Turra couldn't keep his mouth shut.

"I listened, but there was no way I was going to get involved. I thought these guys were all a little wild."

Coming from someone like Alite, that assessment said all you needed to know about the South Philadelphia underworld circa 1994. Turra was moving marijuana, cocaine, and heroin and was also involved in sports betting. Merlino and members of his branch of the mob were asking Turra to pay a street tax, the underworld price for doing business. Turra refused to pay. Or, as his uncle Rocco later explained, "Who was Merlino that we should pay him? If he wants money, let him go out and steal it."

Louie Turra was badly beaten in an after-hours club by members of Merlino's crew. He was humiliated. During the assault, Merlino's henchmen also took his Rolex watch. But Turra still refused to pay. Instead he intensified his efforts to have Merlino killed. Alite heard about some of the plots, which just reinforced his perception of the Turra crew. They were cowboys, he said.

The Turras and nearly a dozen associates would later be indicted on racketeering charges that included drug dealing, murder, and attempted murder. The indictment listed a series of plots to kill Merlino, plots that revolved around hand grenades, machine guns, and even, at one point, a bow and arrow. Most of the defendants in that case were convicted. The three Turras each found a different way out. Rocco, to the surprise of almost everyone in South Philadelphia, became a government witness. He had had enough of the senseless violence, he said. Louie committed suicide by hanging himself in the Metropolitan Correctional Center in Manhattan while awaiting the start of trial. And Anthony, Louie's father, was shot and killed one morning in front of his home as he was on his way to court. Members of the Merlino mob have long been suspected, but never convicted, of that murder.

Alite's name also surfaced in another notorious "hit" that generated intense media attention at the time. The wife of a prominent Cherry Hill, New Jersey, rabbi was killed in her home, bludgeoned to death by an intruder. The murder of Carol Neulander occurred on November 1, 1994. Over the next four years it would be the focus of an intense investigation by the Camden County Prosecutor's Office. At one point word leaked out that investigators had questioned Alite, described as a notorious "mob hit man" then living in Cherry Hill.

"I remember driving home one day with Claudia," Alite said. "She was living in the house on Brick Road. When we pulled up, there were two guys in suits and ties, a white guy and a black guy, waiting at the door."

Alite still laughs when he recounts the story.

"Oh look, Jehovah's Witnesses," Claudia said when she spotted the men.

"That's how naïve she was," Alite said. "I knew right away they were detectives. I told them to come in. They indicated that they didn't think I had anything to do with it, but said they had to question me. I didn't realize it, but sometimes when I went jogging, I would jog past the Neulander house, the house where she was killed. She owned a cake shop and I used to stop in there sometimes. And I used to work out and play racquetball at the same gym where the rabbi worked out. I might have even played a game or two of racquetball with him. I don't remember."

Alite said he was open and honest with the detectives, telling them frankly that he was making too much money on his own to hire out as an assassin. What's more, he said, he would never kill a woman.

"I told them it was either some junkie or it was the husband," Alite said.

Alite was right. It was the rabbi. Fred Neulander was arrested in September 1998 and charged with hiring two men to kill his wife. Both hit men, one a recovering alcoholic whom the rabbi had befriended and was counseling, confessed and cooperated with authorities. They testified at two trials. The first ended with a hung jury, the second with Fred Neulander's conviction for first-degree murder. Neulander is currently serving a life term.

The reason for the murder?

The rabbi was having an affair with a woman who was a prominent radio host in Philadelphia. They met when she asked him to conduct funeral services for her husband, also a radio personality.

He had died of cancer. Their affair began less than two months after the husband was buried. Neulander had promised to marry her, but he thought a divorce would reflect negatively on his standing as a rabbi. Having his wife bludgeoned to death seemed like a more sensible alternative to Neulander, who literally thought he could get away with murder.

While Alite managed to avoid getting entangled in either the Merlino-Turra flap or the Neulander investigation, a traffic stop created more serious problems for him.

"There had been a shooting at one of the clubs on Delaware Avenue," he said. "I was driving back to Jersey over the Ben Franklin Bridge when the police stopped me. They were apparently making random checks and I was driving a car similar to one at the scene."

While he had nothing to do with the shooting, he did have a .32-caliber revolver and some hollow-nosed bullets in his car. He was arrested on weapons counts, a case that eventually was assigned to the U.S. Attorney's Office in Camden. It was a serious problem because Alite had taken a pinch in Queens a few years earlier for gun possession.

"I was in a car with Greg Reiter," he said. "Greg was awaiting trial on drug charges at the time. When police stopped the car, Greg asked me to tell them the gun was mine, not his. He would have violated his bail and would have been sent to jail. I took the charge and ended up getting probation, but it was on my record."

That record enhanced the potential penalties. What's more, at the time of the car stop on the bridge, Alite was free on bail and awaiting trial for the assault on the cops in Mineola. There was little room to maneuver in either case. Alite hired a local attorney, M. W. (Mike) Pinsky, a prominent criminal defense lawyer in South Jersey whose clients included some major players in the Philadelphia crime family. A realist who understood the law and the judicial system, Pinsky counseled Alite to package the two cases, to plead out to both as long as the sentences would run concurrently. What's more, Pinsky was smart enough to arrange for a bigger hit on the gun charge than the Mineola assault, thereby guaranteeing that Alite did his time in a federal facility.

That's the way it played out. Alite got thirty-seven months for the gun charge and fourteen months for the assault.

At one pretrial hearing in Mineola prior to entering his guilty plea, Alite met with Junior in the parking lot outside the courthouse. "He told me John Kelly would take a beating because he had created this problem," Alite said. "I think Junior wanted to make sure nothing would come out about how we had robbed Kelly and stolen his money and his drugs. That's all Junior cared about but he made it sound like he was doing this for me. It was bullshit."

Shortly before he began serving his sentence, Alite heard that Kelly had gotten into a fight at the China Club in Manhattan. He took a bad beating. The guy who tuned him up, Alite said, was Willie Marshall, a friend of Junior's who was part of the Gambino entourage that operated out of Scores, the gentleman's club on the Upper East Side.

Under the terms of his plea deals, Alite was required to turn himself in to federal authorities in Camden in April 1996. His first stop during what would be nearly three years as a guest of the U.S. government was a prison in Fairton, New Jersey, about sixty miles south of Philadelphia. Alite, who had spent time in several county and state facilities, didn't know what to expect. He was pleasantly surprised.

"Most of the state joints I had been in were wild," Alite said. "Crowded and noisy. They're driving me to Fairton and I see the grounds are real nice. It's quiet. They take me to the reception area. It's air-conditioned, clean."

Alite was processed through in a day, given the typical warnings about staying out of trouble, and told that a serious infraction would result in him being sent to the hole—solitary confinement. He was read a list of the names of some inmates and asked if he knew or had a problem with any of them. Several of the names were those of wiseguys whom he knew, but he answered no each time a name was read. He also was shown some photos. He said he didn't recognize anyone, although he would occasionally pause over one photo or another and tell the intake officer, "He looks kind of familiar, but I'm not sure."

Then he was issued his prison clothes.

"A jumpsuit. I asked for an extra large, they gave me a three-X," he said with a laugh. "Sneakers. I asked for a size nine, they gave me elevens."

Alite knew at least a dozen of the inmates in Fairton and had heard of a dozen more. But he wasn't about to tell the prison authorities any of that. Mobsters tend to form their own groups in an institution and in the interest of maintaining order, prison officials often go along with that kind of arrangement. It's a little like assigning college freshmen roommates. It's a random process but one based on pairing individuals with "similar interests." Alite's first cellmate at Fairton was Louis Auricchio.

Within two weeks they were both in the hole.

Auricchio was a wiseguy out of North Jersey connected to the Genovese crime family. He was in his mid-thirties. His brother-in-law was John Lynch, then a prominent New Jersey state senator. Auricchio had been jailed on tax evasion charges in 1989, but that was just the start of his problems. By 1994 he was facing federal and state indictments for murder, extortion, and racketeering. He eventually pleaded guilty and was sentenced to a ten-year federal term and a thirty-year state sentence, which, like Alite's sentences, were to run concurrently.

Among other things, Auricchio had pleaded guilty to an

aggravated manslaughter charge, admitting to the 1988 murder of John DiGilio, a onetime highly regarded amateur boxer and a flamboyant Genovese crime family soldier. DiGilio had been targeted because of his outspoken, high-profile persona. The Genovese still believed in that old-school, make money not headlines philosophy.

DiGilio ended up with several bullet holes in his head, his body stuffed into a body bag later discovered in the Hackensack River. Auricchio had carried out the hit, which, according to some sources, resulted in his formal initiation into the crime family.

"I'm not even in the cell ten minutes and he starts telling me this story," Alite says. "He's having a problem with this kid Bobby Brooks whose dad is with the Lucheses. I said, 'Louis, let me get settled in.'"

Once in population, several other wiseguys got Alite's ear. There apparently was a running feud involving Auricchio and Brooks. Auricchio, a thick, muscular kid with experience as a high school wrestler, was getting the better of the situation.

Alite said he had gotten word from Charles Carneglia to look out for Brooks. Later, in a prearranged phone call, Alite spoke with Brooks's father, who said, "Make sure he [Auricchio] doesn't hurt my kid." It was no different than on the street. Mobsters who were supposed to be tough guys were coming to him for help.

"There's a big difference between a killer and a tough guy," Alite would say several years later. "Some of these guys, they shoot somebody and that makes them a killer. But they don't know how to handle themselves. They can't fight. Or they're afraid to fight. Just 'cause they're a killer doesn't make them a tough guy."

And in prison, it's the tough guy who survives.

"On the street I would try to be a gentleman," Alite said. "If there was a problem, I'd try to reason with someone first. Then, if he didn't listen, I'd hurt him. In prison, when you try to reason with someone, when you talk first, they take that for weakness. In prison, you have to hit first. That's the only way to survive."

Auricchio kept beating on Brooks.

"He was abusing this kid," Alite said. "I asked him to stop. To let it go."

Instead, Alite got word that Auricchio had approached one of the inmates who worked in the kitchen. He asked him to get him a knife. The inmate, who knew Alite from the streets, let him know what Auricchio was planning.

"I didn't know if he had the knife," Alite said, "but I decided to find out. He was in line one night for chow and I walked up to him. I told him to get out of the line. He wouldn't do it. He said, 'I'm not gonna fight you.' I told him he didn't have a choice. I wasn't asking, I was telling him to get out of the line."

Other inmates knew what was going on. They backed away and Auricchio ended up face-to-face with Alite. Alite threw a left and a right. Auricchio slid off the punches, which caught him in the face, but not full force.

"I'm boxing and he's trying to wrestle, trying to get me on the ground," Alite said. "I stayed out of his reach and then hit him whenever I could. He was a strong kid, but he couldn't box. I beat him up pretty bad."

They both ended up in solitary confinement. Alite spent about a month there and then was transferred to a federal prison in McKean, Pennsylvania, about eighty miles north of Altoona and about forty miles east of Lake Erie. It was cold and damp, but in retrospect, he says, it wasn't a bad place to be.

While he didn't realize it as the time, the three-year prison stint that began in 1996 was the initial round of institutional-ization that would dominate his life for the next two decades.

Between 1996 and 2014, an eighteen-year period, John Alite would spend fourteen years behind bars. This would include two years in prison facilities in Brazil, prisons that would make the federal institutions in Fairton, McKean, and later Allenwood, Pennsylvania, seem like four-star hotels.

CHAPTER 15

Three months after he began doing time in a federal prison, Alite got word that John Gebert had been killed. He wasn't surprised. In fact, he had set the hit in motion. His anger and hatred for Gebert was well-known in both underworld and law enforcement circles so he thought it would be a good idea if he was in jail when the murder took place. You can't get a better alibi than that.

Before he left for prison, he had talked about Gebert with a couple of his friends. Alite wanted him dead.

Gebert was finishing up a seven-year sentence for a rape conviction. He had abducted a woman in his car, taking her to a park and forcing her into the backseat where, while several friends looked on, he raped her and forced her to perform oral sex on him. The woman fled, according to the indictment, after Gebert had tired of abusing her. Wearing only a shirt, she ran from the park and was picked up by a passerby who drove her to her boyfriend's home. From there she reported the assault to police. Gebert went on the lam but was eventually arrested and convicted.

He was, from Alite's perspective, a dangerous degenerate.

"Gebert had been on *The David Susskind Show* when he was twelve years old," Alite said. "The show was about juvenile delinquents. He was a criminal his whole life."

The rape conviction only solidified that opinion. Gebert had punked out after the drive-by shooting of the Jamaicans in one of their first criminal acts together. And several years later, he and his brother-in-law, Georgie Grosso, had tried to shoot Alite.

"I wasn't sorry he got killed," Alite would later tell a jury when questioned about the July 12, 1996, murder.

The hit occurred inside Frankie and Johnny's, a bar on Jamaica Avenue. Gebert had been hanging around outside the bar when a car rolled up on him and two shooters jumped out. Gebert ran into the bar and tried to hide under a pool table. The two gunmen found him there and opened fire. An innocent bystander, a mob associate named Carl Capella, was shot by accident. He survived. The two shooters, Dave D'Arpino and Alite's young cousin Pasquale Andriano, later admitted their roles and became cooperating witnesses, helping convict Johnny Burke of murder conspiracy in the Gebert shooting. Burke was also involved in the Bruce Gotterup hit. Peter Zuccaro, another mob associate who claimed that he organized the Gebert shooting, also pleaded guilty and cooperated. Zuccaro's account of the murder conspiracy was somewhat at odds with Alite's version, a fact that the defense jumped on during Junior's 2009 trial. Zuccaro, who was called as a witness for the defense, claimed that he met several times with Alite in 1988 after Ronnie Trucchio okayed the hit. Among other things, Gebert had shot up the PM Pub, which was one of Trucchio's places.

Alite said there were several reasons Gebert got killed but he remembered meeting with Zuccaro on only one occasion where the murder was discussed. He also said that Trucchio had nothing to do with the Gebert murder.

The Gebert homicide was one of the charges Junior Gotti beat in his 2009 case. Alite never disputed the defense argument that he, Alite, had set the murder in motion and that he had his own set of reasons for wanting Gebert dead, not the least of which was to avenge Gebert's attempt to kill him. But Alite insisted that Gebert had been "stamped" for death by Gotti back in the late 1980s and that while it was seven years or more before the hit took place, that didn't change anything.

"Once he [Junior Gotti] said you had to go, you were gone," Alite explained.

He also admitted from the witness stand that he had discussed killing Gebert with Andriano, D'Arpino, and Michael Malone shortly before he headed off to Fairton. Alite said he told them "when I'm in jail, that would be a nice gift."

Alite was in McKean when he heard about the Gebert shooting. Word spreads quickly along the prison grapevine. Inmates are always calling home and anyone from New York would have been told about the shooting by a friend or family member. It was business as usual. Murder was part of the life.

Alite adapted easily to the routine at the federal prison in McKean. He worked out regularly, did some boxing, and tried to spend as much time as possible outdoors in the "yard" getting fresh air and moving around. The weather was cold and there was plenty of snow, which often forced inmates back inside, but overall, he made the best of his stay.

The Gottis, on the other hand, didn't do well in prison.

Their name gave them some cachet, but the aura eventually wore off, particularly in a population of hardened criminals, many from the violent drug underworld. Most of those inmates, blacks and Hispanics, knew about the Mafia from watching *The Godfather* or from their own dealings on the street. But inside a federal institution, they played by a different set of rules. There were always inmates who figured they could enhance their own standing by taking a shot at the Don Corleones of the world.

Alite remembered John Gotti Sr. bitching about his brother

Vinny, who was "punked" in prison by a black inmate who pushed him around and took a gold neck chain from him. Gotti sent Alite to visit Vinny with a crude but understandable message: "If you let a nigger push you around, you're not gonna survive."

"Vinny was a piece of shit anyway," Alite said. "He had pleaded guilty to drug dealing. This was at a time [1986] when Gotti Sr. was saying that no one should plead out. But it was okay for his brother to enter a plea. He was also a predator. He had strangled a girl after getting her high on drugs."

The incident, which occurred in the summer of 1985, was brought up when Alite testified at Junior's trial in 2009. Gotti's defense attorney tried to imply that Alite had raped and strangled a woman at a motel out near JFK airport. Alite told the jury that he and dozens of others in the organization knew the story.

Vinny Gotti had taken the woman, whom he was "dating" at the time, to the Kennedy Inn Airport Hotel, Alite testified. They were doing drugs together and got into an argument. Vinny Gotti strangled her and then got rid of her body. That's what Alite said he was told by another mob associate who said he was there when the woman was killed. The woman's body was found in a garbage pile in the East New York section of Brooklyn. No one has ever been charged in the case.

Alite said he knew the victim's stepbrother, a guy from the neighborhood with whom he used to play softball. Shortly after the woman disappeared, the guy came around the PM Pub asking if anyone knew what had happened to his sister.

He told Alite that she had been with Vinny Gotti on the night she disappeared.

"Did he do something?" the guy asked Alite.

Alite said he lied and told him he knew nothing about it. He also told the jury that in 2006 the *New York Post* ran a story speculating that Junior Gotti was the target of a cold case murder investigation involving the strangulation murder of a Queens waitress, a divorcée with a young daughter, who was last seen partying with his uncle Vinny. When the *Post* story appeared Junior was livid, Alite said, complaining that his scumbag uncle had killed the girl and that he wasn't going to be blamed for it. It was just another piece of the dark and cold-blooded saga that was the Gotti family.

Vinny Gotti, with a shaved, bullet-shaped head but a strong facial resemblance to his brother John, was the black sheep of the family, which is saying more than a little about his character. His career included arrests, but not always convictions, for robbery, rape, and petty larceny. He had been banned by his brother John from mob social clubs, including the Ravenite and the Bergin, because of his drug use. He was jailed in 1986 for cocaine distribution, the charge to which he pleaded guilty. He was sent to prison again in 2012 for the attempted murder of a Queens bagel shop owner. The botched hit was allegedly tied to a loansharking operation that Vinny was then running for the organization.

Vinny was a punk who lived off his family's reputation. And by the mid-1990s, that reputation was beginning to sour. John Gotti brought the same arrogance that he had on the street to the federal prison in Marion, Illinois, where he was serving the life sentences imposed in 1992. It didn't play as well there.

Alite was still in Fairton when he and other inmates learned that Gotti Sr. had taken a beating from another inmate in Marion. Gotti spent most of his time locked in an eight-by-ten cell in the maximum security wing of the prison, then considered one of the toughest in the country. But during a daily walk along a corridor recreation area, according to reports, Gotti had gotten into an altercation with Walter Johnson, a black inmate from Philadelphia who was serving time for bank robbery.

Gotti angrily told Johnson to get out of his way, calling him "a nigger" and "a piece of shit." Johnson moved away to allow Gotti to pass. But the next day they found themselves in the same prison corridor. Before anything was said, Johnson punched Gotti in the face, then jumped on top of him and pummeled him until guards were able to break them up. None of the other inmates out for recreation came to Gotti's aid. At the prison infirmary, when Gotti was asked what happened, he said, "I fell." But reports were that the crime boss was livid. In law enforcement circles, the word was that Gotti reached out to the Aryan Brotherhood, the white supremacist group with a strong prison presence, and offered between forty thousand and one hundred thousand dollars to have Johnson killed. Prison officials, apparently realizing the jeopardy, transferred Johnson to another institution. He completed his sentence and was released before anyone from the Brotherhood could act on the contract put out by Gotti.

The talk inside the prison system, however, painted a somewhat different version of events. Alite was told that the Brotherhood had set the whole situation up as a way to shake Gotti down.

"John had been paying them [for protection] when he first got there, but then he stopped," Alite said. "The Aryans were pissed. They had a guard who made sure Johnson was out there when Gotti went by. They wanted to show Gotti he needed them and that he would have to pay for their protection."

Whatever the truth, the incident took a lot of the luster off the Gotti image. A photo of the bruised and swollen face of John J. Gotti after the beating looked nothing like the handsome Dapper Don that Andy Warhol had captured and that had been plastered on the cover of *Time* magazine.

Alite knew that to survive in prison you had to fight. Early on at McKean he established himself as someone who would not back down if confronted. As a result he did several stints in the hole. But he also had fewer problems with other inmates. His stay also further undermined his relationship with the Gottis, if not the Gambino crime family.

Gene Gotti was serving his time for the federal drug conviction at McKean and at first Alite and he were cellmates.

"He was older and I'd help him out when I could," Alite said. "I used to make sure he had a chair when they were showing movies, things like that. But he had gotten bitter. Angry. He belittled everybody. Used to make fun of guys who did me favors."

Gene Gotti knew about the problems his nephew was having with Alite, but seldom talked about it. Alite understood that in McKean he was an asset, someone Gene Gotti could use. It was no different than on the streets. At that point, despite all his problems with the Gotti family, Alite was still a believer. He was part of the crime family. He also was smart enough to recognize that that affiliation was a benefit behind bars.

The problems began when Gene Gotti started to abuse Joe Gambino, a capo and part of what was then the Sicilian faction of the organization. Joe and his brothers, cousins of the late Carlo Gambino, had been arrested for heroin dealing in the Philadelphia area in the 1980s. Their presence in the Philadelphia–South Jersey area, in fact, had indirectly contributed to the murder of Philadelphia mob boss Angelo Bruno in 1980.

Joe was completing his sentence for drug dealing when Alite came to McKean. The smartest of the Gambino brothers, he was also the most Americanized. He had established himself in the crime family, eventually rising to the rank of skipper. Alite respected Joe Gambino because he never tried to hide who he was or what the life was all about. Unlike the Gottis, there was no bullshit. The Sicilians never had any compunction about dealing drugs. That's where the money was and the Sicilians always went for the money.

"Genie was pushing Joe around and I stepped in," Alite said. "I told him, 'You know the rules the same as I do. You're not supposed to put your hands on another made guy.'"

Gene blew Alite off. His attitude seemed to be, Who the hell is this Albanian telling me, a Gotti, about the rules of our life. The abuse continued.

"He did it in front of other inmates, blacks, Hispanics, the whole prison population," Alite said. "You don't do that kind of thing. It made Joe look weak."

And Alite knew that in any prison situation, an inmate who was perceived as weak was easy prey for anyone.

"I stepped in for Joe Gambino, who is not a tough guy," Alite told a jury. "He was a skipper, but not a tough guy."

Alite slapped Gene Gotti around and told him to back off. The move helped Joe Gambino, who thanked Alite. The mob capo later gave him a gold chain with a religious medal on it. The medal was a cross and an image of the Virgin Mary. Alite, who was not particularly religious (he ended up getting baptized in prison), nevertheless saw the gift as validation. He had done the right thing.

But the incident further undermined his relationship with the Gottis. Now Gene Gotti also wanted him dead.

Junior Gotti, with assistance from his uncle Peter, continued to run the crime family on the streets while Alite sat in federal prison. Junior would occasionally visit his father, a situation that was unique, to say the least. In most instances a jailed mob boss doesn't get to have prison visits with his successor. But the blood relationship trumped authorities' concerns that Gotti, from prison, was using his son to run the Gambino organization.

It didn't take long, however, for Junior to screw things up. Alite could only shake his head when the news broke about the February 1997 raid federal and local authorities staged on an apartment in Ozone Park, Queens, as part of an ongoing investigation into Junior Gotti's operation. Alite recognized the address as the building where, in the basement, he had beaten the boyfriend of Jodi Albanese. In that same basement, according to reports about the raid, authorities found $348,700 in cash, a handgun, a semiautomatic rifle, and a bookkeeper's ledger with a list of nearly two hundred names. These turned out to be individuals who had attended Junior's lavish wedding at the Helmsley Palace Hotel back in 1990. Next to each name was a dollar figure, the amount each individual had given as a wedding gift. A final tally showed that the gifts amounted to more than $350,000.

"I think I was on that list for ten grand," Alite said. "Junior kept cash in that basement and what he would do was continually replenish the supply. Money he made from drugs, gambling, extortions, whatever, would end up in the basement. That's why the cash they found amounted to about the same total as the money in the ledger. Junior figured he could always say the money was from his wedding."

Whether anyone would believe that seven years later the wedding cash was still unspent was, of course, open to speculation. Junior, as Alite learned early on, was not a deep thinker. The media quickly dubbed the discovery an embarrassment and took to referring to Junior Gotti as "Dumbfella." The wedding list and cash were what grabbed most of the attention, but the real screwup from an underworld perspective was another list of names agents found while they searched the basement. There were about a dozen individuals on this list and each was linked to one of three organized crime families in the city. The names, authorities later said, were individuals who had been proposed as mob members. It had become standard procedure for crime families to run the names of their new or potential members past the leaders of other families as a security measure. The idea was to screen members in an attempt to determine if anyone knew any reason why they shouldn't become a member of the secret society.

The standard practice was for the hierarchy of other families to clear those names with their own members and then sign off if there were no problems. It was also standard for the lists to be destroyed. For whatever reason, Junior was saving his.

Now the feds had it and the other families were up in arms.

All of this became public knowledge when Junior Gotti was arrested in January 1998 on charges contained in a sweeping racketeering indictment. The case detailed gambling, loansharking, and extortion schemes, including the shakedown of Scores. It also identified Junior Gotti as the acting boss of the Gambino organization. The indictment and the embarrassing details that came with it effectively ended Junior's reign. He was jailed, but had he remained on the streets, he probably would have been killed. Instead, Peter Gotti, Senior's brother, took over the organization and the Gambinos, however tenuously, remained in the hands of a Gotti.

John Gotti's Rules of Leadership: When charged with a crime, no matter the circumstances, do not plead guilty. It's a sign of weakness.

It was at this time, Junior would later claim, that he decided to end his involvement with the mob. He and his father, in a prison visit that was recorded, argued over his desire to plead guilty to the racketeering charges. Junior insisted that his decision to go against his father's wishes was a clear indication that he was breaking with the crime family.

Junior said that he had decided to plead guilty and that he wanted out. Gotti Sr. told him not to do it. The discussion centered on Junior's desire for "closure," which authorities later said was a coded reference to his desire to enter a guilty plea. Gotti Sr.

had gotten advance warning about why his son was coming to see him and was told that closure was the issue.

He told his son it was not an option.

Gotti Sr. had taken that stance many times, even when an admission of guilt worked to his advantage. Carmine Agnello had helped the Gottis avoid prosecution for jury tampering by obtaining immunity and testifying before a grand jury. Agnello, who couldn't be prosecuted, said he was the one who had approached jurors, not anyone else. The admission stalled the investigation in its tracks. Most defense attorneys and members of the crime family thought it was an ingenious move. Gotti Sr. didn't agree.

At the meeting in Marion, he told Junior that he would never confess to anything. (Early in his career, however, he had entered a guilty plea in the McBratney murder case, but he had either forgotten about that or it was another example of the do-as-I-say-not-as-I-do philosophy that Senior employed in running the organization.)

"I would tell them to go fuck themselves," he said of investigators or prosecutors accusing him of a crime. "If there was a church robbed and I had the steeple stickin' outta my ass, I wouldn't tell them I did it."

Junior, of course, had a different take on the situation.

"I can't do this," he said in a taped conversation from that prison visit that his defense lawyer later played for the jury in his 2009 case. "This is your life. This is not my life."

He left Marion that day without his father's blessing. He later said that he was torn but had decided to go to trial as his father wished. But shortly before the trial began, he changed his mind and told his lawyer to work out a plea. Under the terms of that agreement, he was sentenced to seventy-seven months in prison.

Alite was in a minimum security prison in Allenwood, Pennsylvania, finishing up his thirty-seven-month sentence, when he heard what Junior was saying. He said it was both preposterous and impossible. "You only get out when you die," he said. "Or when you get killed." Of course the Gottis had flouted every other rule and protocol, so it wouldn't have been out of character for Junior to flout this one. But Alite said he knew Junior too well to buy the story Gotti later told to juries and repeated during an exclusive interview on the CBS News show *60 Minutes*. Alite also believed the fact that Junior kept the list of names of made guys was significant.

"Why didn't he destroy the list?" Alite asked. "Because I think he was keeping it as insurance. I think he thought he might make a deal with the feds at some time and that list would be one of the things he could offer."

From the witness stand at Junior's trial, Alite would refer to Junior as the New York version of James "Whitey" Bulger, the Boston mob boss who for years, while dealing drugs, running gambling operations, and committing murder, was also a confidential FBI informant. Alite believes Junior Gotti tried to play the feds the same way Bulger did.

A Philadelphia mob associate who ended up in jail with Junior would later confirm Alite's contention that Junior was still very much a member of the Gambino crime family, Alite said.

Alite had met several members of the Philadelphia mob while he was in Allenwood. John "Johnny Gongs" Casasanto and Ronnie Turchi were both doing time for racketeering. Casasanto and Alite hit it off right away. They were about the same age and had the same approach to life in the underworld. Casasanto was fearless, a genuine tough guy who never backed away from a fight. What he lacked was the savvy and the underworld intuition that allowed Alite to advance and survive. Casasanto would later be transferred to Ray Brook, a federal prison in upstate New York near Lake Placid, where he met and befriended Junior Gotti.

Casasanto's brother Steve would visit Ray Brook and often

returned with messages, Alite said, from both his brother and from Junior Gotti. Gotti might have been telling others that he had "chased" Alite, but the messages that came from Ray Brook were warm and friendly. He told the Casasantos that Alite was his main guy and good friend and that there was nobody better on the streets.

Alite took it all in stride. He knew the move only too well. Gotti was trying to rock him to sleep.

When John Casasanto was released in 2001, he told friends and associates, including Alite, that Gotti suggested he move to New York, where Gotti would make him a member of the Gambino organization. The offer, if true, seemed to fly in the face of Junior's claim that he was no longer involved with the crime family.

Alite would later tell the FBI that he went to Queens to check on Casasanto's story. He met with Peter Gotti, Junior's younger brother, in a deli that Gotti owned and operated. Pete confirmed that his brother was touting Johnny Casasanto for membership, Alite said. (The younger Gotti would deny this when he testified as a defense witness at his brother's 2009 trial.) When he got back to Philadelphia, Alite said he cautioned Casasanto against the move to New York, telling him that it wasn't like Philadelphia and warning him that he'd never survive up there.

Alite was surprised at how naïve some of the Philadelphia wiseguys were about the ways of the underworld. He was used to the backstabbing and treachery. They seemed oblivious. Ronnie Turchi, who was in his sixties and had been around the mob all his life, was another example. He should have known better.

After Allenwood, Alite and Turchi spent time together in a halfway house in Philadelphia before they were both released in the summer of 1999. Alite, who said he bribed several guards, came and went as he pleased, finishing his time in jail reestablishing his connections on the street. Turchi and another local mob associate, a skittish drug dealer named Roger Vella, both hung with Alite in the facility.

Turchi had been the Philadelphia crime family consigliere. Alite had already had some dealings with his son and some other young mob associates. While Turchi insisted everything was fine and that he was looking forward to going home, Alite thought things weren't stacking up right. Turchi had been aligned with mob boss Ralph Natale, who had taken over the Philadelphia mob in 1995 along with Skinny Joey Merlino. Merlino and Natale had met in prison in 1992, when Natale was finishing up a fifteen-year sentence for drug dealing and arson. Natale was sixty-six when he got out and was anxious to make up for lost time. Three years later he was facing narcotics charges and a possible life sentence. By the summer of 1999, he had cut a deal with the feds and agreed to cooperate against Merlino and the other young members of the organization.

Natale was untouchable once he flipped. The feds had him in a protected wing of a federal prison. But Turchi, who had been Natale's top associate, was exposed. At least that's the way Alite saw it.

"He said he was fine," Alite recalled. "He said he had been assured that he'd be welcomed back into the organization, that what Natale had done had nothing to do with him."

"I told him they were gonna kill him," Alite said.

Turchi responded by explaining that guys were already giving him money and helping him get reestablished during his daytime release from the halfway house. He bragged about a new Members Only windbreaker that one of Merlino's guys bought for him. Roger Vella, who was part of the Merlino faction at the time, watched and listened as Alite warned Turchi.

"I looked at him and I knew," Alite said of Vella. "They were setting Turchi up. When I asked Vella about it, he just smiled. But Turchi wouldn't listen."

Ron Turchi was being rocked to sleep.

On October 27, 1999, a few months after he left the halfway house and two days after his wife reported him missing, Ronnie Turchi turned up dead in the trunk of a car parked on a South Philadelphia street. He was naked. He had been beaten and tortured and then shot and killed.

Alite, on the other hand, had a much smoother transition. He came out of the halfway house in July 1999 and got a welcome-home reception from two girls from the neighborhood.

"They took me to a motel," Alite said. "We partied."

CHAPTER 16

Alite returned to South Jersey rather than Queens when he was finally set free that summer. But he was in and out of his old neighborhood on a regular basis. Claudia had moved back to Queens. She was living in Howard Beach with their two sons, John and Matt. Alite spent time with them there. He also was flying down to Tampa at least once a month, where his nightclub, Mirage, had become one of the city's hot spots. He owned two other bars there as well as a valet parking business. Ronnie Trucchio, who in name headed the crew that was operating in Tampa, was also in and out of Florida along with several other associates of the Gambino organization. Money was rolling in. Alite had begun to legitimize himself. He was no longer a major player in the drug game. But the money he had earned moving cocaine was now fueling his other enterprises.

In the South Jersey area, he and two associates took over a business that some local wiseguys, including the son of Ron Turchi, had been running. They had a company that installed towers for cellular phones. There was big money to be made in that business, but they weren't taking advantage of the opportunities. At first Alite suggested that he and some of his associates handle North Jersey and New York. Eventually, he took over the entire operation.

"They weren't very smart and I guess you could say we bought them out," Alite said.

With Claudia back in New York, Alite's ex-wife, Carol, moved into the house in Cherry Hill with Jimmy and Chelsea. Alite spent time with both kids and brought them out to the Voorhees homestead as often as he could. He attended Little League games and taught Jimmy—and John when he would visit—how to box at the outdoor gym and training center he had set up on the property. He usually spent the night there, staying in one of the three houses on the grounds. His parents were living in another. Life was almost "normal," he thought, although his instincts told him otherwise.

"I had a sense that I was being watched," he said. "When I went out, it seemed like there were cars following me. I also knew that I still had a problem with the Gottis, that that was never going to go away."

Alite knew what he had done. There were at least four bodies, maybe more, that he could be held accountable for. And he knew that despite assurances, there were always guys looking to make a deal. It would be easier for someone to give him up than to rat out a made guy. That was the reality. He also had heard that Vito Guzzo had people who were "looking" for him. Guzzo was in jail by this point. He had pleaded guilty to federal racketeering charges in 1998, admitting his involvement in five murders. He was sentenced to thirty-eight years. But Alite knew that it wasn't that difficult to reach out from behind bars to settle a score.

One night, in fact, he believes a team of hit men were lying in wait for him outside Library II, a nightclub on Route 73 a few miles from his property. He and some friends had gone there for dinner.

"This car was there when we went into the restaurant and a couple of hours later it was still there when we came out," Alite said. "I told the guys I was with to get in their cars and box that car in. I didn't know if it was the FBI or if it was someone Guzzo had sent."

He never found out. The car, with tinted windows, skidded in reverse over a grassy lawn, jumped a curb, and sped away from the restaurant parking lot. Alite, in a Volvo, gave chase.

"They were doing a hundred miles an hour," he said. "I chased them for about two miles. They were heading for the New Jersey Turnpike when I lost them. That's why I think it was Guzzo's guys, and not the feds."

Alite's relationship with the Gambino organization was hostile at the time. And he did little to repair the damage. While he was in Allenwood his cousin Patsy Andriano visited him and reported that the brother-in-law of Richie Gotti Jr., a guy named Louie, was shaking down an old lady in the neighborhood whose son owed about three grand in a drug debt. The debtor had, in fact, been Andriano's customer first. Alite sent word back through his cousin, telling Louie to back off.

Instead, Alite later told the FBI, Louie threatened Andriano. He told him that his cousin, Alite, was nobody and that the Gottis had chased him out of Queens. Alite, even though he was on supervised release and prohibited from leaving New Jersey, drove up to visit the old neighborhood and to leave a message for the Gottis.

"I got in touch with a friend of mine in the Bonanno family who knew this kid Louie. They called him Tony Soprano cause he was big, about two hundred seventy pounds, and he smoked cigars. He thought he was a tough guy. I told my friend to get him to the service road off the Belt Parkway in Queens and that I would just happen by."

As planned, Alite drove up, stopped, and got out of the car to say hello to his friend. The mobster in turn introduced him to Louie.

Alite looked puzzled, then pretended that he recognized Louie's name for the first time. With that, he turned angry and began to question him about the shakedown of the old lady and the message he had sent through Patsy Andriano while Alite was in Allenwood.

"At first he acted tough," Alite said. "He said, 'Do you know who I am? Do you know I'm Richie Gotti's brother-in-law?' I told him I didn't give a fuck who he was and I told him that 'Gotti' was the worst name he could have mentioned."

Then Alite punched him, knocked him down, and proceeded to brutalized him.

"I was gonna shoot him," Alite said. "Patsy was with me and I told him to give me the gun he was holding, but instead he took off. He didn't want me to kill him. I would have."

Instead, Tony Soprano took a serious beating.

"I broke his cheek and eye socket," Alite said. "Several of his ribs were fractured and I broke one of his arms."

A few days later, Alite heard from Richie Gotti Sr. He wanted to meet. Alite again went to Queens, this time for what amounted to a street corner sit-down.

"I thought we were friends?" Richie Gotti asked.

"If we were friends," Alite said, "you would have taken care of this problem and I wouldn't have had to do what I did."

They talked for about ten minutes, with Gotti, the brother that John Sr. used to refer to as "pea brain," trying to act like a mob leader. Finally, Alite had had enough.

"You know what," he said. "We ain't friends no more."

With that, Alite demanded a weekly payment of $750 from Louie and his drug partner and left.

"It wasn't about the money," he said. "I think they paid for three or four weeks. They were supposed to give the money to Patsy. I didn't care about the money. I just wanted to make a point. Nobody chased me out of the neighborhood."

Around this time, late 1999, Alite also was subpoenaed to appear before a federal grand jury in Brooklyn. He took Mike Malone, one of his associates, with him because he wanted someone there who could verify what went down.

"I didn't want anyone to think I was cooperating," he said. "But I figured that by talking with them and from the questions they asked, I'd have an idea of what they were up to."

Prior to his appearance before the grand jury, two FBI agents and a federal prosecutor asked to speak with him privately. He insisted that Malone stay in the room. They told him he was not a target. They asked several questions about the Gotti organization and seemed especially interested in Ronnie Trucchio and Joe O'Kane. Alite sparred with them verbally, answering some questions honestly and others with less candor. But he made it clear that he was not willing to become a witness. Alite said when he was placed under oath before a grand jury, he lied, contradicting some of the things he had said privately, then exercising his Fifth Amendment right and refusing to answer any other questions. The session ended abruptly and inconclusively, but it confirmed what Alite knew intuitively. Members of his crew and Junior Gotti and the guys around him were all under investigation. A few weeks later the feds came calling again. It was not what Alite was expecting.

While in Fairton he had become a good friend of another inmate from New York, a guy named Nino. They ended up together again in Allenwood. Nino was in his forties and his wife was in her late thirties.

"Her biological clock was ticking," Alite said. "She wanted to get pregnant, but Nino was doing fourteen years and wouldn't get out for a couple more. He asked if I could help them smuggle in a sperm kit. We did it three or four times after I got out."

It was a relatively simple operation. Alite would pick up the kit from the wife and drive up to Allenwood, where he would meet a guard he had befriended—and bribed—when he was an inmate there. The guard would take the kit in at the beginning of his shift, give it to Nino, and then pick it up at the end of the shift after Nino had "made a deposit." The guard would then turn the kit over to Alite, who remained in the Allenwood area for the day.

"I'd drive it to a clinic in New York where they stored it," he said. "I was paying the guard three hundred, four hundred dollars. No big deal. I think in total I gave him fifteen hundred."

There was, at the time, an ongoing investigation into corruption at the prison, stemming from allegations that guards were taking bribes to smuggle in food, luxury toiletries, steroids, and other drugs. The sperm kit scam was uncovered during that same probe.

In December 2000 Alite got a visit from an FBI agent who told him he was about to be indicted. Alite thought it was the murder and racketeering case he had been anticipating. When he heard it was over the sperm kits, he laughed.

"It was ridiculous," he said. "I never thought I'd end up back in jail for something like that."

The indictment came down a week later. Alite, Nino, and his wife were charged. Looking to protect Nino's wife, Alite told the couple to admit what they had done, to give him up and work out a deal that would keep her out of prison. That's how it played out. They all pleaded guilty and the woman got a year's probation. Alite was sentenced to three months. Nino had the same penalty tacked on to the time he was already serving.

The guard, who got jammed up in the broader probe, cut a deal and cooperated. At one point he called Alite on the phone. It was obvious to Alite that he was trying to tape him. Alite played dumb, said he didn't know what he was talking about, then hung up on him.

The guard ended up being sentenced to two years in prison.

The "contraband" sperm that had been smuggled out became

the focus of a related civil case. The feds had seized the juice after the indictment came down. Nino's wife sued to get it back, but a judge ruled in the feds' favor. Nino's wife never became pregnant.

Once the indictment came down, Alite was placed on house arrest while the case worked its way through the system. And he was on house arrest again after he came out. He did the three months at a federal prison in Loretta, Pennsylvania, where he met and befriended a young Colombian who was serving time for drug dealing. The Colombian was tied to one of the big drug cartels and Alite got the names and phone numbers of several of his associates who were still active in the business in and around Bogotá and Medellín. He wasn't thinking about going back into drug trafficking, but he was thinking about taking a trip.

"I just knew they were going to come for me," he said. "The sperm kit thing was just a way to slow me down. Then, a few months after I'm out, they charged me with a parole violation. I was on parole when we did the sperm kit smuggling."

The result was another three-month sentence, this one at a federal facility attached to Fort Dix, the New Jersey army base. Skinny Dom Pizzonia was there when Alite arrived and Charles Carneglia, convicted in a racketeering case, was on his way. Pizzonia told Alite that Carneglia wanted him dead.

"The day Charles arrived I was waiting for him," Alite said. "I made sure Skinny Dom was with me because I wanted him to hear what I was going to say."

After the usual hugs, kisses, and handshakes, Alite looked at Carneglia and said, "I heard you got a problem with me."

Carneglia acted like he had no idea what Alite was talking about. But then he opened up. The word, he said, was that Alite was a rat, that he had talked with the feds and had been at a proffer session.

"You dumb motherfucker," Alite said before explaining—and

making sure that Pizzonia heard as well. Alite told Carneglia that the only proffer he made was for the sperm kit case and that was so that Nino's wife wouldn't do time.

"If I were cooperating," he told Carneglia, "you wouldn't be here on some half-ass racketeering charge. You'd be here for Louie DiBono's body."

"Don't even go there," Carneglia said.

But the point had been made. Everybody knew something about everybody else. Alite figured it was only a matter of time before it all came undone.

On June 10, 2002, after spending months in and out of prison hospitals battling cancer, John J. Gotti died. The obits that appeared in newspapers and the television reports detailed the infamous life of New York's most famous gangster. Selwyn Raab, one of the premier crime reporters in the country, captured it perfectly in the opening paragraph of a lengthy obituary he wrote for the *New York Times* the next day.

"John J. Gotti, who seized control of the Gambino crime family in a murderous coup, flaunted his power during a flamboyant reign as a Mafia boss, and then spent the last years of his life locked away in a maximum security penitentiary, his gang in shambles, died yesterday at the federal prison hospital at Springfield, Mo. He was 61."

Alite realized that he had been there to see it all. He was a participant in the rise of John J. Gotti and was now watching the fall of the flamboyant mob boss's organization. He decided he didn't want to be around for what came next.

"I started to hear that there was an investigation in Tampa," he said. "I already knew about the one in Brooklyn because I had been subpoenaed to the grand jury there. I had the ongoing problem with Junior and Carmine Agnello and the problem with Vito Guzzo. That wasn't going away."

Alite figured he had very few options.

"If I stayed around, I'd probably have to kill ten or fifteen guys, starting with Junior and Carmine," he said, "and I'd probably end up dead or in jail. That's the way it looked."

He also could have cut a deal then and cooperated, but he couldn't bring himself to do it.

It was around this time that he became friends with an FBI agent from Philadelphia named Dave Gentile. They met at a kids' hockey practice. Alite's son Jimmy, who was eleven, and Gentile's grandson, who was ten, were both playing ice hockey at the time for teams that practiced at the High Ridge Ice Arena in Gibbsboro, New Jersey, not far from Alite's property on Route 73. Their first meeting was casual chitchat about kids and hockey as they watched the teams practice. At first neither knew who the other was. Once Alite learned that Gentile was with the FBI, he decided to tell him about his criminal record and associations. By that time, Gentile, who had done his own due diligence, knew who Alite was.

"I liked Dave," Alite said. "I didn't want to get him in trouble by talking to me."

Throughout this period, as Alite wrestled with what to do and where to go, he would periodically run scenarios past Gentile, who had become a friend. The FBI agent, who had worked some of the biggest mob cases in Philadelphia in the 1980s, said Alite struck him as "looking for someone to talk to."

Over months and during hockey practices, Gentile and Alite did just that.

Alite, in general terms, laid out his situation. Gentile said it looked to him as if Alite would eventually be indicted. That wasn't anything Alite hadn't considered. The FBI agent told Alite his best bet was to go in now, before charges were brought. That way he could get the best possible deal.

"I told him, and I was trying to speak to him as a friend, not an agent, that he might never see his kids again, that he might never see freedom again," Gentile recalled. "I just told him to consider his options."

Gentile also offered to introduce him to a well-known Philadelphia defense attorney, Nicholas Nastasi, who Gentile said might be able to help negotiate an agreement. Alite thanked Gentile, but said no thanks. He was not ready to come in.

"He reverted back to his street sense, to the shield he had used all his life," Gentile recalled. "You know, you can't take a person like John and see a change overnight. I like to think that some of the things we talked about stayed with him and that he ultimately decided to do the right thing and that what we had talked about played some part in that decision."

One day late in 2002 Alite took his father aside and told him he was planning to take off. Matthew Alite told his son he was crazy, that he was paranoid, that nothing was happening. But John Alite knew the streets better than his dad. The safest, the smartest, and the boldest move, he decided, was to leave.

But before he did, he had to put some things in order. He quickly set up bank accounts and channels through which his money could be wired to him anywhere in the world. He used several Canadian banks, believing that it would be more difficult for federal authorities to block the cash flow. Then he spent one afternoon driving up and down Route 73 in Voorhees, stopping at public phone booths to record the numbers. The phone booths were located at a popular diner, at two supermarkets, and at a local gas station. He attached a numerical designation to each booth, numbering them one through seven. Then he met with a trusted associate and laid out his plan.

If he took off, he told his associate, he would call him on his home or cell phone and have an innocuous conversation. If the phone was tapped, there'd be nothing of significance said. But in that conversation, he would always mention a number and time.

"I'd say something like, 'I was working out with three guys yesterday.' Then later in the conversation I'd say. 'I got a dentist appointment at two tomorrow.' That would mean that at two o'clock the next day I was going to call phone number three. He'd go to the pay phone and be there when I called. That way I'd be able to have a serious conversation. That's the way I kept tabs on what was going on."

Some guys go on the run and wind up hiding in a shack in the Poconos or in some sand flea–infested apartment at the Jersey Shore. Alite did it with more style.

He was dating a girl named Rochine at the time and suggested they take a vacation to St. Lucia, one of the islands in the Caribbean. He gave her some cash to buy the plane tickets and told her to make the hotel reservations. They were going to spend a week in the sun. They left in March 2003. They flew out of Fort Lauderdale. It would be three years and nine months before John Alite returned to the United States.

When he came back, he would be in handcuffs.

He and Rochine spent six days on the beach in St. Lucia. As the vacation was drawing to a close, he told her he wasn't going back. After some shouting and some tears, she got on a plane for the return trip to Florida. She had no idea where Alite was headed. And that's the way he wanted it. In fact, he wasn't entirely sure himself.

Looking back on it now, he says, the next six months were controlled chaos. Alite moved in and out of more than a dozen countries. He started in the Cayman Islands, hopped in and out of Cuba and Jamaica, picked up a phony passport in Venezuela, and touched based in Colombia with friends of the drug dealer he had met in the federal prison in Loretta. He lived for a while in

Barranquilla, a beautiful seaside city in Colombia, and also visited Bogotá, Medellín, and Cali. A Colombian girlfriend was one of several beautiful women he spent time with while on the run.

His routine was similar no matter the country. He spoke passable Spanish, which he had picked up on the streets and through his dealings in the drug underworld. He had learned Albanian at home and would eventually pick up a little Italian and more than a little Portuguese while on the run. In big cities like Paris or Rome, if he was just passing through, he would be a tourist and blend in, staying at a good hotel and checking out the sights. If he decided to stay for several weeks, he would seek out a less traveled area of the city, a place a little rough around the edges.

He would work out in gyms, boxing and exercising. He would jog. Partly it was to stay in shape, partly it was to stay alert, to keep his mind and body fresh. He took precautions, but he also realized that he enjoyed traveling. He liked going to new places, speaking different languages, sampling foods, and soaking up the culture. He was living day to day, week to week.

"I decided to enjoy myself," he said. "I knew I could be arrested at any time. I was cautious, but I wasn't going to stop living."

Establishing contacts in the local underworld helped make that possible. So did the large amounts of cash he readily spent.

"I'd go to the bars or strips clubs and meet the girls," he said. "Strippers and prostitutes are great sources of information. And they're usually fun to be around. I had money so that wasn't a problem. And from them I'd get an idea of what was going on, who was running things and how I could maneuver."

In most countries he stuck to the same routine. But in Albania jogging created a problem.

"One of the mob bosses there told me I was crazy," Alite said. "He said it was too dangerous to go out jogging on my own. So he'd send a carload of his guys to follow me whenever I went out for run. They thought I was nuts.

"Any time I went into a country where I intended to stay for a while, I would hire a driver who spoke English. We usually became friends."

In Cuba, he hired a guy named Gustavo to drive him around. Gustavo introduced him to his family and helped him find an apartment. At one point Gustavo's mother offered to marry Alite so that he could stay in the country and perhaps become a citizen. He lived in Miramar, a Havana neighborhood of old stately buildings and modern hotels. He loved it. The climate was great and so were the people. It was like being back in the 1950s. The pace of life was slower and all these old, vintage American cars were on the streets. Except they weren't vintage, they were transportation. He enjoyed walking around the city. Once he stumbled into a plaza where a crowd had gathered and armed soldiers were posted on every corner. A few minutes later, Fidel Castro arrived and proceeded to give one of his classic speeches. Alite couldn't understand it all, but it was clear that Fidel was still touting the communist line as the salvation of the country.

Alite went in and out of Cuba several times. Whenever he got the sense that Interpol might be on his tail, he would head for Havana. It was his way of washing the slate clean, erasing his trail. There was no way for Interpol to track him there. Then, after a few weeks or a month or more, he would head back out. Once he flew out of Havana to Rome. He had been dating a woman named Keenya in Havana and she had gotten residency in Italy. She invited him to visit her there. From Italy he would bounce over to Albania. He made a stop in Greece, then headed to France and Spain. Claudia visited once and they traveled from Paris to Amsterdam and back.

In Barcelona, Spain, he met four young girls from Venezuela who invited him to share the apartment in which they were living. They knew the city and its nightlife. It was perfect. And it turned out to be serendipitous.

"They wanted to take me to this club on the beach called Baja," he said. "We went there one night. The guy that owned it was Albanian. His name was Mojah and he had all these big Bulgarian bodyguards around. I realized right away this guy was into more than just a nightclub. Most of these guys were drug dealers. We started talking. I don't speak Albanian that well, but I can get by."

In typical fashion, the conversation drifted toward who do you know that I might know. George the Albanian's name came up. Not only did Mojah know him, he told Alite, but in fact, "I got a surprise for you."

He took him to an upstairs bar at the club. At the bar sat a somewhat familiar figure wearing a long, black leather coat. This was at the beach in the summer. Alite shook his head as he recognized the character.

"It was Benny, George's brother," Alite said. "Benny told me he had partners in Spain and Italy and they're moving drugs. I think Mojah was part of the business, too."

That night they discussed old times and new opportunities. Benny and Mojah had their eyes on a score, a big gambler, a strapping, six-foot-five Scandinavian named Klaus who was dropping hundreds of thousands of dollars at the local casino. They wanted to rob him and asked Alite to get involved.

"I said I had my own problems," he said. "I didn't need another headache."

Alite passed on the robbery. About a week later he met a woman out walking her dog. They became friends. She worked in the travel industry and asked Alite if he would walk her dog during the day while she was at work. He happily jumped at the chance. It was a way to move around and blend in. Once he got to know her, Alite explained his situation. He was on the run and was looking to obtain another passport or two. The woman's partner had a contact in the government in Senegal. He might be able to help.

Alite's two visits to Dakar, the capital of that West African country, were the only times while he was on the run that he felt unsure of himself, he said.

"I was one of the few white people there," he said. "They hate Americans. And when that horn sounds at noon, they all get down on their knees and start praying. I could disappear there and nobody would ever know what had happened to me."

Money, however, provided a security blanket. He arranged to pay for two phony passports that were processed through an immigration office after hours. On a second trip back, using the same contacts, he got four more. Total cost was about twenty grand, big money in Senegal.

"These were good passports," he said. "The one I got in Venezuela was junk. It might work in some third-world countries, but I was afraid to use it. These were legitimate."

He pasted different photos of himself, different hairstyles and colors, onto the passports. He sometimes struggled to remember the name and birth date on the document that he was using, but he was seldom challenged.

"Especially in South American countries," he said. "Either they were too lazy or they didn't have the technology or they didn't care. Traveling on a train in Europe was when I was most concerned. They would collect the passports. I also worried about traveling with more than one. If they searched my luggage and found a bunch of passports, it would be a problem."

Alite would periodically touch base with people at home, trying to keep abreast of what was happening. Ronnie Trucchio had been indicted on murder and robbery charges in Fort Lauderdale in December 2003, about nine months after Alite took off. That wasn't the case that Alite was expecting, but it confirmed that the feds were all over the Gambino operations in Florida. Junior was still in prison, but there were some strange rumblings about him reaching out to the government. If that were true, it would be a final and fitting conclusion to the Gotti legacy. And Johnny Casasanto, the Philadelphia mobster who had befriended Alite and who had later hooked up with Gotti when they both were in Ray Brook, was dead.

Alite would later tell a federal jury that he warned Casasanto about moving to New York.

"I told him, 'Johnny, you'll get killed in New York. Every corner there's guys, not like in Philly where there's only one crew. And they fight each other all the time.' "

Alite described Casasanto as "a wild kid" who "didn't understand the life, not New York gangster life. He might have understood the mob life in Philly. It's a big difference."

How well Casasanto understood life in his own city is open to question. He had apparently run afoul of the local leadership after returning home from prison. He was involved in several bar fights and confrontations. He was suspected of shooting up the front of a row house owned by the brother of Philadelphia mob boss Joe Ligambi, and he was fooling around with the wife of another jailed mob leader, according to underworld gossip.

Alite told the FBI he had met with Ligambi and two other members of the Philadelphia hierarchy, capo Anthony Staino and underboss Joseph "Mousie" Massimino, in 2001 or 2002. They discussed the cell tower company he had taken over from Ronnie Turchi's son. But they also asked several questions about Casasanto, including reports that while he was in Allenwood with Alite he had informed on several other inmates who were smuggling drugs into the prison. Alite knew about the rumors but offered nothing new to Ligambi and the others. He came away from the meeting with the same feeling he had had when he spoke with Ronnie Turchi as they were about to leave the halfway house.

Like Turchi, Alite figured Casasanto had been marked for death.

"Johnny, be careful, they're gonna kill ya," he said he told Casasanto during one of their last meetings. Casasanto said he'd be fine. But he asked Alite for a favor. He had always admired the gold chain and medal that Joe Gambino had given Alite. He asked Alite if he would trade that chain and medal for the thicker gold chain that he wore around his neck. Alite readily agreed.

"When I gave him the chain and medal, I said, 'I hope this helps you.' I guess it didn't."

On November 22, 2003, the body of Johnny Gongs was discovered in the kitchen of the row house where he lived in a quiet residential section of South Philadelphia. He had been shot in the back of the head. There was no sign of forced entry. Police speculated that someone he knew and trusted had killed him. It appeared Casasanto had let his killer or killers into his home and then turned his back on them as he walked toward his kitchen. The shooting occurred around 1 A.M. Casasanto's brother Steve discovered the body several hours later.

No one has ever been charged with that murder. But from thousands of miles away, Alite could imagine how it went down. It was always someone you trusted, he thought. Nothing was ever going to change. He was more certain than ever that the only things for him back in the United States were a bullet or a prison cell.

CHAPTER 17

John Alite spent three years in Brazil. The first year was "The Girl from Ipanema" meets *Goodfellas*. He loved every minute of it. The next two were hell.

"A friend of mine in the Cayman Islands had introduced me to this woman who was from Brazil," he said. "I started asking her about the country. I knew the weather was great and the women were beautiful. She told me the government was corrupt and it was easy to maneuver. She said she had a cousin named Johnny in Rio who would help me out. But she warned me that he was a real hustler, that he'd try to get over on me. I decided to check it out. I also had some distant relatives who lived in São Paolo so I knew I could visit them when I was there."

Alite traveled by boat from the Caymans to Salvador, the capital of the Brazilian province of Bahia, in the north of the country. Bahia is celebrated for its food, passion, and women in the novels of the great Brazilian writer, the late Jorge Amado. Amado, who grew up there, described Bahia and its people as gritty, passionate, violent, and sensual. Alite said it was all of that and more. He liked Salvador and several other cities he visited in the province but knew he couldn't stay there.

"I liked the people, but they told me I'd never be able to blend in," he said. "They were right. They suggested Rio because there were more tourists and there was more of an international presence."

Within a month he was living in an apartment in Copacabana. His building—most of the other tenants were working girls—was a block from the beach. There was a gym just up the street. There were stores and restaurants and all kinds of people. He happily settled in, following the same routine he had used in other countries. He quickly became known as "American John," a boxer from the United States with what seemed like an unlimited supply of cash.

"Every prostitute in the Copacabana district knew me," he said. "It wasn't because I was a customer. I got to be their friend. I'd loan them money. We'd go out to dinner or to a club. They knew everybody and pretty soon, so did I. And everybody knew me."

He went to the beach almost every day, renting a chair from one of the vendors. He also ran a tab with another vendor who had a cart on the beach out of which he sold sandwiches, cold drinks, beer, and snacks. Alite started buying food for the kids who roamed the neighborhood. In packs they could be dangerous, but he established a relationship early on and never had a problem.

"I used to walk around wearing an eighty-thousand-dollar, diamond-encrusted Rolex watch," he said. "Nobody ever bothered me. If a tourist did that, he'd be beaten and robbed. Those kids used to run in packs. They'd surround someone and take everything. Then they'd disappear in the neighborhood or run back to the slums, the favelas, where they lived. I never got bothered. They knew me."

Alite said he decided to live in Rio the way he had lived in New York. The only difference? The weather was better. He started each morning with breakfast at a local restaurant. After coffee and a bun, he'd sit in the sun for an hour or two and then go for a jog on the beach. He might run four or five miles. In the afternoon he'd work out at the gym. Eventually he started boxing there and got involved with other fighters, training some and working out with others. He also learned some jujitsu.

He was in a great shape and was living well. There were plenty of women, one more beautiful than the next, and most were happy to share a bed with Alite.

He still laughs at the advice one of his Brazilian friends gave him shortly after his arrival. "The best place to learn the language," the guy had told him, "is in bed with a woman."

It was good advice, Alite said, and he was happy to take it.

He made connections with local wiseguys and with members of the Commando Vermelho—the Red Command. He didn't know too much about their history, but he knew they were organized, on the streets and in the prisons, and that if you wanted or needed something done they were the people to see.

At the time, Alite needed very little. He was self-sufficient. He had plenty of cash and knew where he could get more. He would go to bars and clubs at night with some of the girls who lived in his apartment building. Sometimes they would take him into the favelas, where you could spend the night dancing to funky hip-hop music at hole-in-the-wall nightclubs. Located on the hills above the city, these crowded neighborhood slums were unlike anything he had ever seen. Poverty in the extreme.

"I got a better understanding of the country when I went there," he said. "The people were cautious and distrustful at first, but once they got to know you, there was a loyalty that would last forever. In the middle of these slums, gangs controlled each section, there would be these massive open-air markets with food and entertainment, dancing, prostitutes. It was like a carnival."

On the other hand, there were shopping centers in and around Rio that were comparable to those he had seen in Short Hills, New Jersey, and King of Prussia, Pennsylvania. Alite moved easily in and out of those two worlds. And on occasions he would take trips, either to São Paulo to visit his distant cousins or to nearby countries like Paraguay, Uruguay, or Argentina.

"Just short trips," he said. "I wanted to test different ways to get out and what problems there might be. It wasn't very difficult."

The idea was to have a way out if and when that was necessary.

Alite hung out at an Internet café from which he might email someone back home. He also had a cell phone and used his coded system to find out what was going on. The investigations were continuing and periodically he would get reports that someone else appeared to be cooperating. Before he was extradited back to the United States he estimated that two dozen former associates, including his young cousin Patsy Andriano, had given him up.

"I had asked a couple of guys to come with me when I left," he said. "They didn't want to. I knew then that if things got serious they'd cooperate. I think they were already thinking that way."

Alite figured he needed about five years. By that point, he believed, the cases in New York and Tampa would have come and gone, witnesses would have died or disappeared, and even prosecutors and FBI agents would have lost interest or retired. When all that happened, he might go back and try to work out a plea deal. Take a ten-year sentence, do eight, and be back home in Queens with nothing hanging over his head. But he didn't spend a lot of time worrying about that. The sun, the sand, and the lifestyle in Copacabana were perfect. He was happy to live in the moment.

"I just decided to relax, enjoy life, and have some fun," he said. "No worries."

Crime was part of the street scene, but he was smart enough and respected enough to avoid it. He laughs now as he recounts the story of a hapless British couple who happened by his beach one afternoon.

Alite, bare-chested, was doing some pull-ups. He spotted the couple and quickly realized that they wanted someone to take their picture with an expensive camera they were carrying.

"Would you like me to take your photograph?" he asked.

At first they seemed startled that he spoke English. Then they looked him up and down, noted the numerous tattoos that covered his arms, back, chest, legs, and neck, and politely declined.

"There was a local guy sitting on a bench nearby," Alite said. "He was wearing a shirt. I guess they figured he was safe. They asked him to take their picture. I'm doing my pull-ups and I'm watching and I know what's going to happen."

The couple posed and the guy in the shirt took their picture.

"Then he asked them to step back a few paces and he took another shot," Alite said. "Then he asked them to step further back so that he could get more of the beach in the photo. They did. And with that, he took off running with their camera. They called the police, but by the time they got there, the guy was long gone."

A few weeks after establishing his base in Copacabana he was at the beach one day when four girls showed up and took chairs under a tent nearby. He sent drinks over to them and, while still struggling with his Portuguese, struck up a conversation. He was attracted to a dark-haired beauty named Rose. She said she was celebrating her *aniversario*. Alite assumed it was her anniversary and thought she was married. Nevertheless, he got her phone number and asked if she would meet him at the movies—the cinema—that night.

When she didn't show, he called. She came to the movie theater, but struggled to explain. Finally, she stopped a passerby and asked him if he spoke English. Through the tourist, Rose and Alite had their first extended conversation. It was her birthday— that was what *aniversario* meant in Portuguese—and she was spending it with her friends. She had said she would meet Alite at the movies the next night. He hadn't understood. And no, she wasn't married.

Rose was a schoolteacher and went to church two or three times a week. She told Alite early in their relationship that he was not the kind of guy she usually went out with. She thought he was a boxer and his numerous tattoos seemed to indicate that he came from a different world than she was used to. But they hit it off, and over the next six months, they were a couple. Through her he learned to speak Portuguese well enough to hold a decent conversation. He soaked up the culture, sampling some great foods, went to Carnival, and developed an appreciation for *futebol*.

"They take soccer very seriously there," he said. "I was invited by some friends to go to a match one night. It was apparently a very important game. My friends were all fans of [the team] Flamengo. I forget who they were playing, but as we're getting ready to leave for the game, one of the guys called me into another room and handed me a nine-millimeter handgun. He asked if I knew how to use it. I told him I did. He said good, take it with you."

That's when Alite really understood how seriously Brazilians took their soccer.

"I said to my friend, 'Won't anyone check us going into the stadium?' I figured you couldn't bring a gun in. He said the authorities don't bother checking because everybody brought guns. If they checked, he said, there'd be a gunfight."

It wasn't Queens, but there were times when it seemed just like home.

"If you have the time and the money, Rio is a great place to be," he said.

In 2004, John Alite had both. But he stayed too long. He had gotten too comfortable. He knew the ways of the street, but he ignored the obvious. Just as there were hustlers and con men who had befriended him and had helped him make connections in the underworld, there were others—in some cases probably the same guys—who routinely passed information on to the authorities.

Alite had been living in Copacabana for a year. There is no doubt that the police had heard of "American John," the gringo with all the cash who had the moves and the savvy of a gangster. What he didn't know was that an indictment had been handed up in Tampa back in August. He, Trucchio, and four others were charged with racketeering. They were named as part of a Gambino crime family crew operating in Florida that engaged in drug dealing, extortion, robbery, and murder. The indictment was under seal and had not been made public. Trucchio was already in custody for the case pending in Fort Lauderdale. The other defendants were on the street and could be scooped up at any time. The only reason to keep the indictment sealed, it would appear, was to give authorities time to locate Alite.

On November 23, 2004, they did.

Coincidentally, that was the day Alite was planning to leave. He had been told by a few locals—merchants, shop owners, bartenders—that the police had been around asking questions. Nothing specific, but a red flag nonetheless. When Alite asked if they were looking for an American, one of the shop owners said no, that there was no mention of a gringo. But Alite had a feeling and decided to move out. He told several friends that he was planning a trip to São Paulo to visit relatives. In fact, he intended to take a bus and head for Argentina.

"I was going to take a bus that afternoon," he said. "I was going to try to get to Argentina and then maybe from there work my way up to Colombia and Venezuela."

Venezuela, with its firebrand anti-American president Hugo Chávez, was almost as good as Cuba for an American on the run. That was Alite's plan when he bumped into a friend of his named Leonardo, who suggested they have lunch together before Alite left. They headed for a deli/coffee shop that Alite frequented. On the way Leonardo stopped at a pay phone to call his girlfriend.

Alite waited outside the shop soaking up the sun. He was wearing sunglasses and was dressed casually in jeans, a red buttoned-down shirt, and sandals. Normally at that time of the day, the neighborhood would be bustling. Alite suddenly noticed that traffic had stopped. There were no cars on the street. And a helicopter was hovering overhead. Alite felt it before his brain could even process what was going on. There was nowhere to run.

The streets had been blocked off and now a dozen armed soldiers, part of what looked like a SWAT team, were closing in. Their leader, in Portuguese, told him to put his hands in the air and drop to his knees. He just stood there.

"I don't know why, but I didn't move," he said. "Maybe I wanted them to shoot me. I just stood still. I didn't try to run or anything like that. I just wasn't going to get down on my knees."

At that moment, Alite said, he thought of his kids, his three sons and his daughter, and wondered if he would ever see them again. While living on the run he had always told himself that he would eventually get back to the States and be with them. Maybe that was a fantasy. Maybe it was his way of ignoring the obvious, that he had willingly left them behind. But this was different. A bullet to the head would end any chance of him being a part of their lives ever again. In the alternative, a life sentence, which is what he believed he was facing back in Tampa, wouldn't be much better.

Now the Brazilian commander was next to him and had his gun in Alite's chest. With that, Alite dropped to his knees and placed his hands behind his head.

The police closed in, grabbed him, forced him to the ground, and quickly placed him in handcuffs and leg irons. Within minutes he was in the back of an armored car with tinted windows. The drive took about forty minutes. Alite was flanked in the backseat by two heavily armed police officers dressed all in black.

One of them looked at Alite and shook his head, "You are lucky, gringo. We could have killed you. Why didn't you do as you were told?"

Alite didn't answer. Perhaps because he really didn't know.

When the car stopped, he was lifted out of the backseat. He had been taken to a desolate area outside the city and was in the trash-strewn parking area of what looked like an abandoned warehouse. Alite knew this wasn't a prison. As bad as the Brazilian jails were, this appeared even worse. It reminded him of some of the old, abandoned factories in Queens and Brooklyn, places where he and others would take a victim whom they intended to baseball-bat or kill.

Inside the warehouse it was even worse. The smell was horrific, a combination of rotting trash, piss, and shit. Alite was sweating profusely as he was led to an office in the building. Partly it was the heat. Partly it was his nerves. Rats scurried across the floor and swarms of mosquitoes, attracted by the sweat, buzzed around him as he was pushed up a flight of stairs.

He was told to sit in a straight-backed wooden chair in a sparsely furnished office. Shortly after he took his seat, a tall, thin police agent, a Brazilian who apparently worked with or for Interpol, strode into the room and sat behind a desk. He had a file with him, which he perused, then began asking questions. Alite didn't respond. The agent smiled, got up, and casually walked around the desk. He leaned over and whispered in Alite's ear. Alite could smell the tobacco on his breath.

"Listen carefully, gringo," he said. "You are not in America. You have no rights here except the ones I choose to give you. We can do this nicely, as gentlemen, or we can do it my way. And if we do it my way I can assure you that you will be a long time recovering from your injuries."

Alite smiled to himself despite the situation. He had made

the same speech to dozens of guys back in New York, guys he confronted over underworld business, guys who wouldn't pay or who were selling drugs where they shouldn't or who, for whatever reason, had been singled out by one of the Gottis for a beating. Alite knew the agent wasn't making an idle threat. Alite was trying to figure out how to respond when the agent stood up and said, "Just think it over, gringo. I'll be back."

With that, the agent began to walk out of the office.

Alite held up his handcuffed wrists. The agent smiled.

"Yes, the jewelry," he said. "I'm afraid the reports on you indicate that you are a very dangerous man. The cuffs will remain. Think about what I said."

Four hours later, the agent returned. By that point Alite was struggling to control his bladder and bowels, sweat was running down his face, neck, and back, and the handcuffs and leg irons were eating into his skin.

This time Alite responded to the agent's questions. He first complained that he was having trouble understanding because the agent spoke in a dialect, used slang, and talked quickly.

"Bullshit," the agent said. "We have heard you speak on the phone. We know you understand Portuguese."

Alite then realized that he had been right. He was being watched. He told the agent he could understand and speak, but asked him to talk slowly and more distinctly.

The agent smiled.

"Now we are getting somewhere," he said.

The interrogation lasted for another forty minutes. Alite was asked about John Gotti and the American Mafia. He was told that he would be extradited to the United States to face murder charges. And he was asked if, while in Brazil, he had worked with organized crime and had engaged in any criminal activities.

Alite answered truthfully that while in Brazil he had done nothing wrong. He tried to tap-dance around the other questions, but in fact the agent didn't really seem to care. He told Alite there would be a press conference in the morning and that he would be wise to answer any questions posed by the media while keeping in mind that he was a "guest" of the Brazilian government. In other words, the agent explained, say whatever you want about New York and John Gotti, but think twice before you say anything that might embarrass me or my office.

Alite spent that night in a cage somewhere in the basement of the abandoned building. His cuffs and legs irons were removed when he was thrust inside, but that was a small consolation. There was no food. No water. No toilet. A guard was assigned to watch him at all times. The guard paced across the top of the cage. There was nothing else inside, just a concrete floor. Alite's bowels were bursting. He hollered to the guard, telling him he needed to use the bathroom.

"Gringo," came the reply, "you will not be leaving this cell tonight. Do what you have to do. No one cares."

Alite took off his shirt, ripped it in half. He used one half as his toilet. Then he used the other half to wipe himself. When he was done, he threw the soiled pieces of his shirt outside the cell. Then he tried to settle in for what would amount to a long night and his first introduction to the Brazilian prison system.

At first he paced the cage, trying to clear his head. He did some exercises, hoping to relieve the tension and ultimately tire himself out so that he might get some sleep. But the pacing and the sweating attracted what seemed like flocks of mosquitoes, the biggest he had ever seen. Without a shirt, he was an easy target and they attacked continually. When he slowed down and stood still, he was less of an attraction. He tried to curl up on the floor and there he did find some respite from the bugs. But within minutes, rats were scurrying over his legs and feet, nipping at whatever skin was exposed.

And that's the way John Alite spent his first night in custody in Brazil. He would spend two more years in circumstances that were similar, if not as extreme. He had decided not to waive extradition. He had already done some research and knew that the laws in Brazil might be in his favor. If he could find a lawyer and if he could find a court that would give him a fair hearing, he believed he had a shot at winning an extradition fight. The alternative was going back to Tampa, one of the toughest federal districts in the country, to face murder and racketeering charges that could result in a life sentence. Another option, and one that he would explore in detail, was escape and flight. If he stayed in Brazil, there was always a chance that he could find a way out—out of the prison and out of the country.

Alite's arrest stirred a media sensation. There was a press briefing the next day.

Beforehand, the arresting agent again warned Alite about what he might say to the media. Then two guards threw a package wrapped in brown paper at him. Inside were some clothes. He was taken to a dank and dirty bathroom where he was allowed to "wash" at the sink. He ran some water through his hair and over his body, trying not to scratch or irritate the dozens of welts from the mosquitoes and rats that covered him.

The perp walk and the flashing cameras told him that his arrest was big news. He said little during the press conference to incriminate himself, trying to remain as vague as possible. When asked about Gotti, he was evasive.

"Anyone who has ever lived in New York knows who he is," he said. "I knew him from the neighborhood."

He said he had no idea what the charges were that he was

facing back in the United States and denied that he was a member of the Mafia. The only time he was completely honest was when he was asked if the Mafia had sent him to Brazil to set up an organization there.

"I came to Brazil because I love this country," he said. "I love its cities, its mountains, its people. I wanted to live here forever and I was very happy. That's all. No other reason."

The headlines in the local papers screamed the story the next day. INTERPOL PRENDE MAFIOSO QUE SE REFUGIAVA EM COPACABANA was the headline on the front page of *POVO,* a Rio de Janeiro daily. CHEFE MAFIOSO AMERICANO E PRESO NO RIO PELA INTERPOL, read the headline in the *Diário de S. Paulo.*

After the press conference, Alite was taken to a police van and driven to Presidio Ary Franco, one of the most notorious prisons in the Brazilian system. During the ride, two of the Interpol agents tried to scare him.

"Gringo," they said. "You are going to the worst prison in Brazil, maybe the worst in the whole continent." Then they laughed. Alite didn't react. But later another agent said to him quietly, "Gringo, this is no joke. You are going to a terrible place where terrible things happen every day. The worst of the worst. But if you have money to spread around, and I pray to God you do, there are ways to make life bearable. My advice, be very careful. Go slowly. Be stingy with your trust."

CHAPTER 18

When Alite was arrested in Rio, Junior was still in jail. The feds had come with another indictment while Gotti was finishing out his sentence at Ray Brook. The new racketeering charges, handed down in July 2004, focused in large part on the 1992 plot to kidnap and kill Curtis Sliwa. Gotti was denied bail and remained a federal inmate even after he had finished up the seventy-seven-month sentence from his 1998 case.

The Sliwa allegation added a new twist to the tabloid saga that had become the Gotti story. The bombastic self-promoter who founded the Guardian Angels was the perfect victim for a criminal organization that sought celebrity over secrecy. And the trials that followed—there were three, each ending with a hung jury—provided even more fodder.

By this point, of course, Vicky Gotti had turned into an author and a reality TV "star." Her show, *Growing Up Gotti*, purported to offer an inside look at what life was really like for the daughter of the famous Mafia don. Her three teenage sons, their hair heavily gelled, their attitudes Long Island arrogant, were costars.

The show provided all you needed to know about the state of the American Mafia in the new millennium. The "honored society" that had spawned Mario Puzo's classic *Godfather* saga had become the stuff of comic books, talk radio rants, and supermarket tabloids, a caricature of itself, an organization that couldn't even live up to the standards of *The Sopranos*, the then wildly popular HBO series.

Junior was trying to maintain a low profile at the time, insisting that he had left the mob behind. But the new indictment could lead to another extended stay in a federal prison. Even if a jury accepted the argument that he had quit in 1999, he could still be liable for events that happened before that date. And the Sliwa assault certainly fit that timetable. So Junior decided to take a different approach.

In January 2005, as Alite sat rotting in a Brazilian prison, Gotti arranged through his attorneys Jeffrey Lichtman and Marc Fernich to meet with federal authorities to discuss the possibility of cooperating. The proffer session took place on January 18, 2005, at the U.S. Attorney's Office at 500 Pearl Street in lower Manhattan. Gotti was still in federal custody at the time and was probably brought to the meeting by federal marshals.

The story of his flirtation with the feds didn't surface until October 2006, twenty-two months later. That's when Jerry Capeci, writing his popular "Gang Land" column at the time for the *New York Sun,* quoted "sources" who provided details about the meeting, including Junior's version of the Danny Silva murder, the John Cennamo "suicide," and the payoff to a local police detective to keep Gotti's name out of the investigation.

Capeci wrote that the now-retired police detective John Daly did not respond to requests for comment about the allegations. He also noted that back in the early 1990s, Daly had adamantly denied taking a ten-thousand-dollar bribe from Gotti Sr.

In the column, Capeci also quoted Gotti's criminal defense attorney Charles Carnesi, who said that Junior had confirmed the meeting had occurred, but said his client never had any intention of cooperating.

Capeci wrote that Carnesi told him that Gotti "has acknowledged that there was a meeting, but he steadfastly maintains that he did not incriminate anyone in any criminal activity during the meeting, nor did he ever consider cooperating or testifying against anyone. Had it been his desire to make such a deal, his lawyers at the time would have made the deal."

Rather than engage in a debate about what was said and what was intended during the debriefing session, what follows is a replication of the five-page FBI 302 memo from the meeting John A. Gotti and his lawyers had with the feds back in January 2005. Alite, who has read it, said it was a typical Gotti attempt to lay blame on others. He said the version of events depicted by Junior, at least the events that Alite has knowledge of, is a blend of fact and fiction. The allegations in the memo are not being presented as fact for the purposes of this story, but merely to show that Gotti met with authorities and, in a very real sense, was willing to throw the names of others—mobsters, cops, businessmen, and elected officials—into his descriptions of the criminal activities of the Gambino crime family. The names of the businessmen and politicians have been X'd out in this version because they have never been charged with a crime and, if asked, would in all probability deny the allegations. Daly's name remains because he has already been identified in news reports and has denied that he ever took any money from the mob. There are no other changes to the transcription of the memo as it appears here. In fact, the misspelling of the Silver Fox (it was written at the "Sliver" Fox the first two times it was mentioned in the memo) is given as it appears in the document.

It is also interesting to note that while the interview took place in January 2005, it wasn't officially transcribed until a year later. By that point the feds or Gotti or perhaps both sides had decided that a cooperating deal based on the proffer wasn't possible. Alite believes the feds rejected Gotti because they knew he was lying about his own culpability.

FEDERAL BUREAU OF INVESTIGATION

Date of Transcription: 01/16/2006

JOHN A. GOTTI, also known as (aka) JUNIOR (GOTTI, JR.) (Protect Identity) was present at the United States Attorney's Office, Southern District of New York (SDNY), 500 Pearl Street, New York, New York on January 18, 2005 for a proffer session. This meeting was arranged at GOTTI, JR.'S request. Also present were GOTTI, JR.'S ATTORNEYS, Jeffrey Lichtman, Esq., and MARC FERNICH, Esq., as well as Assistant United States Attorneys (AUSAS) Robert Buehler, Joon Kim and Jennifer Rodgers, SDNY.

After GOTTI, JR. and his attorneys read the proffer agreement and the terms of that agreement were explained to them by the AUSAS, GOTTI, JR. signed the agreement. GOTTI, JR. thereafter provided the following information.

The Murder of Danny Silva

In the early morning hours of either March 11th or 12th, 1983, GOTTI, JR., along with friends MARK CAPUTO and ANTHONY AMOROSO, were present at the SLIVER FOX bar located on 101st Street and Liberty Avenue in Queens, New York. At some point, TOMMY Last Name Unknown (LNU) aka "ELFIE" approached GOTTI, JR., who was seated at the bar with a female friend, DONNA (LNU). According to GOTTI, JR., "ELFIE" repeatedly bumped into him. Words were exchanged, one thing led to another and GOTTI, JR. ultimately hit "ELFIE" with a broken glass bottle. GOTTI, JR. then stabbed "ELFIE" with a knife that GOTTI, JR. had obtained from AMOROSO.

According to GOTTI, JR., a melee ensued involving approximately 30 to 40 of the bar's patrons. GOTTI, JR. recalled that among those involved in the melee were: DANNY SILVA, JOHN and GREG MASSA, ANGELO CASTELLI, JOEY CURIO, First Name Unknown (FNU) RILEY and JOHN CENNAMO. GOTTI, JR. stated that DANNY SILVA was stabbed and killed during the melee.

GOTTI, JR. described a meeting which occurred a short time after the incident at the SLIVER FOX, between ANGELO RUGGIERO, SR., and New York City Police Department (NYPD) Detective, JOHN DALY. GOTTI, JR. drove RUGGIERO to the meeting, which took place at the Sherwood Diner located near the Five Towns, on the Queens-Nassau County border. Before the meeting GOTTI, JR. and RUGGIERO discussed the purpose of the meeting. According to GOTTI, JR., RUGGIERO was carrying a brown paper bag containing $25,000 in cash. GOTTI, JR. observed RUGGIERO sit in the rear of the diner and meet with DALY and an unknown white male. RUGGIERO advised GOTTI, JR. that the $25,000 cash payment was made to DALY to get his (GOTTI, JR.'S) name out of the SILVER FOX murder investigation. While GOTTI, JR., did not directly meet DALY, DALY did acknowledge GOTTI, JR. on his way out of the diner, as GOTTI, JR. sat waiting in the car.

Following this meeting with RUGGIERO and DALY, GOTTI, JR. was instructed by his father, JOHN J. GOTTI, (GOTTI, SR.) to leave New York for a while until things "cooled down." GOTTI, JR. left New York for Fort Lauderdale, Florida, where he remained for some time. At some time GOTTI, SR. joined him in Florida and the two eventually returned to New York.

Upon GOTTI, JR.'S return to New York, he learned that JOHN CENNAMO, one of DANNY SILVA'S friends who was present at the SILVER FOX the night SILVA was stabbed and killed, was dead, apparently having hung himself.

GOTTI, JR. provided the following as background:

ANGELO RUGGIERO was 'put on the shelf" by GOTTI, SR. after the murder of JIMMY HYDELL in 1986. HYDELL was tortured and killed by members of the Luchese Organized Crime Family because he (HYDELL) and others had shot and tried to kill ANTHONY 'GASPIPE' CASSO. The Luchese Family learned that RUGGIERO was behind the attempt to kill CASSO and demanded that RUGGIERO himself be killed. GOTTI, SR., who was very close to RUGGIERO, did not have RUGGIERO killed. Instead, RUGGIERO was "put on the shelf."

Prior to HYDELL'S murder, members of the Luchese Family summoned Gambino Family members JIMMY "BROWN"FAILLA and JOE 'BUTCH' CORRAO to the location where HYDELL was being held. According to GOTTI, JR., FAILLA and CORRAO were summoned to that location so that they would be present when HYDELL admitted his and RUGGIERO'S involvement in the attempted murder of CASSO. Prior to the Luchese Family killing HYDELL, FAILLA and CORRAO obtained Gambino Family member DANNY MARINO'S approval to kill HYDELL., because, according to GOTTI, JR., HYDELL was MARINO'S nephew.

Even though RUGGIERO had been "put on the shelf," GOTTI, JR., continued to meet with him in violation of mafia protocol. GOTTI'S father, (GOTTI, SR.) reprimanded him on occasion for meeting with RUGGIERO. GOTTI, JR. learned from RUGGIERO that in the weeks and months after SILVA was killed at the SILVER FOX, CENNAMO put continued pressure on the police department to investigate his (SILVA'S) murder. RUGGIERO told GOTTI, JR. that CENNAMO "pressed" his (GOTTI'S) name in the investigation and his (GOTTI, JR.'S) role in the bar fight that led to SILVA'S murder. RUGGIERO told GOTTI, JR. that he (RUGGIERO) and others had obtained NYPD DD5S [official police department reports] of the SILVA murder investigation from DALY. RUGGIERO then advised GOTTI, JR. that CENNAMO'S death, which appeared to be a suicide, was in fact a murder and that he (RUGGIERO), JOE WATTS and WILLIE BOY JOHNSON had killed CENNAMO on GOTTI, SR.'S orders. RUGGIERO told GOTTI, JR. that DETECTIVE JOHN DALY provided background information regarding CENNAMO which the Gambino family used to locate him.

Several years later, after GOTTI, JR. was arrested on unrelated charges, an additional cash payment was made to DALY when GOTTI, JR.'S name resurfaced in the SILVA murder investigation.

GOTTI, JR. stated that after his father was arrested and remanded to prison [December 1990], GOTTI, JR. frequently met with JOE WATTS, who was a close associate of GOTTI, SR. At one meeting with WATTS at the Lum Chin Chinese restaurant, WATTS admitted his involvement in the murder of CENNAMO. Watts also told GOTTI, JR. that the first "piece of work" he (WATTS) was involved in was the murder of VITO BORELLI in approximately 1980, which he committed with GOTTI, SR.

According to GOTTI, JR. JOHN DALY was assigned to the 106th Precinct during the time he received the payoffs from the Gambino Family and provided information to the Gambino Family about the SILVA murder investigation. GOTTI, JR. added that DALY later went to work for the Queens District Attorney's Office.

Oak Point Garbage Dump

At some point in late 1980's GOTTI, JR and others wanted to develop approximately 28 acres of land located on the Bronx side of the Triboro Bridge. This tract of land was known as Oak Point and at that time was being used by New York City as a garbage dump. GOTTI, JR. and his associates wanted to build modular homes on the property through a company known as Brite Star Homes. In addition to the housing development GOTTI, JR. wanted to get involved in the construction of the Bronx House of Detention on that site. GOTTI, JR. had received assurances that he would be able to sell the prison to the City of New York for twenty million dollars.

According to GOTTI, JR., **XXX**, a partner of GOTTI, JR.'S in this venture purchased the property. GOTTI, JR. advised that bribes were paid to at least two city politicians in order to secure certain city permits required for the development of the project. JOE ZINGARO, a captain in the Gambino Family, had a close association with Bronx politician, **XXX**. GOTTI, JR. gave $20,000.00 in cash to ZINGARO for ZINGARO to give to **XXX**. According to ZINGARO, **XXX** accepted the $20,000.00 GOTTI, JR., using the alias JOHN RUSSO, met **XXX** at a function they both attended at Alex and Henry's Catering Hall in the Bronx.

According to GOTTI, JR., additional bribe money was paid to **XXX** through **XXX**. **XXX** suggested making the payments to **XXX**. According to GOTTI, JR. on at least two different occasions, he (GOTTI, JR.) gave $25,000.00 in cash to **XXX** for **XXX** to give to **XXX**. GOTTI, JR.'S close associate MICHAEL McLAUGHLIN, delivered the money. GOTTI, JR. again using the alias JOHN RUSSO, also met directly with **XXX** at **XXX'S** office. According to GOTTI, JR. the bribes paid to **XXX** did secure whatever permit (s) GOTTI, JR. and his associates needed to obtain for their project.

In addition to the payments described above, GOTTI, JR. paid an additional $100,000.00 to $125,000.00 in cash to various city politicians through **XXX** and the law firm **XXX** in order to 'grease the skids" in the development of the housing project and detention center.

After **XXX** purchase Oak Point, GOTTI, JR. and his associates continued to operate the garbage dump from approximately January 1989 through late August 1989. GOTTI, JR.'S "guys," including McLAUGHLIN, worked at the dump. GOTTI, JR. stated that investigators with the Department of Investigation (DOI) or another New York City investigative agency photographed GOTTI, JR. at the garbage dump on several occasions. Once this photographic evidence of GOTTI, JR.'S connection to the property surfaced, his (GOTTI, JR.'S) investors and business associates no longer wanted to be involved and the project was never completed.

In approximately the spring of 1990, GOTTI, JR. and other Gambino Family members pursued another project involving a garbage dump. This dump was located in Matamoras, Pennsylvania. GOTTI, JR. attended a 'sit -down" with other members of the Gambino Family, as well as high-ranking members of the Luchese Family concerning this project. On behalf of the Gambino Family (which GOTTI, JR. continually referred to as "our family") GOTTI, JR., his (GOTTI, JR.'S) uncle, PETE GOTTI, and SALVATORE "SAMMY THE BULL" GRAVANO met with representatives of the Luchese Family, AL D'ARCO, ANTHONY "GAS PIPE" CASSO and PATTY MASSELLI. According to GOTTI, JR., the deal to purchase and operate this garbage dump fell through.

Queen's District Attorney's Office

GOTTI, JR. also stated that Gambino Family member ANTHONY "TONY LEE" GUERRIERI and his relationship with local politician, **XXX**, the Gambino Family had "influence" with the Queens District Attorney's (DA) Office while JOHN SANTUCCI was the District Attorney. GOTTI, JR. identified **XXX** as the Gambino Family's "go to guy." GOTTI, JR. also advised that after GUERRIERI died, the Gambino Family lost most of their influence with the Queens DA's Office.

Eight months after the proffer session, John A. Gotti was at the defense table as his first trial for the Sliwa kidnapping began. The trial opened in August 2005 in a courtroom in Lower Manhattan. It proved to be one of the best shows in town. Hopeful spectators lined up in a hallway outside the courtroom an hour before the trial began for one of the few available seats inside.

When Sliwa testified, in late August, it was a standing-room-only affair, a perfect storm of the mob and the media. Sliwa, the radio personality on the witness stand. Gotti, the celebrity mob boss, at the defense table. And Vicky, the tart-tongued Mafia princess with the flowing blond locks and heavy eye shadow, sitting in a back row, there to show support for her brother after making an appearance on a morning network TV show to tout the start of a new season of *Growing Up Gotti*.

"I called John Gotti Sr. America's number-one drug dealer," Sliwa said from the witness stand when asked what he had been saying about the Dapper Don during his radio rants back in 1992. But his testimony also included admissions that as the leader of the Guardian Angels he had at times hyped or fabricated details in order to enhance the law enforcement legend of the urban, red-beret-wearing vigilante group. After a mistrial was declared, one of the anonymous jurors told a reporter that some members of the panel had found Sliwa a bit much to take, calling him bombastic and arrogant. The panel had apparently hung 10–2 and 7–5 in favor of conviction on the two counts tied to the Sliwa abduction. But despite their efforts of those voting for conviction, there was no way to break the logjam and the judge ultimately declared the jury hung and the case a mistrial.

A retrial was quickly scheduled. In the meantime Junior was granted bail that September and allowed to go home. He was placed under house arrest and put on electronic monitoring. His family and friends, including his sister Vicky, posted property as security for the $7 million bond on which he was released. He would remain a "prisoner" in his home in Oyster Bay Cove on Long Island's Gold Coast, spending his days with his wife, Kim, and their then five children.

There was no bail for Alite despite attempts by his Brazilian lawyer to convince judges that his client was entitled to it. In fact,

Alite says that had he been granted bail, he would have fled the country. Instead he spent the next two years fighting to survive and trying to escape.

Beatings, riots, and murder were part of the daily routine in the prisons of Brazil. Inmates were divided into factions. Those linked to organizations like the Red Command appeared to carry the most weight, but that was a relative concept depending on the location and the mind-set of other prison authorities. On the lowest level of the inmate scale were poor Brazilians who had no connections, no money, and no way to protect themselves. They were often brutalized by guards, tortured, beaten, and raped.

The prison authorities were also factionalized. There were military police who maintained order along the perimeter of the prison facility, guarding against jailbreaks and, in theory at least, providing the first level of screening for anyone entering the compound. They were heavily armed and politicized. Inside the facility there were jail guards—*functionarios*—and there were trustees. The guards were in charge of order inside the cell blocks. They were aligned with the warden, the deputy warden, or the Red Command. Everyone took bribes and allegiances were constantly shifting. The trustees, on the other hand, were beholden to the warden or deputy warden. They were usually lifers who had cut deals in order to ease the conditions under which they were being held. Most were brutes. Often strung out on drugs or steroids, they were the enforcers for the warden and deputy warden. They would administer the beatings and they would also serve as eyes and ears for the administration inside the cell blocks.

Most Brazilian prisons, like Ary Franco, were overcrowded, vermin-infested hellholes. Toilets were little more than drain holes cut into the floors of the latrines. The holes emptied into old, corroded pipes. Sewage from the upper floors constantly leaked from those pipes that ran along the ceilings of the cells underneath. The smells, the noise, and the hot, humid, fetid conditions created an environment that was beyond miserable.

In March 2005, shortly after Alite began his stay, the BBC, Britain's renowned television network, broadcasted a documentary on prison conditions in Brazil. The report opened with comments from James Cavallaro, a Stanford law professor and founder of the Brazilian human rights organization the Global Justice Center. Cavallaro said he had been in many of the country's prisons and that all presented the same picture.

"They're dark, dreary, wet, and damp," he told the BBC. "Some of them feel like mediaeval dungeons. And it's remarkable—there's the same stench in all of them. Rotting food, urine, excrement, prisoners' sweat. That prison smell is uniform—it's teeming humanity."

Several years later, Alite's Tampa-based defense attorney tried to provide the courts with some insights into what Alite had gone through while an inmate in Brazil. Timothy J. Fitzgerald filed parts of government reports from human rights organizations that were attempting to shed light on the systemic and seemingly unsolvable problems in the jails of Brazil. One of the documents filed by Fitzgerald cited a 2008 Human Rights Report from the U.S. State Department that addressed the horrendous prison conditions. The report read in part:

Prison conditions throughout the country often ranged from poor to extremely harsh and life threatening. Abuse by prison guards, poor medical care, and severe overcrowding occurred at many facilities.

Prison officials often resorted to brutal treatment of prisoners, including torture. Harsh or dangerous working conditions, official negligence, poor sanitary conditions, abuse and mistreatment by guards, and a lack of medical care led to a number of deaths in prisons. Poor working conditions and low pay for prison guards encouraged widespread corruption. Prisoners who committed petty crimes were held with murderers. According to the National Penitentiary Department, in June there were 392,279 prisoners incarcerated, 40 percent more than the system's design capacity, and the number increased approximately 3,000 per month.

Alite also noticed that violence on the street involving gangs like the Red Command spilled into the prisons where one side or the other—law enforcement or gangsters—sought retribution for what had occurred on the outside. A riot in a prison in São Paulo in 2005, shortly after Alite arrived at Ary Franco, was typical. Inmates seized a wing of the prison and proceeded to kill members of another inmate faction. They then cut off the heads of five of their victims and waved them from pikes as they stood on the roof of one of the prison wings.

Survival was a day-to-day proposition. Alite, after overcoming some initial depression, decided he was going to survive. The first connection he made in Ary Franco was with an inmate named Emerson, who was the leader of the Red Command in the cell block where Alite was housed.

Emerson gave Alite his bed after Alite was pushed into a cell in the middle of his first night in Ary Franco. The cell, designed to house a dozen inmates, was home to about forty. Not everyone got to sleep on the stone beds that had been carved out of the concrete walls. Many curled up in corners or on the floor. Emerson ordered another inmate out of the bed in which he was sleeping and took it for himself. The move made it clear to Alite that Emerson was in charge.

The first week was a dismal experience, an emotional and physical assault on his mind and his senses. Alite had no idea if anyone even knew what had happened to him and he had no way to make contact with anyone on the outside. He was dirty and ached from the lack of sleep and the mosquito and rat bites. The cells were also infested with red ants that feasted on the bodies of the inmates during the night. Trying to sleep was a different kind of survival battle until Alite was introduced to the makeshift remedies—creams and skin coverings—that seemed to hold the ants at bay. Alite also found the food inedible. Every meal was the same, a bucket of rice and a bucket of beans to be shared by the inmates in the block.

"The buckets were crawling with bugs," he said. "I couldn't eat it."

Emerson told him he had to. It was the only way to survive. And then he told Alite that it was important to stay strong and alert because there were other "possibilities." It was the first hint that there might be a way to maneuver in Ary Franco the same way he had maneuvered in Fairton and McKean and Allenwood. Money and connections could make things happen. Alite had the money. Emerson had the connections.

"He asked me who I would call if he could, like a magician, make a phone appear," Alite said. "He asked if I could arrange with someone to get some cash to one of the guards at a meeting outside the prison."

Alite saw that Emerson was dead serious.

"I could call someone," he said.

"Then watch, my friend," said the Red Command prisoner.

He and Alite walked casually over toward the latrine area, where the one drain hole that served as the inmates' "toilet" was located. Then Emerson signaled to another inmate, a scrawny kid named Marcello, who, Alite would learn, was one of Emerson's gofers. Marcello went back into the cell, then reappeared with his right arm covered in plastic from his hand to his shoulder.

The covering had been fashioned out of plastic trash bags, but fit more snugly. Emerson looked around, then motioned to Alite to move with him into position, blocking the view of the drain hole. Screened from any guard who might be watching, Marcello got down on his knees, reached into the hole, and after feeling his way around, lifted out a small plastic bag.

"His arm was covered with pieces of shit," Alite said. "It stunk. But inside the small plastic bag was a cell phone."

Marcello cleaned off his arm and the smaller bag, running them under water from a spigot in the corner of the room that served as the inmates' shower area. Only cold water. Inmates helped each other wash by pouring buckets of water filled from the spigot over each other. Buckets of water were also used to "flush" the drain hole.

"You had to pour a bucket into the hole first to scare the rats away," Alite said. "Then you squatted and got done as quickly as you could. The rats might come back and bite you in the ass or legs or balls if you lingered."

The rats had apparently ignored the plastic bag with the cell phone. After he retrieved and cleaned it, Marcello handed the bag to Emerson, who motioned for Alite to follow him to the shower area, a dank corner with walls of uneven concrete covered in scum. Emerson moved toward what looked like a patch of soap on the wall. Using a small Swiss Army knife, he peeled it away and from a small hole that had been hacked into the concrete he pulled out a SIM card. He placed the card in the phone and then he and Alite walked along the walls until the phone lit up. They had made a connection.

Alite made his first call from behind the bars of a Brazilian prison. He would make hundreds over the next two years, using cell phones smuggled into the prison and SIM cards that had been stashed in dozens of locations.

Initially, the calls went to a friend who brought cash and personal items—like clothing, soap, shampoo—to a guard at a prearranged meeting in Copacabana. The guard then brought the money and other items into the prison, taking a small fee for his services. The cash allowed Alite and Emerson to begin bribing other guards in order to improve their living conditions.

Emerson explained how things worked and then introduced Alite to Santana, a black Brazilian guard who would prove to be one of the inmates' staunchest allies. Santana said that anything they wanted could be obtained and brought into the prison . . . for a price. The system he and a few of his guard associates had set up was designed to circumvent a different line of corruption that had been put in place by the warden and deputy warden. The wardens were running what amounted to a black market cantina inside the prison walls, allowing inmates to smuggle cash in and then charging substantial fees for items like toiletries, snacks, vegetables, fruit, and clothing.

Emerson and Alite, through Santana and his network, bypassed the warden's cantina. Alite liked Santana immediately. He was confident and direct. In a corrupt system, he exuded a form of honesty that Alite recognized from the streets. Everyone was in the game, but not everyone was trustworthy. Santana appeared to be someone he could trust.

"If we can get what you want, we get one for you and one for us," Santana said of the smuggling operation. "For example, if you want a pizza, we buy one for you and one for us. And we add a fee that is based on the cost of the item."

Alite can laugh about it now as he describes the first "order" he and Emerson put in through Santana—two Big Macs, two large fries, one large pizza, and a six-pack of beer. Santana, like a waiter in a restaurant, wrote it all down, nodded, and said, "You'll get it when you get it."

Three hours later the order was lowered on a rope by a guard from one of the tiers above. Alite and Emerson sat alone in a patio area off the cell block stuffing themselves. Food and grease from the fries and the pizza ran down their chins as they washed what tasted like a gourmet meal down with bottles of beer. It felt exquisite, an experience comparable to sex, Alite would later say with a smile.

Two hours after their meal, he and Emerson were vomiting and dealing with severe attacks of diarrhea. But it was a price Alite was willing to pay. Slowly, with the introduction of a diversified diet of smuggled food, his system adjusted. Life was becoming bearable.

He also used the phone to call friends and have them begin lobbying for him. Through those connections he got messages home to his parents and had them make additional calls. Alite arranged for lawyers to be hired in both Tampa and Rio to begin fighting the extradition order. He also worked on having more cash sent from the States to those he trusted in Brazil. Several of those calls were made to former associates, some of whom would later claim that he threatened them and tried to extort money. Alite said he was just asking for what was his. In most cases, they were holding money he had earned through his drug dealing, gambling, or legitimate business operations. He rolls his eyes at the notion that any threat he might have made while sitting in a prison in Brazil could have been taken seriously. Alite didn't know if he was ever going to be back on the streets. Any threat he made was a hollow one, a desperate attempt to get money in order to survive. He also instructed his parents to sell his properties in New Jersey and New York in order to generate more cash.

Alite and Santana became good friends, or at least as good friends as two could become under the circumstances. They talked about their backgrounds. Santana, like Alite, had been an athlete.

And they talked about their families. Santana's ten-year-old son had broken his leg playing soccer and it was causing the guard some concern. It was an ugly break and an operation was required to set the bone properly. He worried that his son would wind up crippled. Medical services in public hospitals weren't the best, he explained. Alite wasn't sure if his new friend was looking for help or merely venting about the problem. Within days, after a few phone calls, Alite arranged for a ten-thousand-dollar payment to a private hospital where the boy's leg was properly set.

Santana couldn't thank Alite enough. But he found a way. On two different occasions, the soft-spoken prison guard would save Alite's life.

Around this time, Alite also befriended an inmate named Marco, who had been in the same cell bock. Marco spoke English. He had lived for a time in the Boston area, where he still had family. He was about to be released, but he had problems with some of the guards, who saw him as easy prey.

"He was always walking around reading the Bible," Alite said of Marco. "One day I walked into our cell and saw that two guards had him bent over a bed. They were going to rape him. I chased them away. From that point on, he was my friend."

Once he was released from prison, Marco became one of Alite's go-to guys on the streets. Having few alternatives, Alite decided to trust him and used him as a conduit for the cash that was coming down from New York and Tampa. Marco hired a top extradition attorney and served almost as a paralegal as the lawyer fought the issue through the Brazilian courts. He also, on Alite's orders, arranged to buy a car and a condo for Rose, Alite's Brazilian girlfriend.

With his cell phone access, Alite was also calling former underworld associates and lawyers, including the lawyer for Ronnie Trucchio, who was preparing for the case in Tampa. Alite had been severed from the trial because he was in Brazil. Trucchio was being represented by Joseph Corozzo, the son of mobster JoJo Corozzo.

At that point, Alite was trying to help Ronnie One-Arm and was offering Corozzo advice and information that might work in the defense against the charges. During the conversation, Alite asked Corozzo if he had been in touch with Junior Gotti, who also might have some information that would help.

"We're not sure," Alite said Corozzo responded, "but Junior may be cooperating."

CHAPTER 19

There is a price to be paid for everything that goes on inside a prison in Brazil. The highly successful smuggling operation that Alite and Emerson had set up had not gone unnoticed by other inmates, some of whom were only too happy to inform on them.

Word reached the warden. Some guards were transferred and reprimanded. It wasn't the smuggling that bothered the warden and his deputy. What bothered them was that the bribes weren't making their way into their pockets.

In the end, it always came down to money.

In this case Marcello, the errand boy and gofer for Emerson, would pay the price.

"There was no way the warden would go after Emerson, because he was with the Red Command," Alite said. "And I think he was still uncertain about me."

Alite realized that all the publicity and the talk about his American mob connections were benefits. His ties to Gotti were once again helping him maintain a position in the underworld, this time the chaotic underworld of Ary Franco.

One afternoon, two guards and two trustees came for Marcello. They told him to strip naked, then they marched him off to a dry cell in the bowels of the prison. There he was brutally beaten;

beaten so badly, in fact, that he had to be hospitalized. The word that Alite got from Santana was that Marcello was in critical condition. Alite and Emerson agreed that they had to respond. On the street, Alite's reaction would have been simple and direct. The warden or his trustees would have been beaten or shot. Violence for violence. But that wasn't an option in the prison. Alite came up with a better idea. The word went out from cell block to cell block. Everyone was to stop buying products in the warden's cantina. The warden would feel the beating of Marcello in his wallet. There was no better place to hit him.

That upped the ante considerably. The warden was enraged. And he decided, Mafioso or not, that Alite would be the next inmate taken out for some attitude adjustment. Santana was able to warn Alite in advance. Emerson came up with the idea of the knife wrapped in rags and greased with oil that was inserted in Alite's rectum.

Bomba, the burly trustee, turned out to be the warden's proxy in this now-escalating battle. Like Marcello, he was hospitalized in critical condition after Alite sliced him up. The knife fight led to an internal investigation. Guards loyal to the warden showed up at Alite's cell within the hour looking for the knife. They planned to take Alite out to a place where he would be held accountable. But another contingent of guards, sent by Santana, also jammed into the cell and began to ask pointed questions.

Why was Alite taken to a dry cell to begin with?

Who had authorized it?

Why was a trustee permitted in that cell?

Who started the fight? Who had a knife? Where is the knife? Wasn't the prisoner naked?

None of the guards sent by the warden could answer those questions and it quickly became obvious that a real investigation, which might involve the American consulate since an American inmate was one of the protagonists, would create more problems than it would solve. So the assault on the trustee Bomba was quietly ignored. Alite, as punishment, was transferred to another cell block. But within three weeks he was back with Emerson. Bribes to one of the guards who maintained the inmate rosters allowed Alite to be listed as an inmate in one section of the prison while in fact he was back in the cell block where he had started. By the time he returned, there were three more foreign prisoners in the unit: Leonardo, an Argentine with money; Camilo, a wealthy Portuguese from a prominent family; and Klaus, a tall, blond-haired international drug dealer who looked like a Viking.

Klaus's origin was Denmark. He looked familiar to Alite. All three of the foreigners were soon part of the inner circle. All were using money to bribe guards and improve their living conditions. Now food was coming in for almost every evening meal. There was also beer, and wine, and hard liquor. Videocassettes and cassette players became part of the cell block entertainment, and on occasion, when things lined up right, some friendly guards would smuggle a few prostitutes into the unit for a party. Their fee, of course, included cash and some time alone with the ladies.

The group of inmates was making the best of a bad situation, but the talk was constantly about how to get out. Bribing officials in the court and justice departments was one option that was discussed. Klaus and Camilo were able to make some contacts on the outside and "negotiations" were under way. The foreigners, Alite, Klaus, Camilo, and Leonardo, were each willing to pay $500,000 for what would amount to an authorized escape. Prison and judicial officials at the highest level would provide the phony paperwork that would allow each man to walk out of prison. After that, they'd be on their own. The problem was the officials were asking for $750,000 per prisoner.

So it wasn't a question of if an escape could be arranged but rather a matter of price.

Alite got to know all three of the new inmates, but hit it off best with Klaus. There was something about him. Then one visiting day it hit him. Klaus had said his sister and his business partner were coming to see him. Alite recognized them immediately. She was the woman with the dog in Barcelona and he was the person who helped make the contact in Senegal for his passports. With that, he also remembered the first time he had seen Klaus. Klaus was the tall, blond gambler in the Spanish casino that Mojah and Benny, George the Albanian's brother, wanted to rob.

"I couldn't believe the two of us ended up in the same prison," Alite said.

Ary Franco, despite the benefits that bribes could provide, remained a volatile environment. The warden or deputy warden would order periodic "shakedowns." Guards wearing masks and carrying rifles or machine guns would come through the cell blocks, order all of the inmates to strip naked, and them march them out into the yard.

"They'd spend hours searching and turning the cells upside down," Alite said. "And while that was going on, we had to sit in the yard, our heads down, and wait. It could be ninety degrees or it could be pouring rain. We had to stay there. Anyone who lifted his head up would get cracked. Sometimes it would begin in the morning and wouldn't end till it was dark. If you had to shit or piss, you did it right there. Sometimes instead of the yard, they would take all of us to a room, like a warehouse. There'd be over a thousand inmates. They covered the windows, so it was pitch black and we'd have to just stand in line. Same thing. It would be hours and guys would be relieving themselves right where they stood."

Alite said his Brazilian lawyer would visit occasionally and one time he was accompanied by a Florida attorney who had been hired by Alite's family.

"They told me they were afraid to come into the prison," Alite said. "They said they didn't like it there. I say, 'Try living here.'"

Jealousy and greed, not unlike what Alite had seen around the Gottis, was also part of this new underworld. A "riot" in another section of the prison ended with the warden being shot and killed. Alite and Emerson later learned that the deputy warden had set it all up and that the shooting was actually a hit carried out on the deputy's orders. He apparently wanted to move up the ladder. A new warden, a former military officer, lasted just a few months. He was gunned down on the street while walking with two body guards and his young daughter. Word again came that the deputy warden, who now was placed in charge of the prison, had ordered and paid for the assassination.

The first order of business for the deputy warden, now the top dog, was to bring the foreigners in line. Guards appeared at their cell and ordered a strip search. When they found nothing, one of them threw a bag of cocaine on Camilo's bed and another guard "discovered" the contraband. As they moved to take Camilo into custody, Alite jumped in front and punched the guard. In return, he took a rifle butt to the face. Several of his front teeth were shattered. In the fight that followed, he pummeled one of the guards and took the rifle away from another. The guards retreated, but a large contingent came back a short time later.

Emerson "negotiated" a settlement, agreeing to turn over the rifle in exchange for a promise that no one would be taken out of the cell and punished. The warden's guards agreed, but after they left, Emerson told Alite that they would be back.

"He's full of shit," he said of the guard who had promised there would be no retribution.

The next day Alite and Camilo were stripped and taken to the dry cell. This time Alite had no knife with which to defend himself, but Santana and another contingent of guards were able to intervene. An uneasy peace was established, but the new warden made it clear: he wanted Alite out of his prison.

The extradition process was continuing. Alite was buoyed when his local attorney won a first round in the Brazilian courts, but was stunned to learn that that same court, in an unusual—his lawyer said unprecedented—move, had agreed to reconsider the issue when a superseding indictment was handed up in Tampa.

The case in Florida was a hybrid that made little sense. The alleged racketeering conspiracy included robberies and extortions in the Tampa area, allegations, for example, that Alite and his associates had used threats and force to take over a valet parking business that provided services for restaurants, hospitals, and strip clubs. But the case also detailed murders and attempted murders in New York and robberies in New York, New Jersey, and Pennsylvania carried out by a Gambino crime family crew controlled by Ronnie Trucchio and Alite.

Trucchio and three codefendants went on trial in October 2006. Alite, who was still grappling with his own extradition issues, writing letters to the American consulate complaining about the corrupt prison system and planning an escape if the extradition was upheld, followed the trial as best he could from afar. He was in cell phone contact with someone at least once a week, sometimes more often. He spoke with Trucchio's lawyer, Joseph Corozzo, as the trial drew closer. Alite told Corozzo that he should use a defense that implied that Alite was responsible. But he never expected what happened. Trucchio got permission to make his own opening statement to the jury because Corozzo was tied up in a case in New York. He threw everything on Alite, blaming him for the shakedowns, the robberies, the murders and assaults. All were carried out or orchestrated by the missing defendant, he told the jury.

"I have no idea why I'm here," Trucchio said.

Making his own opening statement was a clever way for Ronnie One-Arm to speak directly to the jury without facing the rigors of cross-examination that would come if he testified in his own defense. Alite figured the opening statement had been cleared by Joseph Corozzo and, by extension, had been run past both JoJo and Nicky Corozzo in New York. Trucchio's comments, looked at from where Alite was sitting, were tantamount to cooperating. He was putting all of the crimes on Alite.

That it didn't work with the jury was of little consequence.

Borrowing a page from Gotti Sr.'s media handbook, Alite decided to fight back. He called a reporter at the *Tampa Bay Times* who was covering the trial. She published an exclusive interview with Alite on November 2, 2006. Alite would later acknowledge from the witness stand that he lied repeatedly to the reporter. Among other things he was quoted as saying, "I'm not the person they're making me out to be. . . . Was I friends with John Gotti? Yes. Am I friends now? No."

But he said he was being truthful when he told her that the extortion charge involving his valet parking company, Prestige Parking, was bogus and built around phony allegations from two business partners who were trying to steal the company from him. In fact, a civil suit filed in federal court in Tampa laid out what Alite said was his claim to ownership and detailed how his partners had conspired to rob him. But Alite was the mobster, not the men he was suing, and Alite believes that played a role in the litigation, which to this day rankles him.

"They robbed me of my company," he said, "and the government helped them do it."

He also told the reporter that while he might have shouted and screamed during the dispute over the valet business, he never intended to hurt anyone.

"I've got a big mouth," he said in the article. "When I yell, I yell. But I'm not a violent person."

That, of course, was a lie. Shootings, beatings with pipes and baseball bats, and stabbings were the way Alite did business. And he would later admit to all of that. But he continues to insist that that was not the way he established and expanded his valet parking operation in Florida.

As 2006 was drawing to a close, Alite was completing his second full year in Brazilian custody. His struggle to survive had shattered his faith in Cosa Nostra. He wanted to believe in the fiction that the Mafia was an organization built on honor and loyalty and that he was a part of it. But when he was being honest with himself, he knew that wasn't true. That, of course, led to more troubling questions. How far would he go and how much would he give up to protect that organization?

Later in the month of November he was abruptly transferred from Ary Franco to Bangu, another federal prison on the outskirts of Rio. Still using his connections with some of the guards, he had a chance to escape during the prison transport.

"They wanted two hundred thousand dollars," he said. "One of the guards said they were ready to stage a phony ambush and claim that I had escaped. But I had to come up with the money immediately."

Alite used a cell phone to call Marco, but his friend didn't answer. Marco was holding more than six hundred thousand dollars of Alite's money at the time. In a desperate alternative, he asked the guards to drive to his lawyer's office. One of the guards went inside to explain the situation to the lawyer. The attorney said he could only come up with fifty thousand dollars on short notice, but would write a note for the rest of the cash, which would be available the next day.

"The guards said it was now or never," Alite said as he talked of his missed opportunity to "escape from hell." When the cash wasn't forthcoming, they continued the drive to Bangu, a sprawling penitentiary complex that was considered as bad, if not worse, then Ary Franco.

"Bangu was not supposed to be for foreign prisoners," he said. "I think I was the first one sent there. The day after I left Ary Franco a riot broke out there [at Ary Franco]. This was at a time when there was all kinds of street violence and retribution. Police were killing innocent kids in the favelas and cops were being shot at on the streets. A journalist we had spoken to was killed after he wrote about the prison conditions and another American, a guy from Washington, D.C., was shot and killed during the riots inside Ary Franco. I had nothing to do with any of that, but they tried to blame me for it. When I got to Bangu, they were waiting."

Alite was greeted by a warden and several guards who stripped him and administered a beating. He was then taken to the hole, solitary confinement, where he remained for several days. But Santana and the Red Command also had influence at Bangu and within forty-eight hours a guard had smuggled him a cell phone. Desperate calls followed and bribes were paid. To the warden's surprise, an order came down within two weeks transferring the "gringo" to Campo Grande, a prison camp in Mato Grosso do Sul, a state in the southwest corner of Brazil on the border with Paraguay. Campo Grande was like the minimum security prison in Allenwood, but with better weather. The inmates, for the most part, were wealthy and politically connected. It was confinement, but with less brutality and not as much stench. The warden was happy to take Alite's cash.

"Marco made most of the payments," Alite said of his friend on the outside. "It cost forty thousand dollars to get me into Campo Grande. We paid another ten thousand for a private cell on the third floor and ten thousand more to have a hole cut in the wall and an air-conditioning unit installed."

Alite also paid a thousand dollars for a conjugal visit with his girlfriend Rose.

"It wasn't a bad place, but I didn't intend to stay," he said. "The air conditioner was installed because I wanted a hole in the wall. I was planning on going out that way. The idea was to get into Paraguay and then make my way to Venezuela. I was depending on Marco and the money he was holding."

But Marco apparently decided his friendship wasn't as valuable as the cash. After helping pave Alite's way to Campo Grande, he effectively disappeared along with the rest of Alite's money.

"I had no one else I could trust," he said. "I didn't want to put Rose in that position. Marco was loyal almost to the end. But when we didn't win the extradition battles in court I think he just figured I'd be sent back to the States and he could pocket the money."

Before Alite could make a break from Campo Grande, the courts in Brazil approved the extradition request of the U.S. Justice Department. On December 24, 2006, John Alite was flown back to Tampa to face the same charges that had resulted in Ronnie Trucchio's conviction and eventual sentence of life in prison.

The trip back to Tampa was in a private jet, a Gulfstream, which Alite figured was at the service of either Interpol or the Justice Department. Once in Florida, he was informed that the U.S. Attorney's Office there was prepared to move forward with a trial that could result in life in prison or the death sentence.

Alite, in one of several angry discussions with the lawyer his family had hired, lashed out at the attorney and the U.S. government. He said he had asked the lawyer to negotiate a deal with the prosecutors in New York. He was willing to plead out and accept a twenty-two-year sentence. But he was not going to cooperate.

Alite, based on what he had been told by his Brazilian lawyer, thought the most time he could face was thirty years. That was the maximum sentence for his charges had they been brought under

Brazilian law and his understanding was that if Brazil agreed to his extradition, which it had done, he could only be sentenced to that maximum penalty. He figured twenty-two years was a strong negotiating point if thirty was the max. But he said he doesn't believe his lawyer ever made the call to New York.

Over the next several weeks, as he was transported from one holding facility to another around the state of Florida, Alite came to realize that "everybody was out to fuck me." What's more, he quickly sized up his situation and saw that Tampa and New York were fighting over who had the rights to the case.

It was classic organized crime versus disorganized law enforcement. And it was one of the reasons, he believes, that Junior Gotti ultimately was able to walk away. The case, in Alite's mind, should have been handled by New York, not Tampa. He said he was subsequently told that Tampa had reneged on an agreement to allow New York to take the case if and when Alite was extradited.

The friction between the two jurisdictions continued over the next two years.

Shortly after being brought back, Alite began to get access to the case documents and quickly realized that dozens of associates had given him up. Years later he would compile a list of those who cooperated against him. There were fifty-three names on two handwritten pages.

He wondered what he was doing and why. Meanwhile, Tampa authorities tried to keep him off balance.

"They kept moving me around," Alite said, "giving me the diesel treatment [a prison expression used to describe a technique in which an inmate is shuttled from one facility to another, usually in an attempt to unsettle him or make him uncomfortable; the mode of transport is a bus that runs on diesel fuel]. Every three days I'm moved. I can't settle in anywhere. I've got nothing to read. And I can't find out what's going on."

A month into the treatment, he was transported to a lockup in Hillsborough. In the cell block was a leader of the Disciples, a Chicago street gang.

"He was a smart guy, very well-spoken," Alite said. "And he told me I didn't get it."

The Chicago gangster had heard of Alite and knew some of his story. The prison grapevine in Florida had broadcast Alite's arrival and followed up with news about who he was and what he had done.

"You're still alive because you were smart and were able to stay ten steps ahead of the guys you were dealing with," he told Alite. "But the game has changed. Everybody's deserted you. They're gonna be laughing while you sit in prison for the rest of your life. You better get with it."

The next day, Alite said, he called his new lawyer, Caroline Tesche, and told her to make a deal. He was ready to talk. Tesche, who later was appointed a judge, set the process in place. When she was appointed to the bench, Timothy Fitzgerald, another Tampa defense attorney, took over the case.

"They were both good to me," Alite said of Tesche and Fitzgerald. "I owe them a lot."

In March 2007 Alite met with federal authorities at the first of what would be dozens of debriefings. This was the initial proffer session where he and his attorney laid out what he would bring to the witness stand. It was a complete package that detailed everything he had been involved in for the Gambino crime family beginning in 1983. The "highlights" included the drug trafficking and the murders of George Grosso and John Gebert.

The meetings continued as Alite was placed in a witness security unit of a local holding facility. He would be brought to meetings and asked questions by prosecutors from Tampa and, eventually, from New York. The alliance between the two juris-dictions seemed fragile at best, and on more than one occasion, Alite said, hostilities broke out. In one of those meetings, an FBI agent from New York almost got into a fight with an agent from Tampa.

"They had to be separated," Alite said.

At several others, the New York team stayed in one room and the Tampa team stayed in another. Notes were passed back and forth, he said, with each posing different questions he was sup-posed to answer. Alite frankly admits he was more comfortable with the New York group and also acknowledges that he knew he had a better chance at a decent sentence if his case were moved there. But it was not to be.

Alite entered his guilty plea in federal court in Tampa on Jan-uary 16, 2008. He was facing a potential life sentence. His coop-eration would be noted at sentencing, authorities told the judge in the case, but no promises had been made.

On July 24, 2008, an indictment was handed up under seal charging John A. Gotti with racketeering, drug dealing, and murder. He was identified as a leader of the Gambino crime family. The indictment charged that at different times Gotti was part of a "ruling panel" that ran the organization for his jailed father and he was the crime family's "defacto boss."

Gotti was arrested on August 5, 2008, and brought to Tampa, where he was arraigned and ordered held without bail. Unlike Alite, he was eventually able to have the case moved to New York, where a dozen other wiseguys, including Charles Carneglia, had been indicted in a separate racketeering case based on informa-tion Alite had provided.

Everyone in the Carneglia case except Charles pleaded out. Both he and Junior Gotti decided to square off against the feds and their star witness in federal court in Brooklyn. The cases were set to begin in 2009.

Alite said he was "a little nervous" when he first testified against Carneglia but that he "couldn't wait" to get on the stand in the Gotti case. Carneglia was convicted and is currently doing life. But in retrospect that was just a preliminary on the fight card.

Alite versus Gotti was the main event.

CHAPTER 20

The trial, which began with jury selection on September 14, 2009, was part criminal justice, part Jerry Springer. And the media was all over it.

The setting was the federal courthouse in lower Manhattan. U.S. District Judge P. Kevin Castel presided. The prosecution team was made up of Assistant U.S. Attorneys Elie Honig and Steven Kwok from the Southern District of New York, Assistant U.S. Attorney Jay Trezevant from the Tampa office, and FBI Agent Ted Otto, who was based in New York and who, much to the chagrin of his FBI counterparts in Florida, correctly was considered the lead investigator in the case.

The defense was headed by Charles F. Carnesi, who was assisted by John C. Meringolo.

After an anonymous jury panel had been chosen, opening statements by the prosecution and defense were delivered on September 21. Eight days later, after testimony from law enforcement witnesses and several other mob cooperators, Alite took the stand. He was brought into court dressed in a gray prison jumpsuit and wearing prison-issue sneakers. He wanted to appear in street clothes—a shirt and slacks, maybe a sport coat or a sweater— but the prosecutors said that wasn't a good idea. They wanted to convey to the jury that Alite was a prisoner, that he was in custody, that he wasn't getting some sweetheart deal for his cooperation.

Alite thought jurors came away with a different impression.

"They thought I was an animal," he said.

It was just another in a long line of disagreements he had with the authorities as the case moved toward trial. Sometimes, during pre-trial debriefing sessions, he would shout and scream. At other times he would just roll his eyes or shake his head. From Alite's perspective, the prosecutors had locked themselves into versions of events provided by cooperating witnesses who had come on board before Alite agreed to testify. In fact, he says he felt he had to "tailor" his story to fit theirs so that what went before the jury was consistent. As a result, Alite believes, the truth sometimes got lost in the telling. In this instance, he just wanted to get on the stand, so he accepted their argument that prison garb was the way to go.

Junior, on the other hand, appeared in court each day prepped out for the jury. On most days he'd be in a business suit, shirt, and tie. Other times it was a sport jacket, shirt, tie, and slacks. His stylish glasses added to the look. He was almost professorial. It was all part of the pitch to the jury that he wasn't a gangster anymore, that he had left the mob in 1999, and that while, yes, he had done some bad things, he had already paid a price with a seventy-seven-month prison sentence. He had broken with his father and wasn't part of the Gambino organization anymore. His lawyer would argue that his name was still a lighting rod that attracted both federal prosecutors looking for a big notch in their guns as well as cooperating witnesses who saw testifying against Gotti as a get-out-of-jail-free card.

Carnesi underlined all of that with a brief but pointed opening statement depicting his client's break with La Cosa Nostra.

"As a young man he looked at his father and saw some charisma and power and was seduced by a certain type of personality,"

Carnesi said. "In the mid-1990s that seduction lost its attraction to him because in the mid-1990s he was starting to grow into a man himself and he started to understand what this was really all about. And even though he was at the very top of that organization, he wanted out.

"Why?" the lawyer asked rhetorically. "Because, you will learn, it was an organization that was based on treachery. It was an organization where more often than not, your best friend suddenly became a threat to you. It was an organization where in fact there was no true loyalty."

John A. Gotti, the defense attorney said, finally saw life in the mob for what it was. And he decided he had had enough.

Carnesi's description of mob life may have been the only thing on which he and Alite agreed. The defense, of course, was portraying Alite and nearly a dozen other cooperating witnesses as the ones who were treacherous. Alite in particular fit the description of the "best friend" who had turned on Junior Gotti, according to the defense's version of the story.

It was, from where Alite was sitting, yet another example of Junior Gotti taking some facts and spinning them to his advantage. The mob, especially the Gambino organization, was the treacherous viper pit described by Carnesi. But it had become that because of Gotti and his father and his uncles. They made millions as a result and Junior was still living off that money and enjoying his position as a mob leader. That was what Alite believed. Convincing a jury would be one of the keys to winning the case.

Carnesi's comments came after Honig had blistered Gotti in his introductory address. The federal prosecutor outlined the three counts that formed the case and provided details about dozens of the allegations, including the gutting of Danny Silva and Gotti's return to the murder scene to mock the dying man as he bled out. While the Danny Silva stabbing at the Silver Fox wasn't a specific charge, it was included as one of the criminal acts in the broad RICO conspiracy count that topped the indictment. The drug dealing, sports betting, extortion, and the murders of Louie DiBono, George Grosso, and Bruce Gotterup were also part of that sweeping charge. Two other counts focused specifically on the drug-related murders of Grosso and Gotterup. Both murders, the indictment alleged, had been ordered by John A. Gotti. Honig painted a picture of Gotti as a "vicious and violent street criminal" who rose to the top of the Gambino crime family.

Honig also talked about the witnesses, including Alite, who would testify for the government. They were part of Gotti's organization and they were criminals, he said. The issue with the witnesses, he told the jury, was credibility.

"I will tell you right up front, you are going to hear things about these cooperating witnesses that you don't like," the prosecutor said. "And you shouldn't like. They are criminals. That is why the defendant had them around him in the first place. You will be called on to decide not whether these cooperating witnesses are likeable, but whether they are believable."

The openings set the stage for what followed, at least what followed in the courtroom. But there was another stage, the media stage, on which the trial also played out. Headlines trumpeted the most sensational testimony on any given day and spectators and family members were often sought out for comment.

Alite spent seven days on the stand, first providing his story under questioning from Trezevant, whose involvement in the trial was part of the compromise worked out between the two warring federal jurisdictions. Everyone wanted a piece of the action and what they anticipated would be their share of the glory. Trezevant questioned Alite for the better part of five days. Then Alite spent parts of two more verbally sparring with Carnesi, Junior's defense attorney.

Gotti's mother, Victoria, was a regular in the courtroom every day. Other family members, including his sister, Vicky, were frequent spectators.

After Alite testified that he had had "feelings" for Vicky and said she had had the same for him, she told reporters, "The only feelings I have for John Alite were that I despised him." Alite continues to take the high road on the Vicky issue. He says that both he and she know what really happened and that it doesn't really matter what anyone else thinks or says. He said he opted not to go into detail about the *Fatal Attraction* scenario that he says is the most accurate description of their relationship. Vicky vehemently denies having any sort of relationship with Alite, fatal or otherwise.

While Vicky Gotti was clearly upset over Alite's testimony and publicly denied his allegations, she nevertheless saw a way to capitalize on the high-profile case. Her memoir, *This Family of Mine*, was published on September 29, 2009, and was in all the city's bookstores as the headlines screamed about the trial.

Alite's stories about corrupt cops also brought angry responses even before he got on the stand. His allegations had surfaced in an FBI report that made its way to reporters prior to the start of the trial. Among other things, Alite alleged two high-profile police officers, Joe Coffey and Bo Dietl, had at different times provided Gotti Sr. or members of his crew with tips and information. The two retired celebrity law enforcement veterans blasted away at Alite, denying the allegations. Coffey, who was considered one of the city's top mob busters, called it "bullshit." Dietl said Alite was a "fucking liar" and "a punk" and said he wanted to take the stand to denounce him.

Every day, it seemed, there were new revelations and accompanying headlines. When Alite testified about all the money he said he and Gotti had earned and about the lifestyle it allowed him to live, the *New York Post* blared: GOODFELLA LIVED LARGE. The story went on to detail Alite's claim that he had earned between $50 million and $75 million for the Gambino organization; that about $10 million had gone into his own pocket and that another $6 million or $7 million more went to Junior Gotti. The cash, Alite said, allowed him to buy fancy cars, expensive Brioni suits, Bruno Magli shoes, and Rolex watches.

The *London Observer* checked in with a story a few days later that included this explanatory subhead: AMERICA IS GRIPPED BY A REAL-LIFE SOPRANOS TALE OF BRUTAL MURDERS AND HIGH LIVING. The piece went on to describe the case as "the Mafia trial to end all Mafia trials."

Alite knew about the buzz the case was creating, but he tried to stay focused. He didn't really care about the headlines. What mattered, he knew, was what the jury thought. He viewed taking the stand as his opportunity to publicly "out" Junior Gotti for the punk and lowlife that he was. It was his chance to put the lie to the Gotti myth. And to do that, he had to convince the jury that he was telling the truth.

His approach was simple and direct. Whenever he was asked a question, he said, he answered honestly. He never tried to sugarcoat anything. And very often he admitted to even more than what he was asked about.

On direct examination, when a federal prosecutor asked him how many people he had shot, he responded, "Me personally? I shot about thirty-five guys. I was involved in probably forty-five shootings. Ten of those I wasn't the shooter."

And when he was asked if, in his plea deal, he had confessed to all his crimes, he answered, "It's impossible. I can't even remember them all."

He also offered quips and asides that he hoped would provide a human side for the jury to consider. Early on his second day on the stand he was asked about the money Johnny Gebert made selling drugs and about a vacation he and Gebert had taken to Puerto Rico in the 1980s. Gebert had paid for the entire trip. Alite was asked if Gebert was making enough money at that time to finance that kind of trip.

"He was making enough money to finance this whole room to go to Puerto Rico," Alite replied.

At another point, when there were questions about Claudia, the woman he lived with for twenty-five years and with whom he had had two sons, he corrected the prosecutor and said she was his "wife" even though they had never been married.

Then he shrugged and looked toward the jury.

"I better call her my wife or I'm gonna be in trouble," he said almost shyly.

Throughout his testimony, Alite came back again and again to the hypocrisy that was the Gotti organization and to the rules of leadership that applied only if the Gottis wanted them to apply and only if the rules didn't affect their ability to make money.

"The life is treachery," he said, unknowingly echoing the opening statement of Carnesi. "John Gotti Jr. [and] his family taught me this life."

Cross-examination by Carnesi led to some fireworks on the stand and, on one occasion, in the courtroom itself. The defense attorney, who in his closing would tell the jury that Alite was the "centerpiece" of the government's case, spent two days trying to discredit the star witness. He hammered away at Alite's criminal history, implying that it was even worse than what he had admitted to. Alite said he wasn't trying to hide anything but that there was no way he could possibly remember everything he had done.

"I committed crimes every day of my life for twenty-five years," he said. "I didn't keep a scorecard."

And while he admitted to most of the crimes that Carnesi

added to the government litany, he clashed with the defense attorney when Carnesi implied that it was Alite who had strangled a woman in a motel after having sex with her. That, Alite said, was an outright lie. It was Vinny Gotti, he told the jury. Everyone knew it. He then went on to explain the background and the events surrounding the murder, as they were told to him by an associate of Vinny Gotti and later by Junior Gotti.

Alite saw the move to link him to the unsolved motel murder as a desperate attempt by the defense to further undermine his credibility with the jury. There was not one shred of evidence linking him to the crime. Everyone knew that Vinny Gotti was responsible, Alite said again.

With the jury already out of the room for a break in that testimony, and as Alite was stepping down from the stand, he says Junior Gotti smirked and mouthed the words "We're gonna kill you."

Alite, flanked by two federal marshals, angrily replied, "You got something you want to say to me?"

With that, Gotti went into a rant.

"You're a dog!" he screamed, according to news accounts in the papers the next day. "You're a dog! Did I kill little girls, you fag? You're a punk. You're a dog all your life. You always were. Did I strangle little girls in motels?"

Alite was hustled out of the courtroom by the marshals. Before the jury was brought back and the trial resumed, Gotti was admonished by the judge for his outburst. He apologized. Later Alite said he was glad the judge got to see the real Junior Gotti. He wished the jury had also had that opportunity.

The outburst made little sense. Who was the "little girl" that Gotti was screaming about? While the motel strangulation was a horrible crime, the victim was a woman in her twenties. Both Gotti and Alite knew that.

The day after the outburst, the New York *Daily News* headline screamed: CHAOS IN THE COURTROOM; JUNIOR GOTTI RIPS MOB TURNCOAT DURING BREAK IN TESTIMONY.

The incident occurred during Alite's seventh day on the stand and the reporters for the *Daily News,* Alison Gendar and Larry McShane, wrote a classic opening line to their story. "And on the seventh day he lost it" was their lead before going on to detail Junior Gotti's verbal confrontation with his chief accuser.

Victoria Gotti, Junior's mother, came to her son's defense and tried to promote the defense's claim that Alite had strangled the woman in the motel room, not her brother-in-law. In typical Gotti fashion, she ignored the threat made by her son and focused instead on his accuser.

"Alite is a pathological liar," she was quoted as saying in a *New York Post* story the next day, "a rat caught in a proverbial trap, caught in his own lies, and he lashed out."

Never mind that it was her son who provoked the incident. Gotti's rules continued to apply even during the trial.

"I think he was just desperate," Alite said several years later as he recounted the incident. "I tried to compose myself after we first shouted at one another. He just went off. To me, it was just another example of John Gotti being the coward that he always was. He thought he was losing the case and he was taking a cheap shot at me. Anyone who knows the two of us knows that if we were together in a room with no one else around, he'd never act like that or say those kinds of things. He'd be afraid of what I would do to him. But he knew I couldn't do anything so he played the tough guy. The next day or the day after, I forget which, the trial started a little late because Junior apparently didn't want to come out of his cell. He was frustrated and scared."

Of all the lies and half-truths that were thrown around by the defense, Alite said, the implication that he was somehow involved in the motel murder is the one that still bothers him.

"I know the woman's brother," he said. "He knows what happened. Everybody does."

Then, in an explanation that his therapist has no doubt heard many times, Alite tried to give perspective to his violent criminal history. Anyone he killed, he said, was in the life, part of the underworld. Everyone who got involved knew the potential consequences. But Alite said he never killed "an innocent person" and never killed women. Street justice, he said, should have taken care of Vinny Gotti when law enforcement couldn't.

"He should have been killed for what he did," Alite said. "I think the only reason he wasn't was because his name was Gotti."

Alite finished testifying on October 8. The trial would run for another month and a half. Kevin McMahon, Peter Zuccaro, Joe O'Kane, young Pete Gotti, and Tim Donovan were among the witnesses called by the defense. All were used to refute parts of Alite's testimony and to put a positive spin for the defense on other things Alite had said. One example: Alite had testified that Gotti had shot McMahon during an angry dispute. McMahon acknowledged he had been shot, but said it was an accident.

Joe O'Kane claimed he was the shooter of Ciro Perrone's nephew during the fight at the Arena, not Junior; that Genie Foster had been beaten by Alite, but not on Junior's orders, and that Junior was "respected" in the neighborhood and "despised" those who used or sold drugs.

On cross O'Kane, who was then serving a life sentence on murder charges tied to the Vito Guzzo crew, admitted that he had been part of a plot to kill Alite for Guzzo. Peter Gotti, Junior's younger brother, refuted the Johnny Gongs story. But during cross-examination, he acknowledged that when he visited his brother in prison, Junior had bragged about beating Jodi Albanese and her boyfriend. Peter Gotti, however, testified that he knew nothing about the boyfriend being brutalized in a basement by Alite. And Donovan, as he had in Tampa, described how Alite and others had forced him out of the valet business. Only this time he was testifying for the defense, not the prosecution.

The issue of Gotti quitting the mob was also the focus of evidence and testimony.

The government played tapes recorded at Ray Brook in 2003 and 2004 in which, prosecutors said, Gotti could be heard complaining about the fact that his uncle Peter and others had taken over the leadership of the crime family and had demoted him to the rank of capo. On one tape he was heard promising to bust their heads once he got out.

The questions that those tapes presented to the jury were clear: If Junior Gotti had really quit the mob in 1999, why would he care about being demoted in 2003? If he was no longer a part of the organization, then how could he have a rank?

The defense countered with the taped conversation of Junior's meeting with his father in Marion, the tape where he said he wanted out. He wanted "closure." The defense also offered part of a government document, an FBI 302 in which an informant—identified only as "individual"—provided details about a meeting in 2006 in which then Colombo family boss John "Sonny" Franzese signed off on a plan to kill Gotti Jr. Franzese told the informant that unnamed leaders of the Gambino organization whom he referred to as the "Howard Beach Crew" had sought his approval for the murder of Junior Gotti.

Carnesi read a part of that 302 for the jury and entered it as evidence.

"On April 3, 2006, individual met with John 'Sonny' Franzese at a restaurant named Bahama Momma's in Northport, Long Island. One of Franzese's nephews was also present. Individual advised that he had previously met with the same nephew at a Dunkin' Donuts several months ago to talk about a painting contract. During the course of the conversation Franzese advised that he had recently met with the Howard Beach Crew (Gambino Cosa Nostra Family) regarding John, Jr. (John Gotti Jr.). Franzese stated that they were very upset about his recent behavior and noted that there is no such thing as quitting the mob. They believed that John Jr. has millions of dollars stashed and that he can't do time. Franzese advised the individual that he gave his consent to kill John, Jr. if they thought it was necessary. Franzese told the individual that the guys from Howard Beach Crew are crazy."

The themes never changed. It was always murder, money, and betrayal. Had Junior "stashed millions"? And were unidentified members of his own crime family—perhaps his uncles—plotting to kill him? There were, of course, no answers. But the document gave the jury something else to ponder and may have helped the "I quit the mob" defense. This was Junior as a target and a potential victim.

Franzese, now in his nineties and back in jail, has long been identified as a throwback, a real gangster, a "man's man," says a mob associate who served time with him in prison in Milan, Michigan. But there is also this somewhat ironic twist to the Franzese piece of the Gotti Jr. story. His own son Michael Franzese, a one-time capo in the Colombo family, allegedly became a cooperator in the late 1980s. He has since turned his role as a Mafia turncoat into an occupation, writing books and giving lectures (for a fee) about his life of crime and his decision to walk away. The title of Michael Franzese's first book? *Quitting the Mob.*

Jury deliberations began on November 11 and encompassed about ten days in total over a three-week period. The anonymously chosen panel had weekends off. There were a few other breaks and an extended five-day hiatus during the Thanksgiving holiday. One of the first notes from a juror came out even before deliberations had begun. The note writer, identified only as Juror #6, asked a favor of Judge Castel. The juror wrote: "Dear Judge Castel, as you know I'm currently unemployed. By serving on this jury I have missed numerous opportunities for employment. I would greatly appreciate if you could please write me a letter of recommendation . . . stating that I have been serving on the lengthy, high-profile John Gotti Jr. trial. This would greatly enhance my chances for future employment."

Judge Castel said he would consider the request after the trial had ended.

Everyone, it seemed, was looking to cash in on the case.

The panel of twelve would arrive each morning at around ten to start the deliberation process. They would usually leave by 5 P.M. The first sign of problems surfaced on November 19 when the foreman sent Castel a note that read: "Unable to reach a unanimous verdict as to counts one, two and three." After consulting with the lawyers and getting a clarification from the foreman that there was no agreement on any of the three counts, the judge urged the panel to continue.

Five days later, on November 24, at around 3 P.M., the foreman sent another note:

"We are unable to reach a unanimous verdict on count one. We are unable to reach a unanimous verdict on count two. We are unable to reach a unanimous verdict on count three."

The judge called the jury in and again urged them to continue trying. The next day he recessed the trial for the Thanksgiving holiday. Deliberations resumed on December 1, 2009. At 3:10 that afternoon the foreman sent what would be the panel's final note:

"Judge Castel, we cannot reach a unanimous decision on any count; we are deadlocked. There is not one member of the jury who believes that we can reach a unanimous verdict on any count."

With that, Castel declared a hung jury and a mistrial. The Gotti camp went wild. A tie was almost as good as a win. Gotti had now faced down federal authorities four times since 2005. All four cases had ended with hung juries. The evidence and testimony just wasn't strong enough to convince all twelve members of any of those four panels.

One of the first things that Carnesi did was move for bail. Junior had been held since the indictment was handed down in Tampa more than a year earlier. Castel granted the request. John A. Gotti Jr. was released later that afternoon on a $2 million bond. As he exited the courthouse, he was swarmed by reporters.

"I want to go home and see my children," he said according to the media reports from that day. "There's a very good chance, thank God, I'm going to have a healthy and happy Christmas with my family."

Four of the jurors agreed to meet with the media to discuss the case. All four remained anonymous and it appeared all four had voted to acquit. According to the stories that appeared in the newspapers the next day, the panel had voted 6–5 with one member undecided to convict Junior Gotti of the RICO charge that topped the indictment. But, the jurors said, the votes had been 7–5 and 6–5 with one undecided to acquit Gotti of the drug-related murders of Grosso and Gotterup.

One juror, according to a report in *Newsday,* also said "the whole jury agreed" that John Alite was the least credible of the government witnesses. The jurors, when questioned, also said they thought the government should not retry Gotti Jr. again.

Enough is enough, they said.

FOR FOURTH TIME, MISTRIAL IN PROSECUTION OF GOTTI said the headline in the *New York Times* the following day. The piece, written by Alan Feuer, said all that needed to be said in the very first paragraph, which noted that for the fourth time in four years a federal jury had failed "to reach a verdict in the epic prosecution of John A. Gotti, enshrining him as a legendary criminal defendant and a mobster even trickier to convict than his father."

John J. Gotti had beaten the feds repeatedly in court, earning the nickname the Teflon Don. But he couldn't beat the feds the last time they came at him and subsequently died in prison. John A. Gotti, who fought the feds to a draw in four straight cases, was going home instead of to prison. On January 14, 2010, he learned that he would not have to square off against prosecutors for a fifth time.

"In light of the circumstances, the Government has decided not to proceed with the prosecution against John A. Gotti," Preet Bharara, the U.S. attorney for the Southern District of New York, said in a brief statement announcing that his office had decided not to retry the racketeering-murder case.

Alite learned of the hung jury while being held in the Metropolitan Correctional Center in Manhattan, not far from the courthouse. He took it in stride. A short time later, he was transported back to Florida to await his own sentencing. That's where he learned Junior would not be retried. There was nothing more he could do. If the feds didn't want to go back into court, then both he and Junior Gotti would get on with the rest of their lives.

"A mistrial is actually a failure in the process," Judge Castel had said in the midst of jury deliberations. "It's not a verdict."

The bottom line, said Alite, is that half the jury voted to convict Gotti.

Johhn Alite was formally sentenced before U.S. District Judge Susan Bucklew on April 27, 2011, in Tampa. Federal prosecutors from both the New York and Florida offices wrote letters praising his "extraordinary" and "substantial" cooperation while asking the judge to depart downward from a sentencing guideline range that at the top would have called for a life sentence.

Alite had pleaded guilty to racketeering—murder charges, admitting his role in four murders, two attempted murders, drug dealing, assaults, gambling, and extortion.

During the sentencing, his Florida lawyer Timothy Fitzgerald recalled that the judge read two impassioned letters sent to her by the daughters of George Grosso and John Gebert, whose murders Alite had confessed to. The letters seemed to carry some weight with the judge, Fitzgerald said. But then he interjected. Grosso and Gebert had tried to kill Alite first, the lawyer told Bucklew. The only reason they were dead and Alite was standing before her was that Alite was a better shot.

Asked by the judge, prosecutors confirmed that was in fact the case.

Like everything else surrounding the John Alite story, the weight you give to facts depends on your perspective.

John Alite was sentenced to ten years in prison. He already

had close to six years in. He was released in the spring of 2012. He opted not to go into the Witness Security Program and has instead returned to New Jersey, where he lives and where he is trying to make a living. He sees a therapist once a week and still struggles sometimes to control himself. Violence was so much a part of his life for so long that he calls it "an addiction." But he says he recognizes that he has to go in another direction.

He is happy to be back around his two sons, John and Matt, and has a cordial, if sometimes strained, relationship with their mother, Claudia. He is estranged from his first wife, Carol. "She hates me," he said. "And I'm not that crazy about her." And he is struggling to work his way back into the lives of their two children, Jimmy and Chelsea.

Alite has several business ventures that he is trying to develop and is still close to many of the friends he had when he was on the streets. He clearly is still rankled by the perception that he was "chased" from his Queens neighborhood by Gotti and his associates. In fact, he has been back there several times since his release from prison. Twice he was accompanied by camera crews. Late in 2013, he was interviewed for a piece on *60 Minute Sports* about New Jersey's efforts to legalize sports betting. As a former bookie, Alite said legalized bookmaking would be a good thing for New Jersey and wouldn't hurt organized crime's illicit business. A film crew for that story accompanied him to Woodhaven, where he showed them around his old neighborhood. A British film crew working on a series about "life after the mob" also spent several days with him in New Jersey and New York in the spring of 2014. Alite tells the same story to anyone who asks: He did what he did. He can't undo it. All he can do is try to move forward, try to be better, try to make sure that his kids, and other kids, don't get seduced by the power and the money that is organized crime.

John A. Gotti has also shared his story with the media,

appearing on *60 Minutes* in February 2011. The hour-long exclusive interview, billed as a *Special Edition of 60 Minutes Presents,* was conducted by Steve Kroft, one of the best reporters on that highly acclaimed program. Kroft interviewed Gotti in his home in Oyster Bay, Long Island.

Gotti's lawyer, Charles Carnesi, was by Junior's side. *60 Minutes* also had to agree that no one else would be interviewed on camera for the piece. Alite has watched segments from the show several times on YouTube. When Alite is mentioned, Gotti refers to him as a "punk," a "dog," and a "miscreant." The interview, which runs for about forty-one minutes, is just more Gotti spin, says Alite. Junior is telling the same story, offering the same half-truths and never coming to grips with who he is or what he has done.

There has also been talk for the past four years about a movie, *Gotti: In the Shadow of My Father,* which would purport to tell the story of the father-and-son mobsters. John Travolta has been mentioned to play Gotti Sr. The project, like so much else in Hollywood, has been on again, off again. But if it ever gets made, with Junior and his sister Vicky as producers, Alite is certain it will be more myth than reality.

John Alite says when he looks in the mirror each morning he knows who he is. He knows what he's done. He does not try to hide from it. But he does try to build on that recognition, on that acceptance of responsibility. He thinks he is becoming a better person. That won't change the horrible things that he did in the past; it won't bring back the people he has killed; it won't ease the pain and suffering of those he has hurt. But by facing up to it all, he believes he can move forward. Alite is at peace with the man he sees in his mirror.

He wonders who it is that John A. Gotti sees in his mirror.

In November 2013, Junior Gotti was in the news again. He said he had been stabbed outside a CVS pharmacy in Syosset,

Long Island, not far from his home. Initial news reports indicated that Gotti, who drove himself to the hospital, told emergency room attendants that he had tried to break up a fight in the drugstore parking lot between two strangers and that one had stabbed him. When police arrived at the hospital, according to news reports, Gotti, who was not seriously injured, politely declined to talk with them.

The incident had occurred around 9:45 P.M. on a Sunday. One news report noted that CVS employees had not seen anyone scuffling. The report also said there was no evidence of a fight in the parking lot. John Alite says he has no idea what happened that night. But he doesn't buy the Good Samaritan spin Junior Gotti tried to sell.

John Gotti's Rules of Leadership: Always manipulate the facts to present a positive image. Perception is reality.

JOHN GOTTI'S RULES OF LEADERSHIP

1. Whenever possible, underlings must take the weight of a crime pending against Gotti or his family.
2. No member of any crew, in the presence of the boss, may wear sunglasses.
3. Members and associates are not to speak to the media. Granting interviews or appearing on television is prohibited.
4. Wives and girlfriends are to remain low-key. They are not to speak in public or call attention to themselves.
5. Whenever possible, use demeaning nicknames to describe underlings. It establishes who is in charge and who is subservient.
6. Drug dealing is prohibited and punishable by death. (Any member or associate dealing drugs must share his profits with the boss.)
7. Always keep underlings waiting. It reminds them who's in control without saying a word.
8. No member or associate is to fool around with the wife, girlfriend, or daughter of another member of the organization.

9. Always acknowledge the presence of the boss first in any public or social setting. In any social setting with members of other crime families, make them come to you to pay their respects. Going to them first is a sign of weakness.

10. Never talk business indoors. The government has "ears." If you are talking business in a car, be sure the radio is turned up loud. Best to talk on the street while walking.

11. When charged with a crime, no matter the circumstances, do not plead guilty. It's a sign of weakness.

12. Always manipulate the facts to present a positive image. Perception is reality.

ACKNOWLEDGMENTS

This story could not have been told without the cooperation and candor of John Alite, who spent hours going over the details with me. The only thing I asked John was to be truthful. I believe that he was and for that I thank him.

Over the years, there have been dozens of law enforcement and underworld sources on whom I have depended for insights and for "reality checks." They were again invaluable in the writing of this book, but for various reasons have opted to remain anonymous. One source and good friend, however, was quoted by name. Dave Gentile, a retired FBI agent who helped dismantle the Philadelphia mob, has always been there for me. I appreciate that in so many ways. He was also instrumental in making the connection between John Alite and me and for that I thank him.

Mark Chait edited this book and did what good editors do. He took a manuscript and made it better. And Tom Pitoniak had the often tedious but necessary job of copyediting this story. He did it with style, class, and grace, which I believe is reflected in the final product.

Finally, I want to thank my wife, Angela, for her love and support. Once again she put up with the crazy hours and every day disruptions that are part of the writing process.